Policy Networks in Criminal Justice

Policy Networks in Criminal Justice

Edited by

Mick Ryan
Professor of Penal Policy
University of Greenwich
London

Stephen P. Savage
Professor of Criminology, and
Director of the Institute of Criminal Justice Studies
University of Portsmouth

and

David S. Wall
Director of the Centre for Criminal Justice Studies
University of Leeds

First published 2001 by
PALGRAVE
Houndmills, Basingstoke, Hampshire RG21 6XS and
175 Fifth Avenue, New York, N. Y. 10010
Companies and representatives throughout the world

PALGRAVE is the new global academic imprint of
St. Martin's Press LLC Scholarly and Reference Division and
Palgrave Publishers Ltd (formerly Macmillan Press Ltd).

ISBN 0–333–75024–1

This book is printed on paper suitable for recycling and
made from fully managed and sustained forest sources.

A catalogue record for this book is available
from the British Library.

Library of Congress Cataloging-in-Publication Data
Policy networks in criminal justice / edited by Mick Ryan,
Stephen P. Savage, and David S. Wall.
    p. cm.
Includes bibliographical references and index.
ISBN 0–333–75024–1
    1. Criminal Justice, Administration of—Great Britain. 2. Pressure
groups—Great Britain. 3. Policy networks—Great Britain. I. Ryan,
Mick. II. Savage, Stephen P. III. Wall, David, 1956–

HV9960.G7 P65 2001
364.941—dc21
                                                    2001021607

10   9   8   7   6   5   4   3   2   1
10   09 08 07 06 05 04 03 02 01

Printed in Great Britain by Antony Rowe Ltd, Chippenham, Wiltshire

To
Joan Ryan
Nicholas P. Savage and
Harrison, Sophie and James Wall

Contents

List of Abbreviations

ACC	Association of County Councils
ACLEC	Advisory Committee on Legal Education and Conduct
ACOP	Association of Chief Officers of Probation
ACPO	Association of Chief Police Officers
AMA	Association of Metropolitan Authorities
BMA	British Medical Association
CCCP	Central Council of Probation Committees
CICB	Criminal Injuries Compensation Board
CJA	Criminal Justice Act
CoLPA	Committee of Local Police Authorities
CPO	Chief Probation Officer
CPOSA	Chief Police Officers' Staff Association
CPS	Crown Prosecution Service
ECHR	European Court of Human Rights
GCHQ	General Communications Headquarters
HL	Howard League for Penal Reform
HMIC	Her Majesty's Inspectorate of Constabulary
HMIP	Her Majesty's Inspectorate of Prisons
LAA	Local Authority Association
LARIA	Local Authorities Research and Information Association
LGMB	Local Government Management Board
MCC	Magistrates' Courts Committee
MCSI	Magistrates' Courts Service Inspectorate
MIS	Management Information System
MSC	Manpower Services Commission
NACRO	National Association for the Care and Resettlement of Offenders
NAPO	National Association of Probation Officers
NCCL	National Council for Civil Liberties
NCE	NACRO Community Enterprises Ltd
NCIS	National Criminal Intelligence Service
NCT	NACRO New Careers Training
NVQ	National Vocational Qualification
OFT	Office of Fair Trading
PAC	Penal Affairs Consortium
PACE	Police and Criminal Evidence Act

PGA	Prison Governors' Association
PMCA	Police and Magistrates' Courts Act
POA	Prison Officers' Association
PRI	Penal Reform International
PROP	Preservation of the Rights of Prisoners
PRT	Prison Reform Trust
PSA	Police Superintendents' Association
QC	Queen's Counsel
RAP	Radical Alternatives to Prison
RCCJ	Royal Commission on Criminal Justice
RCCP	Royal Commission on Criminal Procedure
SAMM	Support After Murder and Manslaughter
SNOP	Statement of National Objectives and Priorities
WIP	Women in Prison
WISH	Women in Special Hospitals

Notes on the Contributors

John Benyon is Professor of Politics at the University of Leicester and was Director of the Scarman Centre at the University of Leicester from 1987 to 1999. He is also convenor of the UK Political Studies Association's Specialist Group on the Politics of Law and Order, which he co-founded with Adam Edwards in 1993, and has been Treasurer of the Political Studies Association since 1992. He has published widely on urban crime and disorder, race and policing, international police co- operation and local crime prevention. His books include *Scarman and After* (editor, 1984); *The Constitution in Question* (editor, 1991) and *Debates in British Politics* (with D. Denver and J. Fisher, 2001). He is currently researching the politics of gun control and the politics of law and order, including the impact of elected mayors on local policing and crime prevention.

Sarah Charman studied at the University of Wales, Bangor for both her undergraduate and postgraduate degrees. She was formerly a Research Associate and is now Lecturer in Criminology at the Institute of Criminal Justice Studies, University of Portsmouth. She has published variously on the role of pressure groups in criminal justice policy-making, the role of the Association of Chief Police Officers and the politics of criminal justice policy. Sarah is co-author of *Policy and the Power of Persuasion* (with S. Savage and S. Cope, 2000).

Stephen Cope is a Principal Lecturer in Public Policy in the School of Social and Historical Studies, University of Portsmouth. He has researched widely into and published extensively on matters relating to policy networks and governance. He is currently working on a research project on regulating public services in Britain. He is a co-author of *Policing and the Power of Persuasion: the Changing Role of the Association of Chief Police Officers* (with S. Charman and S. Savage, 2000).

Jane Creaton is Senior Education Officer at the Bar Council. Pre-viously, she has worked as Lecturer in Criminal Justice Studies at the Institute of Criminal Justice Studies, University of Portsmouth and as a Research Officer at the Centre for Criminological Research, University of Oxford. She has written about DNA profiling and forensic science, and the treatment of vulnerable witnesses in the criminal justice system.

Adam Edwards is Senior Lecturer in the Department of Social Sciences, Nottingham Trent University. He is also Director of the Economic and Social Research Council's research seminar series on 'Policy Responses to Transnational Organised Crime', Chair of the Home Office working group on Community Safety and Crime Prevention Curriculum Development and adviser to the Government Office of the East Midlands on the Statutory Crime and Disorder Partnerships. His research interests include: crime prevention, organised crime, local governance, and the transferability and evaluation of crime control policies.

Ben Fitzpatrick is a lecturer in the Centre for Criminal Justice Studies, Department of Law, University of Leeds. His research and teaching interests lie within the field of the criminal law and criminal justice processes. He has published articles and chapters of books on 'Holding Centres in Northern Ireland' (with C. Walker, *European Human Rights Law Review*), 'Provocation' (with A. Reed, *The Transnational Lawyer*) and also 'Disclosure' (in C. Walker and K. Starmer (eds), *Miscarriages of Justice: a Review of Justice in Error*, 1999). With P. Seago and D. Wall, Ben recently completed research for the Lord Chancellor's Department on the impact of new public management upon the Magistrates' Courts.

Mike Nash is a Principal Lecturer in Criminal Justice at the University of Portsmouth. He has a particular interest in the probation service and was formerly a senior probation officer. His research interests include criminal dangerousness, criminal justice policy and the changing role of the probation service. He has published widely in these areas and his first book, *Police, Probation and Protecting the Public*, was published in 1999.

Mick Ryan is Professor of Penal Politics at the University of Greenwich, London. An active member of the Penal lobby he is a former chair of INQUEST, the subject of his most recent book, *Lobbying from Below: INQUEST in Defence of Civil Liberties* (1996). He jointly edited *Western European Penal Systems* (1995), and with Tony Ward wrote the first international study of private prisons, *Privatization and the Penal System: the American Experience and the Debate in Britain* (1989).

Stephen P. Savage is Professor of Criminology and Director of the Institute of Criminal Justice Studies, University of Portsmouth. He has researched into and has published widely on the politics of criminal justice and policing. His books include *The Theories of Talcott Parsons*

(1981); *Public Policy under Thatcher* (ed. with L. Robins, 1990); *Public Policy in Britain* (ed. with R. Atkinson and L. Robins, 1994); *Core Issues in Policing* (ed. with B. Loveday and F. Leishman, 1996 and 2000); *Policing and the Power of Persuasion: the Changing Role of the Association of Chief Police Officers* (with S. Charman and S. Cope, 2000); and *Public Policy under Blair* (ed. with R. Atkinson, 2001).

Peter Seago is Senior Lecturer in Criminal Law in the Centre for Criminal Justice Studies, Department of Law, University of Leeds. He is also a serving lay magistrate and was awarded the OBE in 1998 for his services to the administration of justice. In addition to conducting research on the judiciary and publishing a range of articles and commentaries, his books include *Criminal Law* (with A. Reed, 1999); *Readings in Criminal Law* (ed. with R. Weaver, J. Burkoff and A. Reed, 1998); *Criminal Law* (fourth edition, 1994) and *Cases and Materials on Family Law* (with A. Bissett-Johnson, 1976).

Peter Starie is Senior Lecturer in Politics at the University of Portsmouth. His research interests cover a range of subjects from international political economy to political theory. He has written about policy networks in relation to a wide variety of issue-areas, including the IMF and police reform. He has recently written about globalisation and European economic integration.

Clive Walker is a Professor in the Department of Law and Head of the Department of Law at the University of Leeds. He was formerly Director of the Centre for Criminal Justice Studies at Leeds. He has written extensively on criminal justice, civil liberties and media issues. His books have focused upon terrorism: they include *Political Violence and the Law in Ireland* (1989); *The Prevention of Terrorism in British Law* (second edition, 1992); and upon miscarriages of justice, including the books, *Justice in Error* (1993) and *Miscarriages of Justice* (1999). He is also a co-editor of *The Internet, Law and Society* (ed. with Y. Akdeniz and D. Wall, 2000).

Sandra Walklate is currently Professor of Sociology at Manchester Metropolitan Universty. She is author of many books on policing and victims. These books include: *Introducing Policework* (with M. Brogden and T. Jefferson, 1988); *Victimology: the Victim and the Criminal Justice Process* (1989), *Gender and Crime* (1995); *Understanding Criminology* (1997); *Critical Victimology* (with R. Mawby, 1993); *Zero Tolerance or*

Community Tolerance? (with K. Evans, 1999); *Gender, Crime and Criminal Justice* (2000). She worked actively with Victim Support on Merseyside during the 1980s and has worked with police officers on Merseyside, Greater Manchester and West Yorkshire on the issue of 'domestic' violence.

David Wall is the Director of the Centre for Criminal Justice Studies at the University of Leeds. He has written about, researched into and taught the subjects of policing, access to criminal justice, the courts process and also crime and the internet. He is currently conducting various funded research projects into a variety of policing, courts and cybercrime issues. His books include: *The Impact of PACE: Policing in a Northern Force* (with K. Bottomley, C. Coleman, D. Dixon, M. Gill, 1991); *Access to Criminal Justice: Legal Aid, Lawyers and the Defence of Liberty* (ed. with R. Young, 1996); *The British Police: Forces and Chief Officers 1829–2000* (with M. Stallion, 1999); *The Chief Constables of England and Wales* (1998); *The Internet, Law and Society* (ed. with Y. Akdeniz and C. Walker, 2000); *Crime and the Internet* (ed., 2001).

Chas Wilson is a Senior Lecturer in Criminology at the University of Portsmouth. He has particular interests in and published widely on comparative prison systems, international human rights law and prisoners' rights in both British and European prison systems; is currently interested in the implications for prisoners of the Human Rights Act 1998 and is currently working on the contribution and achievements of penal reform groups in Britain, with a particular focus on the Penal Affairs Consortium.

1

Analysing Criminal Justice Policy-Making: Towards a Policy Networks Approach?

Stephen Cope

This chapter examines the increasingly fashionable and salient concept of policy networks as a way of understanding criminal justice policy-making. More broadly, network analysis has been an increasingly prominent form of analysis in understanding economic, political and social life (Knoke, 1990; Law, 1992; Castells, 1996). Indeed Castells argued that 'as a historical trend, dominant functions and processes in the information age are increasingly organized around networks' (1996: 469). Networks are often portrayed as alternative forms of coordination to those of hierarchies and markets (Thompson *et al.*, 1991; Maidment and Thompson, 1993; Jackson and Stainsby, 2000). In ideal terms, whereas the principle of command underpins hierarchies and that of competition underpins markets, it is the principle of cooperation, stemming from shared interests and interdependence, that underpins networks. In reality, of course, a specific system may be characterised by a mix of these three coordinating principles, with perhaps one such principle dominant (Hay, 1998: 39). A network is simply a set of relations between interconnected actors; or, as Castells stated, 'a set of interconnected nodes' (1996: 470), and, as Knoke and Kuklinski wrote, 'a specific type of relation linking a defined set of persons, objects or events' (1991: 175). However, within the burgeoning literature on network analysis there is more agreement on defining than on delineating a network. For example, Castells stressed that networks 'are open structures, able to expand without limits' (1996: 470), and Jackson and Stainsby noted that they 'are clusters of relationships which span indefinite ranges of space and time' (2000: 11); but Frances *et al.*, argued that many networks 'are highly exclusive of outsiders' (1991: 14). Networks, as will be argued later, can be both open or closed, though their 'boundary specification' is problematic and often 'poorly understood' (Knoke, 1990: 235). The question of determining what actors are inside (and for that matter, outside) a given network is critical in network analysis. Following Thompson, a network constitutes 'a specific set of relations making up an interconnected chain or system for a defined set of elements that forms a structure' (1993: 51). This chapter argues that the criminal justice system can be analysed as a network, and in particular, a policy network, and that such network analysis offers useful insights into how criminal justice policy is made.

There is now a rich vein of literature on policy networks, reflecting the embeddedness of network analysis in policy analysis as well as socio-logical analysis (Coleman and Skøgstad, 1990; Marin and Mayntz, 1991; Marsh and Rhodes, 1992a; Smith, 1993; Knoke *et al.*, 1996; Kickert *et al.*, 1997a; see Bogason and Toonen, 1998; Marsh, 1998a). The policy net-works approach has been used extensively by political scientists as a way of understanding policy-making in government (particularly, intergov-ernmental relations and pressure group–government relations). This chapter accounts for the rise of the policy networks approach by asses-sing its contributions to understanding the policy-making process; illus-trates this approach by examining the policing policy network; and evaluates the policy networks approach by assessing its strengths and weaknesses as a way of explaining policy-making.

The rise of policy networks

From government to governance

The rise of the policy networks approach coincided with the rise of governance, both as an empirical trend and as a theoretical perspective. In the words of Pierre (2000: 3):

> Governance has a dual meaning; on the one hand it refers to the empirical manifestations of state adaptation to its external environ-ment as it emerges in the late twentieth century. On the other hand, governance also denotes a conceptual or theoretical representation of co-ordination of social systems and, for the most part, the role of the state in that process.

Rhodes argued that Britain is no longer a unitary state but a '"differ-entiated polity"'... characterized by functional and institutional specialization and the fragmentation of policies and politics' (Rhodes, 1997 : 7). Governance reflects the view that Britain is no longer governed from one place (if indeed it ever was), but instead is governed from many places. The traditional, and largely hierarchical and monolithic system of government, as depicted by the Westminster model, has been challenged as a result of globalisation, Europeanisation, privatisation and decentralisation (Jessop, 1993; Peters, 1993; Rhodes, 1994; Rhodes, 1997; Weller *et al.*, 1997; Cope, 1999). Following Pierre and Stoker (2000: 29–30):

> Governing Britain – and indeed any other advanced western democratic state – has thus become a matter of multi-level governance. To understand the challenge of governing requires a focus on multiple locations of decision-making – in both spatial and sectoral terms – and the way in which exchanges between actors in those locations are conducted and managed.

There is thus a highly complex and dynamic set of interdependent and consequently interconnected actors, cutting across different levels of government and different sectors of society, involved in governing. Governance, according to Kooiman, 'takes place in interactions between actors on micro, meso and macro levels of social-political aggregation' (1993: 41). Governments do not govern on their own; they increasingly rely on other actors to govern society. Gamble wrote (2000: 110–11):

> The separation of governing as a process from government, a particular agent, explains the popularity of the term, governance. Governance denotes the steering capacities of a political system, the ways in which governing is carried out, without making any assumption as to which institutions or agents do the steering.... The state is always involved in governance, but often in an enabling rather than a directing role, helping to establish and sustain the institutions in society, including crucially markets, which make steering possible.

For Rhodes, networks are 'central to the analysis of governance' (2000: 54), and governance can be seen as 'self-organizing interorganizational networks' (1996: 660). Governance, then, is all about steering a myriad of networks, consisting of a maze of interconnected actors. It is 'a new process of governing' (Rhodes, 1997: 46).

From networks to policy networks

Policy networks are specific forms of networks within governance. The policy networks approach originated in an attempt to explain relations between central and local government (Rhodes, 1988), and between government and pressure groups (Smith, 1993). It stresses the importance of disaggregating the policy-making process into discrete policy sectors. Benson defined a policy sector as 'a cluster or complex of organizations connected to each other by resource dependencies and distinguished from other clusters or complexes by breaks in the structure of resource dependencies' (1982: 148). The power-dependence model of interorganisational relations is central in understanding the policy networks approach. This model assumes that all organisations are dependent on others for resources, and, therefore, organisations need to exchange resources for them to achieve their goals; such exchanges of resources involves bargaining within and between organisations (Rhodes, 1981: 97–133). This interdependence facilitates the construction of policy networks, because actors within a policy sector are dependent upon each other for resources and are thus connected together as a network.

The policy networks approach acknowledges that policy- making is not uniform across government, because network structures vary considerably between policy sectors. The number of interested policy actors, their goals and resources, and their consequent relations will depend significantly upon the different traditions, routines and environments of policy sectors, as well as issues within policy sectors (Harrop, 1992: 123–217, 273–77; Hughes, *et al.*, 1997; Marsh and Rhodes, 1992a; Smith, 1993; Gray, 1994: 120–133; Marsh, 1998a; Cope and Goodship, 1999). For example, the criminal justice policy network is increasingly multi-level, with the increasing influence of local authorities, private security industry, professional associations, pressure groups, the media, the European Union, the Council of Europe and, to a far lesser extent, the United Nations, thus making the network more resistant to a central steer. In contrast the social security policy network is hardly multi-level; central government (mainly the Department of Social Security and the Treasury) largely steers the array of local social security agencies in a centralised and hierarchical manner. As policy-making has become more complex, governments rely increasingly upon professional associations, pressure groups, think-tanks and private sector companies for the formulation and implementation of policies. Indeed Weir and Beetham argued that 'organised interests and professional groups play a significant and often dominant role in government policy-making' (1999: 271).

Following Kickert (1993: 275):

> The control capacity of government is limited for a number of reasons: lack of legitimacy, complexity of policy processes, complexity and multitude of institution etc. Government is only one of many actors that influence the course of events in a societal system. Government does not have enough power to exert its will on other actors. Other social institutions are, to a great extent, autonomous.

Furthermore, government is not monolithic, and within government there exists many agencies, both elected and appointed, operating at different levels (e.g. local, regional, national, international), and with different goals and resources. In the words of Smith (1993: 50):

> It is not the state that acts but state actors within particular parts of the state. the state does not have a unified set of interests. Different state agencies have various interests, and individuals within those agencies may also have conflicting interests.

Government is thus fragmented, making the task of centrally steering government itself difficult. For example, within central government there is much conflict between the Treasury and spending departments (such as the Home Office) over public expenditure decisions. Central government is limited to the extent that it can steer the criminal justice system (especially the courts and police service that enjoy a high degree of operational independence within their respective remits). This fragmentation within government reflects the lack of control that the core executive can exert over government. The core executive comprises 'all those organisations and structures which primarily serve to pull together and integrate central government policies, or act as final arbiters within the executive of conflicts between different elements of the government machine' (Dunleavy and Rhodes, 1990: 4). The core executive (embracing such actors as the Prime Minister's Office, Cabinet Office and Treasury) can only attempt to 'police the functional policy networks' (Rhodes, 1997: 14). The core executive is relatively weak, not strong, because 'power-dependence in policy networks is a cause of executive segmentation' (Rhodes, 1997: 15).

As a result of segmented government and fragmented governance, a myriad of relationships of mutual dependence exist between actors within government and between government and non-government actors within a policy sector, involving exchanges of resources in the making of public policy. Following de Bruijn and ten Heuvelhof, a policy network is 'an entity consisting of public, quasi-public, or private actors who are dependent on each other and, as a consequence of this dependence, maintain relations with each other' (1995: 163). A policy network consists of a set of interdependent actors sharing a common broad interest and operating within a functionally defined policy area. Policy networks thus become '(more or less) stable patterns of social relations between interdependent actors, which take shape around policy problems and/or policy programmes' (Kickert *et al.*, 1997b: 6).

Different types of policy networks

Policy networks have been categorised and differentiated according to interests, membership, resources and dependencies. Rhodes developed a typology of different kinds of policy networks along a continuum ranging from a policy community to an issue network (1988: 235–366). He identified five different types of policy networks: policy communities, professional networks, intergovernmental networks, producer networks, and issue networks – see Table 1.1.

Policy communities are the most integrated type of policy network. They are characterised by limited membership of policy actors, involving perhaps a single government agency and a few privileged 'insider' interest groups insulated from other actors (including the public), and they 'are based on the major functional interests in and of government'

Table 1.1 Types of policy networks

Type of network	Characteristics of network
Policy community	Stability, highly restricted membership, vertical interdependence, limited horizontal articulation
Professional network	Stability, highly restricted membership, vertical interdependence, limited horizontal articulation, serves interest of profession
Intergovernmental network	Limited membership, limited vertical interdependence, extensive horizontal articulation
Producer network	Fluctuating membership, limited vertical interdependence, serves interest of producer
Issue network	Unstable, large number of members, limited vertical interdependence

Source: Adapted from Rhodes and Marsh, 1992: 183.

(Rhodes, 1990: 304). A policy community displays much continuity of policy, frequent interactions between participating policy actors, a high degree of consensus between actors, an exchange of resources between actors, and a 'positive-sum game' with all policy actors increasing their influence. Policy is thus made in a stable and regulated environment within which policy communities 'routinise relationships by incorporating the major interests to a "closed" world' (Rhodes, 1988: 390). For example, the judicial policy network constitutes a policy community in that policy is traditionally made by an exclusive and small set of actors, namely, the Lord Chancellor's Department, the Home Office, the courts' system, the Crown Prosecution Service and the legal professions (Raine and Willson, 1993). Only occasionally and sporadically is this relatively closed network of 'insiders' open to 'semi-outsiders' (such as the police, prison, probation and social services) and 'outsiders' (such as pressure groups and the mass media), and often only when a perceived crisis has occurred – for example, a miscarriage of justice – within this otherwise routinised world of judicial policy-making. That this policy network is a state-dominated policy community should not be surprising given that 'the maintenance of internal order through coercion and political socialisation is a primary state function' (McLeay, 1998: 110).

Issue networks are the least integrated type of policy networks. They are characterised by a 'large number of participants and their limited degree of interdependence' (Rhodes, 1990: 305). The membership of issue networks is fluid with actors freely joining and leaving the policy arena. An issue network displays a lack of continuity of policy, erratic interactions between participating actors (especially between government agencies and interest groups), a low degree of consensus between actors, a limited exchange of resources between actors, and a 'zero-sum game' with some policy actors gaining influence at the expense of other actors. Relations between government and pressure groups are more likely to be characterised by informal consultation and lobbying, conflict between policy actors, policy instability, and even 'policy messes' (Rhodes, 1988: 87). Issue networks embody 'relationships that are distinguished from the general pressure group universe' because their participating groups possess 'some interest in the area and minimal resources to exchange' (Smith, 1993: 65). They thus display regularised (albeit informal rather than formal) contact between many loosely connected actors. An example of an issue network would be that which emerged over gun reform in the aftermath of the Dunblane massacre in the mid-1990s. The Snowdrop Campaign was launched by many parents of the gunned-down children to restrict the possession and use of guns, which enjoyed considerable popular support and media attention. The issue also attracted other interested actors, such as the Home Office, police service, and political parties, as well as the gun, sports and civil liberties lobbies. This inclusive and open network was characterised by a conflict of goals between many of the actors, and once the issue disappeared from the political agenda, after the Labour Government implemented some limited gun reform measures, the network also disappeared (though perhaps to return if and when another shooting-spree takes place).

A policy community exhibits characteristics of continuity, consensus, limited membership, significant resources held by all actors, and a relative balance of power between actors; and an issue network displays instability, conflict, wide and relatively open membership, an imbalance of resources, and unequal power between actors. The characteristics of these two types of policy networks are illustrated in Table 1.2.

Table 1.2   Characteristics of policy networks

Dimension	Policy community	Issue network
Membership		
Number of participants	Very limited, some conscious exclusion	Large
Type of interest	Economic/professional	Wide range of groups
Integration		
Frequency of interaction	Frequent, high quality	Contacts fluctuate
Continuity	Membership, values, outcomes persistent	Fluctuating access
Consensus	All participants share basic values but conflict present	A degree of agreement
Resources		
Distribution of resources within network	All participants have resources. Relationship is one of exchange	Some participants have resources, but limited
Distribution of resources within participating organisations	Hierarchical leaders can deliver members	Varied and variable distribution and capacity to regulate members
Power	There is a balance among members. One group may be dominant but power is positive-sum	Unequal power. Power zero-sum

Source: Smith, 1993: 60; Adapted from Marsh and Rhodes, 1992b: 251.

A policy community represents a relatively closed, consensual and tightly knit network of policy actors. An issue network embraces a relatively open network of actors loosely bound together by their (often competing and conflicting) interests being affected by a particular policy. Rhodes presented the different types of policy networks along a continuum, with policy communities at one end and issue networks at the other end. Professional networks, intergovernmental networks and producer networks, as intermediary networks, fall between these two ends of the continuum. This schema suggested a decreasing degree of integration from policy communities to issue networks, but Rhodes later accepted that this continuum may be confusing because these intermediary networks may display similar characteristics as policy communities or issue networks (Rhodes, 1997: 39). The distinction between policy communities and issue networks is based upon 'their integration, stability and exclusiveness' – see Table 1.3, whereas professional networks, intergovernmental networks and producer networks differ according to 'which interest dominates them' Rhodes, 1997: 39.

There is a further terminological dispute within the literature on policy networks, which is not surprising given the '"Babylonian" variety of different understandings and applications of the policy network concept to be found in the study of policy-making' (Börzel, 1998: 254). Dowding noted that the terms, 'policy community' and 'policy network', were not used consistently in the literature, thus resulting in terminological confusion (1995: 140). Some writers, such as Marsh and Rhodes (1992a), used 'policy network'; and other writers, such as Wilks and Wright (1987), used 'policy community' as the generic label. However, the debate over terminology is misleading, and amounts to 'a phoney war of words hiding a deeper conflict over the nature of social explanation and the role of state theorizing' (Dowding, 1995: 140). However, it is Marsh and Rhodes's usage of the terminology that has become 'accepted currency' (Jordan, 1990: 335), and consequently

Table 1.3   Continuum of policy networks

Policy community	Issue network
stable membership	fluid membership
highly insular	highly permeable
strong dependencies	weak dependencies

Source: Peterson, 1995:77.

Wilks and Wright's usage should be resisted. Thus, policy communities and issue networks are types of policy networks. These terms represent ideal-types, and consequently, it is important to apply them empirically to test their usefulness. The next section examines the policy networks approach in understanding the making of policing policy.

The policing policy network: a case study on police reform

The policy networks approach would begin by identifying the actors involved in the making of policing policy. The policing policy network consists of (at least) the following key actors:

- the Home Secretary
- civil servants responsible for policing in the Home Office
- National Criminal Intelligence Service (NCIS)
- National Crime Squad
- MI5
- HM Inspectorate of Constabulary
- Audit Commission
- police authorities
- Association of Police Authorities
- chief constables and other police officers
- Association of Chief Police Officers
- Police Superintendents' Association
- Police Federation
- European Police Office (Europol)

In times of stability, characterised by routine policy-making, these actors are the 'insiders' of the policy-making process. Parliament, the judiciary, the mass media and the public are the 'outsiders', influencing the policing policy agenda sporadically and normally only when policy-making has become unsuccessful, more politicised or crisis-ridden. The policing policy network exhibits the characteristics of a relatively tightly integrated and state-dominated policy community. However, this policy community is part of the wider criminal justice policy network, embracing a series of interconnected and overlapping policy communities and issue networks (such as judicial and penal policy networks comprising actors like judges, lawyers, probation officers, prison officers, social workers, academics and journalists). Moreover, as successive governments have adopted a multi-agency approach to tackle crime the policing policy network is increasingly connected to key actors in other criminal justice networks, furthering the creation of a single criminal justice policy network. For example, in 1991 the Home Office established the Criminal Justice Consultative Council, comprising actors drawn from central government, the courts and the police and social services, as a way of 'sorting out the "rubbing points" in the system' (Hoddinott, taken from McLeay, 1998: 126). Furthermore, Rose claimed that under one former Home Secretary, Michael Howard, the Association of Chief Police Officers 'found itself in the unfamiliar position of actually being asked to draft Government policy' on certain criminal justice matters (1996: 327; see also Savage *et al.*, 1996: 103). McLeay claimed that 'the autonomy of the traditional policing policy state network has been challenged; "policing" has increasingly been subsumed into the broader sector of "criminal justice", introducing further influential agencies and, moreover, groups outside the state', and, as a possible consequence, 'policing policy in future becomes part of this wider sectoral network' (1998: 131). A policy network thus both comprises of sub-policy networks and forms part of wider supra-policy networks.

The police play a key role in policy-making because governments need their consent for many policies to be implemented. Ritchie commented that 'the Association of Chief Police Officers (ACPO) and the Police Federation are consulted about policing policy and new legislation ... [and are] ... seen as vital partners in the policy-making process' (1992: 204). However, in the early 1990s the previous Conservative Government attempted to restructure the policing policy network by overriding the traditional consultative mechanisms of making policy, and generally wanted to impose rather than negotiate reform. Leishman *et al.* argued that the Government 'attempted to use "despotic power"', involving the capacity to implement its policy without consultation and negotiation with affected groups; rather than "infrastructural power"', involving the capacity to intervene in society via its interdependent relationships with groups' (1996: 18–19; on the distinction between despotic and infrastructural power, see Mann, 1984). It introduced fixed-term contracts and performance-related pay for senior police officers, established new police authorities with increased patronage powers exercised by the Home Secretary, set national policing objectives to be achieved by the police, strengthened the role of the HM Inspectorate of Constabulary, and increased opportunities for the privatisation of policing functions (Leishman *et al.*, 1995, 1996; Cope *et al.*, 1996).

These reforms represented an attack upon the police, which constitute a significant part of the highly integrated and relatively powerful policing policy network that traditionally exercised a dominant influence over policy-making. However, many reform measures were dropped or diluted because of parliamentary and police resistance (Leishman *et al.*, 1995). For example, the then Home Secretary, under pressure from the police, conceded that fixed-term contracts should be introduced only for senior and not all police officers and that he should not appoint the chairpersons of police authorities. The implementation of police reform was less than smooth, mainly because of resistance from the police (especially the Association of Chief Police Officers and Police Federation), supported by many in Parliament and local government. The Conservative Government was unable to stand firm against this campaign not least because of its small parliamentary majority.

The case study on police reform demonstrates that the Conservative Government was unable to implement fully its reform plans because of resistance from elsewhere within the policing policy network. It illustrates the interdependent world of the policing policy network embracing a few relatively powerful actors who together shape policing policy. The failure of the Conservative Government to get its reforms through Parliament can be understood by using the policy networks approach. The policing policy network is highly integrated as witnessed by the ease with which many of its constituent parts were welded together to block the reforms. The Home Office, and especially the Home Secretary, were left stranded as other formidable parts of the network mobilised political support amongst politicians and the media against its proposals. The mobilisation of the many actors within the policy network was facilitated by the hierarchical structure of the police, popular concern over rising crime rates, the small parliamentary majority of the Conservative Government, and government dependence upon the police to implement law-and-order and other policies. The reforms represented an attempt by the Conservative Government to restructure an obdurate policy network. However, the strength of the police within the policing policy network and the consequent weakness of the Conservative Government meant that the police reforms were always likely to be (at least temporarily) blocked. The case study demonstrates the difficulties in implementing reform in a policy arena dominated by a highly integrated and relatively closed policy community.

The fall of policy networks?

The policy networks approach has become the dominant approach in understanding policy-making in government. It is superior than the largely arid constitutional and institutionalist accounts of policy-making that stress the role of institutions (such as the cabinet and civil service) in the making of policy (Smith, 1999). These accounts, such as the sterile debate on prime ministerial versus cabinet government, largely fail to capture the complexity and interdependence of actors involved in shaping public policy. Neither the prime minister nor cabinet governs, for example; but instead a series of interconnected policy networks comprising interested and interdependent actors drawn from inside and outside government shape policy, though mediated by the core executive. Policy-making in government is fragmented, though there is interdependence within the fragments. The policy networks approach acknowledges such fragmentation between policy sectors and the influence of key actors transcending government and non-government agencies in shaping policy. The approach appreciates the myriad of formal and informal relations between interdependent actors within the complex world of multi-level governance.

Though the policy networks approach provides useful insights into how policy is made (and not made), there is an emerging critique of its validity (Dowding, 1994, 1995; Kassim, 1994; Mills and Saward, 1994; Klijn, 1996; Evans, 1998; Hay, 1998; Peters, 1998; Hay and Richards, 2000). Dowding believed that the term, 'policy network', is 'essentially metaphorical' relying on a set of images to visualise relations between actors within a policy network (1995: 137). Börzel argued that 'the concept of policy networks as a specific form of governance does not constitute a proper theory' (1998: 263). The policy networks approach is useful in understanding the policy-making process, but there are limits to its usefulness. It is far better at describing than explaining policy change. The approach is useful in making sense of a seemingly complex and chaotic policy-making process, often characterised by inclusion and exclusion of actors, interdependence of actors, and exchange of resources between actors. However, the policy networks approach cannot provide answers to questions about the formation of preferences of actors and the distribution of resources between actors. For example, it failed to explain why the Conservative Government wanted to reform the police but was insufficiently powerful to fully implement reform. The policy networks approach is useful in understanding how things get done (or not done) but not very useful in understanding why things get done (or not done). Nonetheless, the approach captures, by describing without explaining, the complexity and interdependence of the policy-making process. There is much empirical evidence that policy networks exist as sets of 'relatively stable relationships which are of non-

hierarchical and interdependent nature linking a variety of actors, who share common interests with regard to a policy and who exchange resources to pursue these shared interests acknowledging that co-operation is the best way to achieve common goals' (Börzel, 1998: 254). However, this evidence only confers the policy networks approach with descriptive and not explanatory power. The final part of this concluding section surveys the main criticisms levelled at the policy networks approach and evaluates the responses from proponents of the approach.

The rescue of policy networks?

Notwithstanding a few definitional and methodological quibbles, there are three key lines of argument against the policy networks approach, which have, to varying extents, been countered by its crusading supporters. Critics of the policy networks approach have argued that the approach does not pay sufficient attention to the formation of policy networks, networking within policy networks, and transformation of policy networks.

First, how do policy networks form? There was an assumption in the earlier literature on policy networks that policy networks were given entities; they just existed. This assumption was far more apparent in the discussion of the more stable policy communities than the more fluid issue networks. However, there was little discussion, never mind explanation, of how and why policy networks form. Baggott noted that the policy networks literature offered 'little explanation of how policy networks emerge' (1995: 26). Following Hay and Richards, the idea of a network 'is neither a neutral nor an uncontested concept' (2000: 12). They argued that 'decisions to participate in networks are, in some sense, strategic' (2000: 13), and posited the following three strategic and contextual conditions for network formation (2000: 17):

(i) the recognition of the potential for mutual advantage through collective (as opposed to individual) action, i.e. a positive-sum game for all those participating in a particular network form;
(ii) the recognition of the potential for enhancing the strategic capacities of participant organizations through the pooling of strategic resources ...;
(iii) the recognition and/or establishment of the conditions of network feasibility...

This criticism, though valid, does not make the policy networks approach redundant, rather it highlights a significant omission in the earlier literature, which, to a certain extent, has been rectified in the later literature. Marsh and Smith admitted that policy networks 'are structures that cannot be treated as given' and 'are inscribed with other structural divisions' (2000: 7). For example, in a study of transnational local authority networking, Benington and Harvey argued that a complex set of factors accounted for the formation of such networks including the recognition of mutual benefits by those participating actors, such as the European Commission and local authorities (1998: 159–163). Similarly Nunan explained the formation of the packaging waste policy network as a result of the Department of the Environment, as the lead actor responsible for implementing the European Community's directive on packaging and packaging waste, consulting with only a limited number of actors drawn from the packaging industry and excluding other actors that held divergent views to those of the packaging industry, until the embryonic policy network was established (1999: 627–9).

Secondly, how do policy networks work? In the earlier literature little attention was paid to the dynamics of policy networks. Writers instead spent more time mapping out the key actors, and their relations, within a given policy network, and noted the interdependence of the identified actors (especially within policy communities). Such entrenched interdependence, it was argued, was a significant obstacle to government-sponsored reform, because governments cannot govern alone. However, more recent literature has paid far more attention to the 'nuts-and-bolts' of the workings of policy networks. For example, more recent literature has looked at the networking strategies of key actors within policy networks (Kickert *et al.*, 1997a; Bogason and Toonen, 1998; Nunan, 1999; Cloke *et al.*, 2000; Hay and Richards, 2000; Rhodes, 2000: 72–6); and examined methods to identify and measure relations within policy networks (John and Cole, 1998; Milward and Provan, 1998; Marsh and Smith, 2000).

However, the policy networks approach is meso-level in that it examines relations between actors within the state, and also between state and non-state actors, in making public policy (Marsh, 1998b: 15). The approach is firmly consistent with the neo-pluralist tradition from which it stemmed, that stresses the significance of pressure groups in the policy-making process and the importance of disaggregating the state to explain policy-making. The policy networks approach is weak at understanding how individual actors set goals and exchange resources in their pursuit of goals. For example, Dowding argued that 'the explanation lies in the characteristics of the actors' within a policy network and not with the characteristics of the network itself (1995: 142). Moreover, the policy networks approach, though seeing policy networks as 'structures of resource dependency' (Marsh, 1998b: 11), is weak at placing such structures within wider structures (such as economic structures) that shape patterns of power-relations between actors within policy networks. Increasing globalisation, Europeanisation, privatisation and managerialisation of policy-making have had a significant impact on policy networks (including the criminal justice policy network) (Cope, 1999), yet the policy networks approach largely regarded these developments as exogenous factors impacting upon a policy network, without unravelling how these factors actually impact upon a network and, moreover, how actors within a network impact upon these so-called exogenous pressures. For example, the new public management-reform agenda facing the police service to a significant extent emanated from the Association of Chief Police Officers (Savage *et al.*, 1996, 1997), thus blurring the extent to which managerialisation of the police service is an exogenous or endogenous factor. The approach, if it is to fully explain policy-making within governance, needs to embrace more micro-level and macro-level forms of theoretical analysis. Following Marsh, the policy networks approach 'has little utility as an explanatory concept unless it is integrated with macro-level and micro-level analysis' (1998b: 15). This multi-theoretic form of analysis is beginning slowly to take shape (Börzel, 1998; Daugbjerg and Marsh, 1998; Hay, 1998; Marsh, 1998c: 192–7; Hay and Richards, 2000; Marsh and Smith, 2000).

In response to this criticism, Marsh and Smith developed a dialectical model of policy networks, acknowledging that 'networks are structures which constrain and facilitate agents' and that 'the culture of a network acts as a constraint and/or opportunity on/for its members' (2000: 5). However, unlike the earlier exposition of the policy networks approach that tended to assume that network structures largely determine policy outcomes (Marsh and Rhodes, 1992b: 262; Rhodes and Marsh, 1992: 197), they argued that both structures and agents matter. They noted that 'outcomes cannot be explained solely by reference to the structure of the network; they are the result of the actions of strategically calculating subjects', but they added that 'these agents are located within a structured context, which is provided by both the network and the broader political and social-structural context within which the network operates and those contexts clearly affect the actor's resources' (2000: 6–7). The dialectical model of policy networks acknowledges that (Marsh and Smith, 2000: 9–10):

- The broader structural context affects both the network structure and the resources that actors have to utilize within the network.
- The skill that an actor has to utilize in bargaining is a product of their innate skill and the learning process through which they go.
- The network interaction and bargaining reflects a combination of the actor's resources, the actor's skill, the network structure and the policy interaction.
- The network structure is a reflection of the structural context, the actor's resources, the network interaction and the policy outcome.
- The policy outcome reflects the interaction between the network structure and network interaction.

Marsh and Smith explicitly argued that relations between actors within a policy network, the structure of a policy network and the wider structural context surrounding a policy network are 'interactive or dialectical' (2000: 10), thus accepting that micro-level and macro-level, as well as meso-level, forms of analysis are necessary in understanding how policy networks work.

Thirdly, how do policy networks change? In the earlier literature it was easy to leave with the impression that policy was made by a relatively exclusive set of interdependent and entrenched actors within a policy network, and that because policy-making was closed, routinised and stable, policy change was very difficult. Hay and Richards observed that policy networks are often portrayed as 'static, indeed torpid phenomena' (2000: 2), and that a policy network is often seen as 'a static and invariant structure' (2000: 4). This impression was not consciously sought by the proponents of the policy networks approach, who have long noted, particularly within issue networks, that policy change takes place as a result of both endogenous and, moreover, exogenous pressures (Marsh and Rhodes, 1992b: 257–61; Rhodes and Marsh, 1992: 193–7; Smith, 1993: 76–98). However, what was problematic was not the misplaced criticism that the policy networks approach denied that change takes place, but that the approach fails to sufficiently explain change within policy-making. If change is brought about by endogenous and/or exogenous pressures, then, the policy networks approach lacked theoretical power to explain such changes, not least because 'the distinction between exogenous and endogenous factors is difficult to sustain' (Marsh and Smith, 2000: 7). As a meso-level approach, it found itself in 'no-man's land'; it did not have the conceptual tools to explain policy change and consequently failed to understand how policy networks sponsor, resist and react to change by precisely specifying 'the mechanisms through which change occurs' (Smith, 1993: 97). In response to this static representation of policy networks, Hay and Richards developed a strategic-relational model of policy networks that recognised 'the observable sequence of network formation, development and termination' (2000: 5). Marsh and Smith offered a dialectical model of policy networks recognising 'a dialectical relationship between the network and the broader context within which it is located' (2000: 7). Both of these refinements of the policy networks model represent significant advances in understanding and explaining change within policy networks.

In conclusion, the policy networks approach is a very useful way of understanding policy-making within governance. However, its earlier conception was flawed, as outlined above, and in response to these (and other) criticisms the policy networks approach has been significantly refined. By drawing on other theoretical perspectives, plus some 'back-pedalling', the later conceptions of the policy networks model provides a relatively robust and sophisticated theory of policy-making. The policy networks approach, as a result of concerted empirical application and considerable theoretical critique, has moved from descriptive to explanatory analysis. More generally, Bevir and Rhodes used an anti-foundational approach as a way of rescuing the policy networks approach, which reduces academics to story-tellers rather than truth-spreaders, and argued (1999: 227–8):

> an anti-foundational epistemology does not treat institutions as given facts. It is a commonplace observation that even simple objects are not given to us in pure perceptions but are constructed in part by the theories we hold true of the world. . . . The social science model of networks treats them as given facts. . . . An anti-foundational approach posits that networks cannot be understood apart from *traditions*. The individuals whose beliefs, interests and actions constitute a network, necessarily acquire the relevant interests and beliefs against the background of traditions. . . . In short, an anti-foundational approach turns the current approaches to networks on their head, by insisting that networks are enacted by individuals in part through the stories they tell one another, and cannot be treated as given facts.

Rhodes further argued that 'governing structures can only be understood through the beliefs and actions of individuals' (2000: 86). The policy networks approach, therefore, is simply 'a narrative interpreted through tradition' (Bevir and Rhodes, 1999: 230), which may be challenged by other stories but there is 'no expectation there will be the one "true" account' as all stories are 'provisional' (Rhodes, 2000: 85–6). Rhodes conceded that defining governance as 'self-organizing inter-organizational networks is . . . stipulative', and the policy networks approach relies on the construction and application of 'an ideal type' (2000: 66). The task ahead is less about furthering the narrative of policy networks, and more about comparing rival narratives and constructing meta-narratives as a way of understanding policy-making. However, the policy networks approach is a very useful antidote to the belief that governance is government; more often government is only part of governance, and sometimes governance is 'governing without Government' (Rhodes, 1997: 47). The policy networks approach challenges and indeed rejects the simplistic and misplaced belief that governments govern. The extent of government within governance of, say, criminal justice is an empirical question.

References

Baggott, R. (1995) *Pressure Groups Today* (Manchester: Manchester University Press).

Benington, J. and Harvey, J. (1998) 'Transnational local authority networking within the European Union: passing fashion or new paradigm?' in Marsh, D. (ed.), *Comparing Policy Networks* (Buckingham: Open University Press).

Benson, J. K. (1982) 'A framework for policy analysis' in Rogers, D. L. and Whetten, D. A. (eds), *Interorganizational Coordination* (Ames: Iowa State University Press).

Bevir, M. and Rhodes, R. A. W. (1999) 'Studying british government: reconstructing the research agenda', *The British Journal of Politics & International Relations*, 1(2).

Bogason, P. and Toonen, T. A. J. (eds) (1998) 'Comparing networks', *Public Administration*, 76(2).

Börzel, T. A. (1998) 'Organizing babylon – on the different conceptions of policy networks', *Public Administration*, 76(2).

Castells, M. (1996) *The Rise of the Network Society* (Oxford: Blackwell).

Cloke, P., Milbourne, P. and Widdowfield, R. (2000) 'Partnership and policy networks in rural local governance: Homelessness in Taunton', *Public Administration*, 78(1).

Coleman, W. D. and Skøgstad, G. (eds) (1990) *Policy Communities and Public Policy in Canada* (Toronto: Copp Clark Pitman).

Cope, S. (1999) 'Globalisation, europeanisation and management of the British state' in Horton, S. and Farnham, D. (eds), *Public Management in Britain* (Basingstoke: Macmillan Press – now Palgrave).

Cope, S. and Goodship, J. (1999) 'Regulating collaborative government: towards joined-up government', *Public Policy and Administration*, 14(2).

Cope, S., Leishman, F. and Starie, P. (1997) 'Globalization, new public management and the enabling state: futures of police management' *The International Journal of Public Sector Management*, 10(6).

Cope, S., Starie, P. and Leishman, F. (1996) 'The politics of police reform', *Politics Review*, 5(4).

Daugbjerg, C. and Marsh, D. (1998) 'Explaining policy outcomes: integrating the policy network approach with macro-level and micro-level analysis' in Marsh, D. (ed:) *Comparing Policy Networks* (Buckingham: Open University Press).

de Bruijn, J. A. and ten Heuvelhof, E. F., (1995) 'Policy networks and governance' in Weimer, D. L. (ed:) *Institutional Design* (Boston: Kluwer).

Dowding, K. (1994) 'Policy networks: don't stretch a good idea too far' in Dunleavy, P. and Stanyer, J. (eds), *Contemporary Political Studies 1994: Volume One* (Belfast: Political Studies Association of the United Kingdom).

Dowding, K. (1995) 'Model or metaphor?: a critical review of the policy network approach' *Political Studies*, 43(1).

Dunleavy, P. and Rhodes, R. A. W. (1990) 'Core executive studies in Britain', *Public Administration*, 68(1).

Evans, M. (1998) *Policy Networks: A British Perspective* (York: Department of Politics, University of York).

Frances, J., Levačiĉ, R., Mitchell, J. and Thompson, G. (1991) 'Introduction' in Thompson, G., Frances, J., Levačiĉ, R. and Mitchell, J. (eds), *Markets, Hierarchies and Networks: The Coordination of Social Life* (London: Sage).

Gamble, A. (2000) 'Economic governance' in Pierre, J. (ed:), *Debating Governance: Authority, Steering, and Democracy* (Oxford: Oxford University Press).

Gray, C. (1994) *Government beyond the Centre: Sub-national Politics in Britain* (Basingstoke: Macmillan Press – now Palgrave).

Harrop, M. (ed.) (1992) *Power and Policy in Liberal Democracies* (Cambridge: Cambridge University Press).

Hay, C. (1998) 'The tangled webs we weave: the discourse, strategy and practice of networking' in Marsh, D. (ed.) *Comparing Policy Networks* (Buckingham: Open University Press).

Hay, C. and Richards, D. (2000) 'The tangled webs of Westminster and Whitehall: the discourse, strategy and practice of networking within the British core executive', *Public Administration*, 78(1).

Hughes, G., Mears, R. and Winch, C. (1997) 'An inspector calls? regulation and accountability in three public services', *Policy & Politics*, 25(3).

Jackson, P. M. and Stainsby, L. (2000) 'Managing public sector networked organizations', *Public Money & Management*, 20(1).

Jessop, B. (1993) 'Towards a Schumpeterian workfare state?: Preliminary Remarks on Post-Fordist Political Economy', *Studies in Political Economy*, 40: 7–39.

John, P. and Cole, A. (1998) 'Sociometric mapping techniques and the comparison of policy networks: economic decision making in Leeds and Lille' in Marsh, D. (ed.), *Comparing Policy Networks* (Buckingham: Open University Press).

Jordan, A. G. (1990) 'Sub-governments, policy communities and networks: refilling the old bottles?', *Journal of Theoretical Politics*, 2(2).

Kassim, H. (1994) 'Policy networks, networks and European Union policy making: a sceptical view', *West European Politics*, 17(4).

Kickert, W. (1993) 'Autopoiesis and the science of (public) administration: essence, sense and nonsense', *Organization Studies*, 14: 261–78.

Kickert, W. J. M., Klijn, E-H. and Koppenjan, J. F. M. (eds) (1997a) *Managing Complex Networks: Strategies for the Public Sector* (London: Sage).

Kickert, W. J. M., Klijn, E-H. and Koppenjan, J. F. M. (1997b) 'Introduction: a management perspective on policy networks' in Kickert, W. J. M., Klijn, E-H. and Koppenjan, J. F. M. (eds) *Managing Complex Networks: Strategies for the Public Sector* (London: Sage).

Klijn, E. H. (1996) 'Analyzing and managing policy processes in complex networks: a theoretical examination of the concept of policy network and its problems', *Administration and Society*, 28(1).

Knoke, D. (1990) *Political Networks: The Structural Perspective* (Cambridge: Cambridge University Press).

Knoke, D. and Kuklinski, J. H. (1991) 'Network analysis: basic concepts' in Thompson, G., Frances, J., Levačiĉ, R. and Mitchell, J. (eds), *Markets, Hierarchies and Networks: The Coordination of Social Life* (London: Sage).

Knoke, D., Pappi, F. U., Broadbent, J. and Tsujinaka, Y. (1996) *Comparing Policy Networks: Labor Politics in the U. S., Germany, and Japan* (Cambridge: Cambridge University Press).

Kooiman, J. (1993) 'Governance and governability: using complexity, dynamics and diversity' in Kooiman, J. (ed.) *Modern Governance: New Government–Society Interactions* (London: Sage).

Law, J. (1992) 'Notes on the theory of the actor-network: ordering, strategy, and heterogeneity', *Systems Practice*, 5(4).

Leishman, F., Cope, S. and Starie, P. (1995) 'Reforming the police in Britain: new public management, policy networks and a tough "old bill" ', *The International Journal of Public Sector Management*, 8(4).

Leishman, F., Cope, S. and Starie, P. (1996) 'Reinventing and restructuring: towards a "new policing order" ' in Leishman, F., Loveday, B. and Savage, S. P. (eds), *Core Issues in Policing* (Harlow: Longman).

Maidment, R. and Thompson, G. (eds) (1993) *Managing the United Kingdom: An Introduction to its Political Economy and Public Policy* (London: Sage).

Mann, M. (1984) 'The autonomous power of the state: its origins, mechanisms and results', *Archives Européennes de Sociologie*, 25(2).

Marin, B. and Mayntz, R. (eds) (1991) *Policy Networks: Empirical Evidence and Theoretical Considerations* (Boulder, Col.: Westview Press).

Marsh, D. (ed) (1998a) *Comparing Policy Networks* (Buckingham: Open University Press).

Marsh, D. (1998b) 'The development of the policy network approach' in Marsh, D. (ed.), *Comparing Policy Networks* (Buckingham: Open University Press).

Marsh, D. (1998c) 'The utility and future of policy network analysis' in Marsh, D. (ed.), *Comparing Policy Networks* (Buckingham: Open University Press).

Marsh, D. and Rhodes, R. A. W. (eds) (1992a) *Policy Networks in British Government* (Oxford: Clarendon Press).

Marsh, D. and Rhodes, R. A. W. (1992b) 'Policy communities and issue networks: beyond typology' in Marsh, D. and Rhodes, R. A. W. (eds), *Policy Networks in British Government* (Oxford: Clarendon Press).

Marsh, D. and Smith, M. (2000) 'Understanding policy networks: towards a dialectical approach', *Political Studies*, 48(1).

McLeay, E. (1998) 'Policing policy and policy networks in Britain and New Zealand' in Marsh, D. (ed.), *Comparing Policy Networks* (Buckingham: Open University Press).

Mills, M. and Saward, M. (1994) 'All very well in practice, but what about the theory?' in Dunleavy, P. and Stanyer, J. (eds), *Contemporary Political Studies 1994: Volume One* (Belfast: Political Studies Association of the United Kingdom).

Milward, H. B. and Provan, K. G. (1998) 'Measuring network structure', *Public Administration*, 76(2).

Nunan, F. (1999) 'Policy network transformation: the implementation of the EC Directive on packaging and packaging waste', *Public Administration*, 77(3).

Peters, B. G. (1993) 'Managing the hollow state' in Eliassen, K. A. and Kooiman, J. (eds), *Managing Public Organizations: Lessons from Contemporary European Experience* (London: Sage).

Peters, G. (1998) 'Policy networks: myth, metaphor and reality' in Marsh, D. (ed.), *Comparing Policy Networks* (Buckingham: Open University Press).

Peterson, J. (1995) 'Decision-making in the European Union: towards a framework for analysis' *Journal of European Public Policy*, 2(1).

Pierre, J. (2000) 'Introduction: understanding governance' in Pierre, J. (ed.), *Debating Governance: Authority, Steering, and Democracy* (Oxford: Oxford University Press).

Pierre, J. and Stoker, G. (2000) 'Towards multi-level governance' in Dunleavy, P., Gamble, A., Holliday, I. and Peele, G. (eds), *Developments in British Politics 6* (Basingstoke: Macmillan).

Raine, J. and Willson, M. (1993) *Managing Criminal Justice* (Hemel Hempstead: Harvester Wheatsheaf).

Rhodes, R. A. W. (1981) *Control and Power in Central – Local Government Relations* (Aldershot: Gower).

Rhodes, R. A. W. (1988) *Beyond Westminster and Whitehall* (London: Unwin Hyman).

Rhodes, R. A. W. (1990) 'Policy networks: A British perspective', *Journal of Theoretical Politics*, 2(3).

Rhodes, R. A. W. (1994) 'The hollowing out of the State: the changing nature of the State in Britain', *The Political Quarterly*, 65(2).

Rhodes, R. A. W. (1996) 'The new governance: governing without government', *Political Studies*, 44(4).

Rhodes, R. A. W. (1997) *Understanding Governance: Policy Networks, Governance, Reflexivity and Accountability* (Buckingham: Open University Press).

Rhodes, R. A. W. (2000) 'Governance and public administration' in Pierre, J. (ed.), *Debating Governance: Authority, Steering, and Democracy* (Oxford: Oxford University Press).

Rhodes, R. A. W. and Marsh, D. (1992) 'New directions in the study of policy networks', *European Journal of Political Research*, 21(1/2).

Ritchie, E. (1992) 'Law and order' in Harrop, M. (ed.), *Power and Policy in Liberal Democracies* (Cambridge: Cambridge University Press).

Rose, D. (1996) *In the Name of the Law: The Collapse of Criminal Justice* (London: Jonathan Cape).

Savage, S. P., Charman, S. and Cope, S. (1996) 'Police governance, the association of Chief Police Officers and constitutional change' *Public Policy and Administration*, 11(2).

Savage, S. P., Cope, S. and Charman, S. (1997) 'Reform through regulation: transformation of the public police in Britain', *The Review of Policy Issues*, 3(2).

Smith, M. J. (1993) *Pressure, Power and Policy: State Autonomy and Policy Networks in Britain and the United States* (Hemel Hempstead: Harvester Wheatsheaf).

Smith, M. J. (1999) 'Institutionalising the "eternal return": textbooks and the study of British politics', *The British Journal of Politics & International Relations*, 1(1).

Thompson, G. (1993) 'Network coordination' in Maidment, R. and Thompson, G. (eds), *Managing the United Kingdom: An Introduction to its Political Economy and Public Policy* (London: Sage).

Thompson, G., Frances, J., Levačiĉ, R. and Mitchell, J. (eds) (1991) *Markets, Hierarchies and Networks: The Coordination of Social Life* (London: Sage).

Weir, S. and Beetham, D. (1999) *Political Power and Democratic Control in Britain* (London: Routledge).

Weller, P., Bakvis, H. and Rhodes, R. A. W. (eds) (1997) *The Hollow Crown: Countervailing Trends in Core Executives* (Basingstoke: Macmillan).

Wilks, S. and Wright, M. (eds) (1987) *Comparative Government–Industry Relations* (Oxford: Clarendon Press).

2
The Bobby Lobby: Police Associations and the Policy Process

Stephen P. Savage and Sarah Charman

Introduction

There are particular sensitivities regarding the interface between British policing and the political process. Unique in the public services, policing is, at least in principle, governed by the constitutional doctrine of 'operational independence' generally referred to as *constabulary independence* (Lustgarten, 1986). While the primary thrust of this doctrine is to inhibit any attempt by external political authorities to seek to control or even influence policing policies – these are to be the exclusive province of chief police officers themselves – the *discourse* surrounding constabulary independence (Savage *et al.*, 1999) draws a more general demarcation line between the world of policing and the world of politics. Not only must politics not impinge on policing but also the police must not become embroiled in politics. The apparent *quid pro quo* of constabulary independence is the notion that the police should not in turn dabble in political affairs. However, not only is the concept of constabulary independence itself hugely contentious (Lustgarten, 1986), the idea that the British police have managed to stay aloof from politics is, to say the least, problematic.

In this chapter we trace a specific area of the involvement of the police in 'politics': the role of police associations in influencing *policy* relating to policing in particular and criminal justice in general. Against a backcloth of *non-intervention* in politics, the police have, in a variety of ways, positioned themselves as key players in the game of policy agenda-setting and policy formation. This has not always been the case. Indeed we shall argue that the 'Bobby Lobby', the more or less cohesive 'pressure group' or, more accurately 'pressure *groups*', that represent the police service, have been relative latecomers on the policy-shaping scene. More particularly, we shall demonstrate the extent to which the most senior police association, the Association of Chief Police Officers (ACPO), has developed from a fairly loose confederation of members with limited impact on the wider policy agenda, to a strategic, organised and effective force with a growing track record of policy successes. In this respect we draw from our recent research on ACPO[1] and from ongoing work on the politics of criminal justice policy-making (Charman and Savage 1999).

We shall begin with an examination of the constitution and role of each of the police professional associations before moving on to analyse the internal and external policy networks which have functioned in relation to police and criminal justice policy-making.

Rank and representation: professional associations in the British police service

An understanding of the role of representative associations within the British police service must begin with *rank*. As with the structure of police management, there is a rigid correspondence between the organisational composition of police representative associations and the rank structure of the service. The existence of a rank-based framework of professional representation has a key role in the determination of relative influence and the distribution of power within the 'police lobby'. This does not necessarily always run in the expected direction. Four bodies now reflect this framework: the Police Federation, the Police Superintendents' Association (PSA), the Association of Chief Police Officers (ACPO) and the Chief Police Officers' Staff Association (CPOSA). CPOSA was, in effect, an off-shoot of ACPO; we shall in this context deal with them together. These organisations have their counterparts in Scotland but, based on our research, we shall be considering the situation in England, Wales and Northern Ireland. Additional research needs to be undertaken to understand more about the situation in Scotland.

The Police Federation: strength in numbers?

The Police Federation acts as the body representing the 'rank-and-file' of the police service. It represents and is organised around the ranks of constable, sergeant, inspector and chief inspector. There are Central Committees for each rank, which combine to form the Joint Central Committee, the executive body of the Federation. The Federation was established as a statutory body under the Police Act 1919 in an attempt by the then Government to crush the rise of the illegal trade union which had emerged during World War I (Judge, 1994). In a real sense the Federation acts as the 'rich relative' of the police representative associations because of its sheer size and concomitant resources: it has a membership in excess of 120,000, a heavily staffed full-time Secretariat and press office, two sponsored Members of Parliament who act as spokespersons for the organisation and a monthly journal, *Police*, which presents itself as the 'Voice of the Service' (as we shall see, a claim much disputed by ACPO). Its own resources, based largely on flat-rate levies on all members, are enhanced by the arrangement whereby Federation functionaries are allowed to undertake Federation business on full- or part-secondment from their police force, effectively force sponsorship of Federation activities.

The Federation has traditionally held a position of notoriety among commentators on the police, particularly those on the left. This has rested largely on what has been seen as the complimentary 'law and order' discourses of the Federation and the Conservative Party: if the Church of England was seen as the 'Conservative Party at Prayer', the Federation could be seen as the 'Conservative Party in uniform' (Reiner, 1985). The high point in this regard, and possibly an early sign of the future blurring between policing and politics, was the infamous campaign by the Federation in the run-up to the 1979 General Election in support of 'law and order', seen by many as an open invitation to the electorate to vote Conservative (Reiner, op. cit.) . There is no doubt that the Federation has been the most *vociferous* of the police associations and has been ever ready to state its preferences on all manner of issues and not just those relating directly to policing. Beer (1955: 39; quoted in Jordan and Richardson, 1987) felt that it was more important to study the groups that had quiet but regular access to government rather than a focus on the 'noisy threats and loud demanding claims' of other groups. Yates refers to this as 'silent politics' (1982: 87; quoted in Jordan and Richardson, 1987). Therefore what is less clear is how *effective* it has been in influencing the policy agenda. While some have viewed the Federation as a darkly subversive force of reaction (Scraton, 1985), others have been more sceptical. Kettle, for example, argued that the Federation tends towards '. . . tilting at windmills, forever launching grand schemes which have no real chance of fulfilment . . . ' (Kettle 1980: 32). Brogden in a similar vein stated that 'The Federation raises issues in the public domain as a substitute for direct access to the corridors of power' (Brogden, 1982: 95).

In the wake of Federation campaigns subsequent to these judgements such assessments of the effectiveness of the Federation as a lobbying body may need to be revised. In a recent study by McLaughlin and Murji (1998) it has been argued that the Federation has over time enhanced its capacity to put its own particular version of the 'police view' across and in doing that has managed to transform its representative status. It has shifted, they claim, from being a 'toothless tiger' to becoming an influential and powerful pressure group (op. cit., 371). They present this transformation as being two-pronged. On the one hand the Federation has enhanced its *private lobbying* skills and activities. This includes direct briefing to politicians; issue-based lobbying of Members of Parliament; the creation of Federation-funded special 'advisers' in Parliament (now involving one Member of Parliament from each of the Labour and Conservative Parties – before it was just one); targeted lobbying at 'neutral' or sympathetic opinion formers; 'off-the-record' briefings to selected journalists; and the formation of *strategic alliances* with other groups on specific issues – as we shall see later, this has included the other police associations.

On the other hand, McLaughlin and Murji argue, the Federation has pursued a programme of *public campaigning*. This has included strategies such as:

(i) Protest meetings; (ii) issuing press releases; (iii) establishing a higher media profile for their annual conferences and making them more 'media' friendly; (iv) vociferous campaigning against various 'anti-police' critics; (v) submitting evidence to public inquiries, commissions and committees; and (iv) placing advertisements in newspapers to appeal to the general public on particular issues.

(ibid.)

In this respect McLaughlin and Murji trace the role of the Federation through a range of campaigns, including those linked to police pay, 'law and order' and penal policy, police complaints procedures and police powers and capital punishment (op. cit., pp. 375–386). However, even these highly public campaigns look tempered in the light of the Federation's activities during the debate on 'Sheehy'. In 1992 the then Home Secretary, Kenneth Clarke launched an inquiry into 'police roles and responsibilities', a root-and-branch review of police functions, pay and conditions of service. The inquiry reported in 1993 with a highly controversial set of recommendations for reform of the service (Home Office, 1993a). We shall return to the case of Sheehy later, when we consider police association activities around the wide-reaching police reform agenda which was formed under the Conservatives in the mid-1990s. At this point what is of note is that prior to and after the Sheehy Report was published the Federation was seen to employ the full panoply of lobbying machineries as a means or resistance and opposition to the emerging framework for reforms of police pay and conditions. This included the use of a public relations company to lobby the media, a huge protest gathering at Wembley (with over 20,000 officers in attendance), strategic alliances with other police associations, commissioned research involving academic consultants and an elaborate programme of media advertising warning of the threat posed by Sheehy to the 'fundamental traditions of British policing', including statements of support from high profile political figures (McLaughlin and Murji, op. cit., pp. 392ff.). The fact that Clarke's successor Michael Howard was at pains to distance himself from the main thrust of Sheehy, such as the support for fixed term contracts for police officers and performance related pay (Leishman *et al.*, 1996) was due in part at least to the Federation's energies in lobbying against Sheehy at every point. If ever there was a campaign which the Federation felt to be successful, it was that surrounding the Sheehy agenda. From our own research one senior member of the Federation saw the Sheehy campaign as a watershed in the organisation's lobbying capacity:

'we came of age in ... [our] ... political lobbying style ... we took on lobbyists as well as communication groups in London, so we knew who to target'.

(E51)

If the Federation has traditionally been the most *vociferous* of the police staff associations – and it can certainly enforce that with the huge resources at its disposal – what is less clear is whether it stands as the most politically *effective* of the police staff associations. As we shall see later, in recent years *ACPO* has laid claim to that mantle. In terms of policy networks, what is at issue here is the *relative* power and influence of the police associations, what might be called the 'horizontal' distribution of power *between* those associations. Increasingly integral to this distribution are the articulations of rank and the growing significance of a divide, both cultural and functional, between 'management' on the one hand and the 'workforce' on the other, a divide exacerbated by the rise and rise of 'new public management' (Leishman *et al.*, 1996). With reference to the relationship between the Federation and ACPO, a senior Federation member interviewed as part of our research referred to ACPO's attitude as 'the philosophy that "I'm the boss and you're the workers"'' (E51). In this respect we can now move on up the 'rank hierarchy' and consider the role of the PSA.

The PSA – 'piggy-in-the-middle'?

The PSA was formed in 1920 and currently has a membership of approximately 1,500 officers of the ranks of superintendent and chief superintendent (a membership much reduced over recent years with the shedding of superintendent's posts as part of the drive to 'de-tier' police management). The work and activities of the PSA have not attracted a great deal of attention from observers of British policing, perhaps some recognition that the organisation in a sense sits 'in between' its sister associations. It cannot compete easily with the size and resource-base of the Federation nor can it boast the level of seniority of ACPO. Brogden has expressed it thus:

> Neither the master or servant, the Police Superintendents' Association can at most only make a marginal contribution to the development of the power of the police institution within the state.
>
> (Brogden, 1982: 64)

The PSA in this sense suffers a structural weakness as the 'piggy-in-the-middle' of the police staff associations. However, we should be careful not to underestimate the influence which the PSA has had on policy-making, particularly in recent years. The police reform agenda of the mid-1990s, embracing everything from police pay and conditions of service through roles and responsibilities to police accountability, created fertile ground on which all of the police associations could set out their wares and the PSA was no exception. This was soon coupled with a growing tendency of politicians to take heed of the 'police view' on all matters relating to criminal justice policy, a tendency symbolised above all by the then Home Secretary Michael Howard but matched speech-by-speech by his opposite number in the Labour Party, Jack Straw. What emerged was an environment in which the associations found themselves being courted by senior politicians bent on appearing to support the forces of law and order (Charman, and Savage 1999). As doors were being opened the PSA was quick to step inside.

It is never clear whether an organisation's 'success' in the lobbying business is due to environmental factors – in this case an environment more receptive to the 'police view' – or factors relating to the organisation itself such as the growing 'professionalism' of its representative capacities. Government through its policy changes may adopt ideas and suggestions from a pressure group but this does not translate into success for the group. Pluralists, in particular, tend to ignore the notion of ideology within politics (Smith, 1990, 1993), a group's policy ideals may 'fit in' with the ideology of the government – who then is success-ful? For example consider the supposed 'success' of the Institute of Directors during Thatcher's period as Prime Minister (Holliday, 1993). If success within pressure group activity is, in part, having coincidental interests then the resources of that group (financial or otherwise) become less relevant. In that case, Ryan argues that it is not the resources of the group that are important but its 'clout' (1978: 13). This has as many implications for the large and heavily financially resourced Federation as it does for the smaller and less well financially resourced PSA and ACPO.

It has been argued (as with the other police associations) that the PSA has 'geared up' its lobbying activities and political skills in recent years. A senior PSA role holder interviewed as part of our research argued it thus:

> In recent years, not to put too fine a point on it, we've [the Super-intendents' Association] moved from a fairly benign officers' dining club, more than anything else, to becoming a ... proactive organisa-tion which is able to exert considerable influence not only on po-licing but on conditions of service ... and the criminal justice system generally. ... We have had to turn around from basically being inno-cuous ... to being what we consider we are now, a major influence on policing in general.
>
> (E31)

The implication here is that in so far as there has been an increase in the PSA's influence over policing and criminal justice policy, this has not simply been the result of a more receptive environment but is also an expression of a more proactive and concerted organisational approach to the art of lobbying. Of course, we need to be cautious about such claims; there is perhaps an inbuilt tendency of senior role holders of an organisation to portray that organisation as being more effective than it had been in the past – it is in a sense self-supporting to do so! However, there does seem to be a plausible case here. Certainly in terms of *media* exposure, the PSA did score quite heavily in the law and order debates of the mid-to late-1990s.

It was certainly noticeable that the President of the PSA throughout this period, Brian McKenzie, made more radio and television appearances than either of his equivalents in the Federation and ACPO. This was clearly something of which the PSA was proud, as our interviewee in this area made clear:

> A recent example is where Dimbleby wanted someone on his programme and it was Brian McKenzie, our President, who went on as opposed to somebody from the Federation or somebody from ACPO.
>
> (E31)

This competitiveness can also be seen by ACPO who have argued,

> when was the last time you heard Fred Broughton [Federation Chairman] on *Today*?
>
> (E11)

However, while we would argue that appearance on *Question Time* or Radio 4's *Today* programme is not in itself a performance indicator of media effectiveness, it is difficult to deny that the President of the PSA or one of his colleagues were frequently allowed air space and column inches to state their views and preferences on a wide range of issues, some of them only indirectly concerned with policing. It was apparent as well that the 'PSA line' on such matters had a tendency to find its way to the ears of senior politicians. Undoubtedly part of the reason for this rested with the personal media skills of McKenzie himself. The fact that on retirement he was made a life peer by the new Labour Prime Minister could be seen as some measure of that! It will be interesting to see whether this high profile scheme of the PSA will be able to continue with a different character at the helm. Nevertheless, there is an important *organisational* phenomena here which could be significant to pressure group analysis, at least as it applies to the police.

We have made the point that the PSA lacks both the size of the Federation and the seniority of ACPO, factors which together could act to diminish its 'clout' in pressure group terms. However, these very 'disadvantages' could in other senses act as sources of organisational strength. There are group theorists who believe that organisation is far more important than size (Richardson and Jordan 1979) and those who argue for the importance of small groups (Grant, 1984). Smaller groups can be more effective than larger groups because of the pressure to contribute in a small group whereas in a large group anonymity can result in inaction (Olson, 1971). So on the one hand the *smallness* of the

PSA can enable it to move quickly, particularly in rapid response to a crisis or the sudden emergence of a new policy agenda – something that was happening frequently during the police reform era of the mid-1990s. What this means is that, unlike a large and complex organisation like the Federation, which represents tiers of police ranks with potentially conflicting interests, the PSA does not have to 'refer back' to the central Executive before any commitment is made or any view expressed. A high degree of autonomy is granted to key role holders in taking the lead on key issues, as the senior PSA respondent stated:

> What actually happens is that we are given the discretion by the National Executive Committee to make decisions on the hoof.
>
> (E31)

On the other hand this very discretion benefits the PSA relative to ACPO precisely because of its *lack of seniority*. As we shall see, a crucial feature of ACPO as an organisation is the constraining effect of the discretionary powers of individual chiefs over the formation and adoption of 'collective' policing policy. Because of the doctrine of 'constabulary independence' (Savage *et al.*, 1999) chiefs frequently assert their right to individually judge each and every matter of policing policy and decide upon its merit. The whole machinery of ACPO policy-making is skewed to take heed of this 'right of *chiefs*'. One consequence of this is that the President of ACPO and even the ACPO Executive would never take it upon themselves to formulate ACPO policy without full reference back to the full committee of chiefs – Chief Constables' Council – and even policy thus approved can be subject to non-compliance by individual chiefs. What this means is that the sort of 'policy-making on the hoof' open to the PSA and the Federation would be unthinkable in the context of ACPO. Olson (1971) argued that groups which existed for reasons in addition to their pressure group role (for insurance, access to facilities, employee protection, etc.), as the Federation and the PSA do, required less consultation than other groups. His 'by-product' theory stated that leaders of these groups can act without the consent of its members in the knowledge that members will tend not to leave the organisation in protest. Salisbury (1984) supplements this by adding that leadership of these groups is more autonomous and that the actions of these leaders are less likely to be justified for membership approval. The result is a 'captive membership' (Olson, 1971: 133). We shall return to this issue concerning ACPO later. At this point what is of relevance is that this 'discretionary freedom' gives the PSA a distinct advantage in responding immediately to new agendas, particularly in terms of responding at short notice to media requests for comment and a 'party line' on this or that matter of policing and criminal justice policy. It enables the Association to keep itself in the media spotlight at times when ACPO would be forced to adopt a low-profile or non-committal stance. It would be interesting to determine the extent to which this pressure-group variant of the theses that 'small is beautiful' has resonance for other policy sectors.

It is, however, only in recent years that this organisational advantage in so far as it exists has been brought to bear. As with the Federation's 'coming of age' in terms of lobbying skills and activities, the Sheehy agenda appears to have been the major spur for this. The PSA had much at stake with Sheehy: one of the central proposals of the Sheehy Report was to abolish the rank of Chief Superintendent, one of the two ranks represented by the PSA. The reform agenda more widely pointed to the 'thinning out' of middle management within the police service – a process which was directed more than anything at the superintendent level of the police organisation. The PSA were spurred into action as a result and were forced at short notice to sharpen their lobbying skills. This entailed the adoption of a higher media profile, mainly through the public presence of the PSA's President, as we have seen, together with direct lobbying of politicians and members of the House of Lords – who happened to have in their ranks a small number of retired senior police officers (who were also to prove useful to ACPO). The main focus of this campaign was on retaining the middle management ranks threatened by Sheehy. Ironically, it could be argued that it was the Federation rank of chief inspector, rather than the rank of chief superintendent – for both were seen as disposable in the Sheehy Report – which was to become the PSA's success story. It has been claimed that, in effect, the PSA were given a choice between the two by supporters in the Lords ('one or the other could be saved') and in the end the association opted for the chief inspector rank:

> We saved the rank of chief inspector. Absolutely down to the Superintendents' Association that was... when the *Police and Magistrates' Court Act* wanted to abolish the ranks, we argued long and hard that was a step that shouldn't be taken. We wish we could have saved the chief superintendent rank as well but we weren't successful. We certainly saved the chief inspector rank.
>
> (E31)

While the other associations may also claim some responsibility for this 'success', there seems little doubt that the noise created by the PSA had at least some impact on the eventual policy outcome. This taste of the lobbying action became an acquired one. As was to be the case with ACPO, as we shall see, the police-focused successes over Sheehy were to act as a spur to more wide-ranging and diffuse campaigns by the PSA. The Association successfully campaigned for the establishment of a 'paedophile register', a local listing of sex offenders convicted of offences against children which could be used to monitor their movements and actions of those listed. The PSA also took a lead role in the shaping of gun controls and in particular controls on the possession of handguns (in the wake of the massacre of 16 children in Dunblane, Scotland). In both cases the PSA was quick to pounce on the opportunities presented by huge public concern and high intensity media coverage of the issues and stamp its mark on the emerging policy agendas. Relative success had bred relative success.

These cases notwithstanding, it is important not to overstate the PSA's role in the policing policy network. It is perhaps best to depict the PSA as more of a 'policy-sniper' than an 'policy-shaper', able to score on specific but relatively marginal targets but not well placed to take a leading role in police policy-making more generally. It is *ACPO* which has positioned itself most effectively in this role.

The ACPO: the view from the top

If the Federation has acquired notoriety in the eyes of some for its vociferous and *high profile* campaigning (typically in pursuit of anti-liberal causes – opposition to new police complaints procedures, support for capital punishment, etc.), ACPO has attracted critical attention over its *covert* activities. The concern over ACPO has been less about 'tub thumping' than about 'behind the scenes' agenda-setting and lobbying. For example, Geoffrey Robertson, writing in the late 1980s, claimed that:

> ACPO . . . has become the most powerful club in the country, promoting policies agreed amongst its members, resisting attempts to introduce measures for accountability and *actively entering the political arena*. . . . It reports directly to the Home Secretary, and has the capacity to become a centralised intelligence agency, without any charter to limit its operations.
>
> (Robertson 1989; 24–5; emphasis added)

The image painted here is of an organisation working concertedly but discreetly in the corridors of power to shape the policy agenda in what it considers to be its best interests. This was a common reading of the role and activities of ACPO throughout the 1980s, particularly in relation to controversies over local accountability of the police (Jefferson and Grimshaw, 1984; Scraton, 1985). We have challenged this view as an overstatement of the capacity of ACPO, at least in the past, to act cohesively and effectively in pursuit of any apparent goals (Savage, *et al.*, 1996). Our own research has revealed that, on the contrary, ACPO's history has been one of *disunity* rather than cohesion (Savage and Charman, 1996). This applied both to ACPO's ability to hold its own members together in adopting common policing policies across individual police forces (Savage, *et al.*, 1996) and its capacity to conduct united and strategic campaigning in terms of its external representational activities. ACPO members revealed to us their concerns that all too often ACPO had been side-stepped and outmanoeuvred when it came to public campaigning, particularly in comparison to their main rival for media attention, the Federation. For example, one commented that:

> when something happened they [the media] would go to the Federation and whoever was the Secretary of the Federation would speak for the country's police service.
>
> (M38)

That the body representing the 'rank-and-file' could enjoy more media attention than ACPO, representing the 'police elite', was clearly a cause of much frustration:

> we get infuriated by the Federation being known as the voice of the service.
>
> (M15)

If this was the case, it has become less a source of concern over time. Most ACPO members were of the view that in recent years ACPO had managed to position itself much more effectively in terms of media exposure and political impact. Again, this is presented in terms of the relative influence of ACPO in relation to the Federation. As one member stated:

> I think ACPO is now far more powerful and influential in terms of the media than it ever was. I think the Home Secretary and the media are

far more likely to go to talk to the President [of ACPO] about the issues of the day than they would to talk to the Chairman of the Federation.

(M18)

We would argue that both in terms of the *relative* influence of ACPO as a campaigning group *vis-à-vis* the Federation and the *absolute* effectiveness of the organisation in shaping the policy-agenda, ACPO has become a much bigger player in recent years. More specifically, as we shall make clear later, ACPO has managed to shift from the position of relative *outsider* in the policy process to one very much as an *insider* (Grant, 1989). This transformation became most apparent during the police reform agenda of the mid-1990s, but has its roots in the key organisational changes which took place some years before.

It has been stated that ACPO, at least as far as its own members were concerned (Savage and Charman, 1996), had traditionally been a somewhat fragmented and disunited body unable to 'get its act together' (ibid.). This situation was to change with a number of developments which took place from the late 1980s onwards which were to have a significant impact on ACPO's capacity to launch effective campaigns and run lobbying activities. The first was the creation of what we have termed the 'presumption in favour of compliance', an important internal reform which enabled ACPO as a body to more effectively bring its members 'into line' and thus 'professionalise' ACPO by making it more cohesive. This was due mainly to the Presidency of Peter Wright, Chief Constable of South Yorkshire in the 1980s and past President of ACPO (1988–89). Faced with the scenario in which individual chief constables frequently departed from 'ACPO policy' and forged policy within their own force irrespective of ACPO's own national policies, Wright argued that there were some areas of policing policy where it was essential to have consistency across the service and not a multitude of different policies force-by-force. He established the principle that once a particular policy at committee level had been duly discussed and then ratified at Chief Constables' Council, a chief would be bound by that policy in his or her force unless that chief wrote to the President of the day explaining the reasons why this was not possible. This shift was most significant as a step towards the greater influence of ACPO over *internal* policy-making, i.e. in terms of increasing the influence of ACPO over its own members by bringing chiefs more and more into line over force-level policy formation and moving away from permissiveness in ACPOs approach to policy-compliance (Savage and Charman, 1996; Charman *et al.*, 1998; Savage, Cope and Charman, 1997). However, the 'presumption in favour of compliance', by asserting the importance of a collective approach to policy-making, also enabled ACPO to present a 'party-line' to the *external* world, something crucial to public campaigning.

Following closely on the heels of this development was the second key organisational development within ACPO, the establishment of a permanent Secretariat of ACPO. For one past president of ACPO, this was seen as vital:

> you'd find yourself with a letter, probably dictated two weeks previously but not posted or shifted down for various opinions or signatures, requiring you to respond in about three days and that was part of the reason why I saw a need to try and strengthen the Secretariat...
>
> (P09)

Established in 1989 on the recommendations of a Home Affairs Select Committee and with the strong support of the then Home Secretary Douglas Hurd, the full-time Secretariat, part funded by the Home Office, began to more professionally coordinate the work of the Association and harmonise its internal and external processes. One dimension of this is *media management*, organised through the ACPO Information Office. This Office manages responses to requests from the media for information and comment and also maintains close links with information offices around the forces with the aim of presenting a 'common face' to the media and with developing a more *proactive* approach to media management. The origins of this could be found in a paper written by ACPO in the mid-1980s entitled *A Clearer Voice for ACPO*, which had stressed the 'mistakes of the past' and which argued for a much more proactive approach to media relations. It acknowledged ACPO's past 'delayed, diversified or sometimes non-existent response to media demands' and warned of the dangers of a slow response to the media:

> Delay allows inaccuracies in stories to become established in the public mind and other voices are heard instead. These may be the voices of staff associations, with a particular angle to push or lacking in some aspects of finesse...

This was a clear enough reference to ACPO's media key rivals, the Police Federation. It took some years before the paper's message was put into effect. This stressed the need for an information base of statistics, common lines of criticism and agreed lines of response. Each ACPO committee, it was argued, should have a media strategy item placed on every agenda. A list of agreed media 'voices' was also seen as essential and the report continued in this vein right through to the recommendation of news release headed stationery. In 1994 the establishment of the Media Advisory Group, a free standing body with a link to the Presidential team made clear ACPO's commitment to an informed media strategy. Tactically, this has included the national distribution of 'fact sheets', for example, a series entitled *Your Police*, the first one *A Service to Value* which presented the case that the police service is good 'value for money' and which was aimed at increasing public support for the police, at a time when economies and efficiency-savings within the police were creeping up higher on the Government's agenda (ACPO, 1994). Following on such diffuse campaigns was the publication of the more strategic document *In Search of Criminal Justice*. This set out, in effect, a 'shopping list' of the criminal justice changes ACPO wished to see introduced, including advance disclosure of the main platform of the defence case and changes to the rules of evidence to admit previous convictions and hearsay, measures heavily opposed by civil liberties bodies and criminal lawyers (ACPO, 1995). The publication of this document signalled more than any other the arrival of a *proactive* campaigning strategy for ACPO in place of the primarily reactive approach of earlier ACPO activities. Following on from this, ACPO produced *In Search of Justice: Three Years On*, which provided a progress report of the 'shopping list' plus some new proposals which included thirty-one recommendations for the future of the criminal justice system (ACPO, 1998). We shall return to this issue later.

In addition to the newly empowered Information Office, the media management strategy within ACPO embraced programmes of media training for its members, such as 'Media Skills', 'Broadcasting Skills' and 'Facing the Press'. This new approach to the media enabled ACPO to 'compete' more effectively with the Police Federation whose media and public relations machinery was already firmly in place. This process also involved persuading reluctant ACPO members that they could comment on an issue that was not only related to their force area. This has meant that increasingly ACPO members have been made available to respond to media requests, so that the media do not simply have to turn to the Federation, who were always be there to offer what one member called 'red meat'!

However, a third recent organisational development within ACPO may prove to be the most significant in the long term, at least in terms of ACPO's position as a police pressure-group: campaigning: the split of ACPO into two distinct bodies, a 'staff association' and a 'professional body'. Until 1994 ACPO acted both as a staff association, concerned with its members pay and conditions of service, and a body which developed policing policy and which represented the 'professional' view of the police. Pressure for change within the organisation had been apparent for a considerable amount of time but it was only in late 1993 that a paper was submitted to the ACPO Autumn Conference with firm recommendations and agendas for reform. The paper was presented by the General Secretary, Marcia Barton and was entitled, *'The future structure of ACPO – professional advisers, staff association or both?'*. The thrust of the paper and indeed the rationale behind the move was that better co-ordination was needed of the work of the Association and that the professional appearance of ACPO to outsiders needed to be improved, especially with regard to the Home Office. There was a need to improve the role and status of ACPO as a professional body; the need for a clearer distinction between the professional and staff association; a better way of doing business with the Home Office and the need for funding arrangements to enable both functions to be carried out adequately. Splitting the organisation into two quite distinct bodies which would create 'clear blue water' between the staff and professional wings was presented as the main option in this regard. After much debate, proposals to split the organisation and enhance the central Secretariat were put to the membership and were endorsed. 'ACPO' would from this point focus on the 'professional/policy' side of policing while the CPOSA was to be responsible for pay, conditions and so on. Underpinning support for the split was the acceptance of the logic of distinguishing, for the sake of the outside world, chief officers' professional *interests* (i.e. pay and conditions) from professional *'judgement'* (i.e. policy decisions and policy preferences). With this framework established, ACPO could then present the case that while the Federation and the PSA acted primarily with their own 'interests' at heart when they adopted their position on this or that policy, ACPO, now free from such 'vested interests', was the only body genuinely concerned with the service *as a whole*. In the discourse of public campaigning ACPO could claim that it alone had its hands 'clean' of narrow, sectoral interests. We shall return to this later.

   The final organisational development within ACPO, although one related to more specific circumstances (ie the police reform agenda of the mid-1990s), has been the establishment of *strategic alliances*. With policy arenas becoming increasingly overcrowded, governments are more than happy to reduce the nmubers of groups that they need to consult. Close knit policy communities have extremely restricted access so the fewer the groups within them the more successful the policy community is likely to be (Smith, 1993). McRobbie (1994) lists 'alliances' as one of the four requirements for pressure politics. These 'strategic alliances' have been established with other national bodies, in furtherance of campaigns around policing and criminal justice issues. These alliances involved a number of sectors (including 'internal' alliances with the Federation and the PSA over the Sheehy agenda), but most notably, ACPO chose to work closely with the local authority associations (LAAs), such as the Association of County Councils (ACC) and the Association of Metropolitan Authorities (AMA), during the debate over aspects of the Police and Magistrates' Courts Act 1994 (PMCA). This Act offered plenty of scope for ACPO and the LAAs to find common ground – most obviously, over the threat to the 'local' element in the accountability structure (Loveday, 1995). In this respect the leadership of ACPO effectively 'bought into' the established political skills and political networks of the LAAs as it sought to amend certain dimensions of the planned reform of the police authorities. One past president interviewed as part of our research said:

> We didn't have any experience in lobbying at all in the Houses of Parliament; the ACC and the AMA had considerable experience in that and so we worked well with them...which created this enormously powerful alliance of interests, and that still exists.
>
> (PO4)

As we shall see later, there are certain ironies associated with such alliances (not least because they entailed ACPO 'getting into bed' with former adversaries!), but it does seem to be the case that they have had a longer-term effect on ACPO's capacity to undertake public and political campaigning, as the above statement implies. Political skills were acquired during the police reform debate of the mid-1990s which ACPO was to employ again.

An overall assessment of the status of ACPO within the police policy-network would, on the basis of the developments outlined above, point to an incremental but relatively short-term process by which the organisation has enhanced its capacity to influence the police and criminal justice policy agenda. In comparison with the reactive and often disorganised and inhibited approach to pressure-group activity which characterised the 1980s, ACPO has developed into a much more proactive and concerted lobbying machine as the 1990s have progressed. Undoubtedly the heated environment of the police reform agenda of the mid-1990s helped to boost that process of development, but it was a process which, as we shall see, was well underway already.

Looking across the three police associations as they have operated during the 1990s there appears to be a common theme. Each body claims to have enhanced its own capacity to lobby and campaign on the policing and criminal justice front and to have competed more effectively with the other police associations within the policing policy network in the battle to represent the 'police view'. In this respect two notes of caution should be stated. Firstly, there is something of an 'organisational imperative' for senior figures within representative bodies to claim to have overseen a process of 'professionalisation' of that body. This can take the shape of comparing a relatively unsuccessful past with a much more effective present, which in turn reflects posi- tively on the figures who were at the helm during that process. We should for this reason be circumspect about such claims; analysis must assess the evidence that such enhancement has taken place. Secondly, we should not underestimate the extent to which the environment of the early to mid-1990s was one in which the 'police view', however and by whoever it was articulated, was virtually guaranteed to have been well received (Charman and Savage, 1999). The political contest between the Conservative and Labour parties in the long run-up to the 1997 General Election was one which frequently embraced 'law and order politics' (ibid.); the parties competed for the title of 'toughest on crime' and in that environment the 'police view' was one sought out at every point. As a consequence the police associations were courted by senior figures in both of the main parties, who were more than ready to appear at the annual police association conferences and pledge their support for the police. In this respect whether any increased 'influence' of the police associations is due primarily to their own endeavours or to a more receptive environment is a question we should constantly bear in mind.

These issues notwithstanding, we shall now proceed to draw more general conclusions about the role of the police representative associ- ations within the police and criminal justice policy network.

Caught in the act: police capture of the policy agenda

We would argue that the police staff associations and ACPO in particu- lar, have, over the past decade or so, managed to relocate their position within the criminal justice policy network. The 'Bobby Lobby' has enhanced its status as a player with influence over the policy agenda and, significantly, that influence has extended beyond the *policing* policy agenda and has penetrated more effectively than before the wider *criminal justice* policy agenda. The pattern which the relocation of the police lobby has taken is directional: it takes the form of a three-stage movement, from *agenda-resistance*, through *agenda re-shaping* to *agenda setting*. This movement has been uneven and does not lend itself easily to periodisation, but it is, we would argue, a movement evident in *policy outcomes*. We shall argue this case in two ways. First, we will attempt to identify the *policy networks* which have configured the policy agendas in question. Secondly, we shall examine the *discourses* which have been employed as instruments in the policy-shaping process, discourses which constitute part of the *technique* of policy-shaping.

From agenda-resistance to agenda-setting: forming the policing policy network.

If there has been a discernable movement in the effectiveness of the police lobby, that has been due largely to the role adopted by ACPO within the police staff associations as increasingly the lead body in the representation of the 'police view'. By means of the organisational mechanisms outlined earlier, ACPO has strategically and successfully relocated itself within the policing and criminal justice policy-networks to occupy a position more centre-stage than had ever been the case. In that sense the path of ACPO's ascendancy involved two major steps. First, ACPO set out its stall *internally* by deliberately attempting to present itself as *the* police professional association. The split within ACPO between the 'staff association' and 'professional' wings of the organisation's roles referred to above was a crucial element in that strategy. By seeming to separate out the 'professional police view' from 'vested interests', ACPO could more easily distinguish itself from the other police associations whose interventions and posturings could, when convenient, be labelled as sectoral and interest-driven. According to this logic, only ACPO – now stripped of its organic connection with its own members' interests in terms of pay and conditions – could advance itself as the only essentially *'professional'* police association, one which could thus speak on behalf of the *whole* service. It was also, of course, the *senior* association in terms of police rank. In terms of gaining legitimacy, these rationalisations could be powerful instruments. The second step was *externally* oriented. It was to move the organisation from a *reactive* approach to policy-shaping to one that was increasingly *proactive*. As pressure group theorists have long argued, in order to be 'successful' groups need to be organised in two ways – internal organisation and organisation in terms of contact with government (Richardson and Jordan, 1979). Not content with being more or less effective in combatting policy-agendas set in motion by other parties outside of the police service, ACPO began to adopt an approach which more and more took the initiative in policy formation. We shall develop this argument by means of specific areas of police-related public policy and present the activities and ACPO and to a lesser extent the other police associations in terms of three configurations of policy-shaping as they have emerged during the 1990s. These cannot be easily or accurately articulated in a temporal framework as they were to an extent co-terminus; however, the incremental and directional nature of the shifts in question allow some form of periodisation.

Phase one: agenda resistance

There is little doubt that the policing policy agenda which emerged during the early 1990s constituted a serious threat to the status quo of the British police service. Having enjoyed very much a privileged position within the public sector throughout the 1980s in terms of levels of funding and non-interference in the management of its affairs, there were clear signs that government had now reached the point of 'the party's over'(Savage and Nash, 2001). Conservative ministers were beginning to become restless that there appeared to no clear 'pay off' for the years of generous funding directed at the police service and pointed to continuing rises in recorded crime as evidence that the police were failing to deliver. It was in this context that Kenneth Clarke took over as Home Secretary. Clarke was noted for his refusal to treat public sector professional bodies with kid gloves and was quite prepared to 'tough it out' with what he clearly saw as bastions of self interest. This was apparent in his approach to his first Police Federation conference as Home Secretary in 1992, when he threatened to undermine tradition by not attending. He said to the Federation Chairman:

> I didn't go to the teachers conference, not the BMA's. I don't have to go to yours. I've looked up my legal obligations towards the Federation. I am only obliged to consult you. No more no less.
> (Quoted in Judge, 1994: 468)

This 'cooling down' of relationships between the Conservatives and the police was to become more apparent with the police reform agenda which emerged, initially at least, under Clarke. As has been mentioned, amongst other things this entailed the Sheehy Inquiry on police pay and conditions which set out to challenge in fundamental ways some of the basic arrangements for the employment of police officers. The absence of any police representative on the Sheehy team signalled the tone of the Inquiry; quite clearly the police service was in for a shock. In policy terms this was to take the form of recommendations for *fixed-term contracts* for officers and support for schemes to introduce *performance-related pay*, both designed to strengthen the 'right to manage' within the police and overhaul the rewards and sanctions framework of the service.

There is little doubt that the police representative bodies had been 'side-stepped' by Sheehy and forced onto the defensive; the new agenda was dominated by employment philosophies which took little notice of tradition and showed no sympathy with precedent. However, the speed and effectiveness with which they responded to the agenda thus *imposed* was to prove crucial. In this respect what was at issue was the capacity to launch a campaign of *agenda resistance* and in that sense the police associations did so by means of an *intra-organisational policy network*. ACPO, the Police Federation and the Superintendents' Association, operating as an *internal policy network*, began to work together to challenge, oppose and undermine the Sheehy agenda. Fixed term contracts and performance related pay were to be the main targets of this campaign. Joint platforms and shared information and research furthered the capacity of the associations to lobby against the introduction of such measures within the police, on the grounds that they would fundamentally alter the type of service which has been the tradition of British policing (McClaughlin and Murji op.cit.). That the Conservatives eventually dropped both schemes (at least for all non-ACPO tanks) bore witness to the effectiveness of that campaign – although the subsequent arrival of Michael Howard as Home Secretary, noticeably more 'pro-police', played its part (Savage and Nash, 2001). ACPO itself played a key role, as one ACPO member interviewed expressed it:

> When we were most under attack from Sheehy...you saw ACPO as a fairly strong lobby breaching the political line...we did I think become a very strong political lobby at all levels...with local MPs and local politicians and very successfully so.
>
> (M06)

Whichever way, there is little doubt that Sheehy forced the police associations into what another member described as 'on the back foot defending our position' (P06). What was at issue here was their ability to *resist* agenda set by others. The early- to mid-1990s were also to witness the capacity of the associations, and ACPO in particular, to *shape* or at least *re-shape* agendas.

Phase two: agenda re-shaping

Alongside the reform agenda directed at police officers' pay and conditions was another, overlapping agenda concerned with the structures of *police governance, police management* and *police roles and responsibilities.* During the early to mid-1990s two major reviews were undertaken which set out to challenge in radical ways the reorganisation of British policing, the White Paper *Police Reform: A Police Service for the 21st Century* (Home Office, 1993b) and *Review of Core Ancillaries and Responsibilities* (Home Office, 1995), known generally as the Posen Inquiry. The White Paper and Posen were intended to undermine the status quo of British policing in different but fundamental ways; both were to be blunted by the concerted efforts of the police associations in general and ACPO in particular.

The White Paper was concerned primarily with the question of police governance and set in motion what was to become the Police and Magistrates' Courts Bill (1993) and eventually the PMCA. It is difficult to overstate the strength of opposition to the White Paper's key proposals and to doubt that they sent shock waves throughout the police establishment and beyond. The two central issues were on the one hand the plans to reform the local police authorities by reducing them in size and by replacing part of the directly elected element by 'independent members', and on the other the plan to create new powers for the Home Secretary to set out 'national objectives' for the police service. These proposals opened up the Government to attack (Loveday, 1995) that it was guilty of both diminishing the *local* nature of policing, by reducing the involvement of local councillors on the police authorities, and at the same time by *centralising* controls over the police through the new powers of the Home Secretary not only to set national objectives but also to select the chairs of the new police authorities. Senior police officers saw in these proposals therefore a dual threat to their position: the Home Secretary would be able to *impose* policing objectives and thus reduce their own discretion to determine policy; the externally appointed chairs to the police authorities could overturn established working relationships between chief officers and their local chairpersons, relationships which had allowed considerable autonomy to those chief officers.

The response of chief officers to the emerging agenda was concerted and effective. As has already been stated, ACPO sought out and formed *strategic alliances* with LAAs and key figures in both Houses of Parliament to put pressure on the Government to pull back from some elements of the Police and Magistrates' Bill. With their partners in the campaign they forced concessions from the Home Secretary over the selection of chairs to the police authorities – these would now be selected locally – and the setting of national objectives, which would now only be formed after formal consultation with chief officers themselves. These were seen as at least partial victories over the policy agenda as originally set out. The 'lobbying' had paid off, as one member put it:

> the new Police Act had a lot more teeth and a lot more danger in its draft form . . . there was an awful lot of lobbying which went on with local MP's and local politicians and . . . very successfully so. Probably quite worryingly so from the Home Office perspective.
>
> (M06)

There appeared to have been a subtle shift in comparison to the response to Sheehy: ACPO were now *re-shaping* the policy agenda and moving on the *offensive* as a campaigning body. A central mechanism of this was the *policy network* involving ACPO, the local authority associations and key allies in the Houses of Parliament. Without this network it is difficult to imagine that the Home office would have been forced to concede in the way it did on central platforms of its legislative plans.

The re-shaping process was to become even more apparent in relation to Posen. The Inquiry set out to identify policing functions which were 'core' in the sense that they could only be undertaken by sworn police officers and those which could be classified as 'ancillary' and which potentially could be undertaken by other bodies and agencies, perhaps through 'out sourcing'. Chief officers initially saw in this agenda the spectre of 'stripping' down the police service and of the privatisation of policing functions; again a campaign was launched by ACPO, using the same allies assembled against the PMCA, to counter this threat. What transpired was that, almost by a process of stealth, ACPO managed to position itself in the Inquiry in such a way as to gain a significant degree of *ownership* of the eventual recommendations contained in Posen. Key ACPO members were granted full participation in the proceedings and allowed not only to comment on but to take an active role in the drafting of particular sections of the Inquiry Report. Indeed, ACPO effectively provided much of the 'research' on which the final recom-

mendations of Posen were based. ACPO's own preferences on core and
ancillary functions were clearly evident in the final report (see Leishman, *et al.*, 1996). As with PMCA, the final outcome of the Posen agenda
was considerably less threatening to the status quo of policing than
might have been the case. It is appropriate to view this as a process of
agenda-reshaping rather than straightforward *agenda-resistance*; ACPO
was in this case fully and actively on the *inside* of policy-formation
and not, as with Sheehy, forced to defend *ex post facto*.

The successes over the PMCA and Posen were, however, over concessions forced from agendas *imposed* on the police service. Throughout
and subsequent to these campaigns ACPO was also moving strategically
into the business of *agenda-setting*.

Phase three: agenda-setting

There is something of a paradox in the lobbying track record of ACPO
and the other police associations as it unfolded through the 1990s. In
relation to issues pertaining directly to the police service, such as pay
and conditions, roles and responsibilities and police governance, they
were forced on the defensive and managed at best to re-shape agendas
set by others. Yet in relation to areas less within their remit of responsibility and control the police associations have to some extent been more
successful in actually *setting agendas* for others to respond to. Nowhere is
this more apparent than in relation to the highly controversial debate
over the *right to silence*. The background to this lies with ACPO's handling of the Royal Commission on Criminal Justice (RCCJ, 1993), known
generally as the Runciman Commission.

ACPO's tactical response to the launch of Runciman, set up in the
wake of a series of miscarriages of justice in the 1979s and 1980s, contrasts sharply with the organisation's earlier approach to the Royal
Commission on Criminal Procedure (RCCP) set up almost a decade
before, again a response in part to concerns over abuses of police powers
and the miscarriages of justice which followed. ACPO did submit evidence to the *RCCP* on issues like police powers and the rights of suspects
but it did so more on the basis of stated *preferences* than on the basis of a
constructed *case*. There was no apparent strategic or tactical approach to
the emerging agenda, more a defensive and negative *resistance* to the
proposed changes to police powers which were winning support within
the Commission. It was not until the Commission's recommendations
were drafted into legislative from that ACPO and the other police associations really began to mobilise. With Runciman, however, ACPO
adopted a very different strategy: it decided to *steer* the agenda, to

some extent, in the direction which it preferred and to operate *pro-actively* by deciding both what it wanted out of the Commission and how it was to achieve it. This was reflected in the use of 'evidence' and 'research' in support of its preferences, something which had clearly not been employed in response to the RCCP. One Past President of ACPO compared the two different approaches as well:

> whereas a couple of years ago we would have probably grumbled about what we saw as major deficiencies in the criminal justice system, now we proactively try to get something done about it.
>
> (Respondent P01)

Research thus becomes a tool in the this 'proactive' approach is to setting agendas. This signalled a departure from from past practice, as another past president explained:

> if you look at the Royal Commission on Criminal Procedure . . . there is a critic in that report saying that they were concerned that the evidence given by the police was largely anecdotal . . . was not based on sound research. I think the Runciman Commission . . . would say they were impressed by the evidence that was prepared by the police because it was extremely well prepared, was based on good research and indeed there was a marked absence of anecdotal evidence . . .
>
> (Respondent P05)

The effect, according to this respondent, was evident:

> we have evolved a much more professional approach to this in that we research it ourselves very thoroughly, we debate an area of change that we think we would like to see and then we market it to government, to members of Parliament whatever, to try to achieve that change.
>
> (Respondent P01)

The central target in this strategic campaign was the *right to silence*. The police service had long held that the unfettered use of the right to silence had given excessive protections to suspects of crime and that this had led in turn to the manipulation of the criminal justice process by 'guilty' defendants. The launch of Runciman, among other things, was taken as an opportunity to fight for the abolition of the unfetterred right to silence. ACPO set out in this direction by assembling research evidence in support of its case and by constructing powerful counter-arguments to the traditional objections to interference with this right. It had even prepared a drafting of the statute which could be part of the legislation replacing the existing case-law on the right to silence. A member of ACPO's Secretariat learned the skill of statute writing in order to assist ACPO in this aim. ACPO knew what it wanted to achieve and marshalled the case to win over enough of those who needed to be convinced, a case supported with a targeted media campaign, again attached to documented research and evidence in favour of the proposals. As it transpired, Runciman did not accept the case, but the case that was marshalled did receive partial support and, subseqeuntly, the amendment to the right of silence was enacted through the Criminal Justice and Public Order Act 1994. In *In Search of Criminal Justice: Three Years On*, ACPO voiced its approval of this change in law:

> The changes in the law around the right to silence were in particular welcomed by ACPO, who had pressed for some considerable time for such a change as a counter to 'ambush defences' which were becoming increasingly prevalent.
>
> (ACPO, 1998: 3.5)

We would argue that what was involved in this context was a process of *agenda-setting* and a strategic approach to that process. In some respects it left other more 'established' criminal justice pressure groups, such as the legal professions, floundering. ACPO, rather than the legal professions, had the 'ear' of government and had as such manoevered itself *within* the governmental policy network. It had become an *insider* pressure group (Grant, 1989), arguably for the first time. Grant (1984) argues that a decision needs to be taken by both the government and the pressure group before insider status can be granted. Grant rests the majority decision with the government who make this decision based on three factors – whether the group is needed for implementation purposes, whether the pressure group represents many people and whether the pressure group will play by the rules (*ibid*: 138). Nevertheless, pressure group politics is concerned with the exchange of resources and in the case of ACPO, they are in a strong bargaining position. However despite the fact that ACPO have not always adhered to the rules of the game and have not always maintained a 'strategy of responsibility' (Grant, 1984: 134), they have been granted insider status and have themselves adopted an insider strategy. They are a strong, 'resource-rich' (Maloney *et al.*, 1994: 23) group whose participation, vitally, is needed for policy implementation.

Table 2.1   Three Configurations of Policy Formation

Policy influence	Policy area	Policy networks
Agenda resistance	Fixed-term contracts Performance-related pay	ACPO and Police Federation/PSA (Intra-organisational network)
Agenda re-shaping	PMCA (appointment of Chair of Police Authority) Performance measurement	ACPO and LAAs (AMA, Committee of Local Police Authorities, CoLPA) Her Majesty's Inspectorate of Constabulary (HMIC) Audit Commission
Agenda setting	Right of silence Intrusive surveillance	Direct influence over Home Office and 'hostile' networks (legal professions)

What we have mapped out here are *three configurations of policy formation* within the policing policy network. They do not fall neatly into a temporal framework but rather involve overlapping and at times consequential processes. We can portray them in tabular form (see Table 2.1), with additional areas of policing policy other than those examined here.

We would want this framework to be seen as *context-* and *time-bound*. While there may be a general process of 'movement' here, *from* agenda-resistance *to* agenda-shaping, this should not be seen as an immutable process. It was revealing that ACPO's subsequent campaign over the police use of intrusive surveillance (Savage *et al.*, 1997) largely failed to achieve its objectives. In 1996 ACPO had set out to gain statutory powers for chief police officers to decide on the propriety of intrusive surveillance by the police of private premises, very much in the 'agenda-setting' mould. It fought a campaign which employed many of its recently acquired political skills and which at one point appeared to have gained cross-party support. However, at the eleventh hour Labour support was withdrawn – after heavy lobbying by those old hands the legal professions – and, given the frailty of the Conservative's majority in Parliament, the case was lost. Some members of ACPO saw in this a sense of 'one-battle too many' and the need to 'turn down the steam' after a run of successes (ibid.). However, it may also have signalled something of a reversal of fortune. The heavily 'pro-police' atmosphere which cut across party lines in the run up to the 1997 General Election may well have given way to a more even handed, perhaps even dismissive, approach to ACPO by the Labour Home Secretary. This reversal has been fairly rapid. In 1997 commentators were bemoaning the attention that ACPO was receiving:

> Labour . . . increasingly appears to be listening to a few select voices. In the criminal justice area the tough-on-crime policy translates as hearing the demands only of the Association of Chief Police Officers.
>
> (Donovan, 1997)

By 1998 Jack Straw was arguing that single issue pressure groups had taken over control of the Labour Party in the 1980s and he was not going to let that happen again. He would instead be concentrating his attentions on 'local communities and their elected representatives' who were worth 'a thousand pressure groups' (Straw, 1998). By 2000, Straw had turned full circle by announcing that no increase in police numbers would make a difference unless officers were operating at levels of maximum efficiency. In order to fulfil this aim, rigorous and extensive inspections would be aimed at all basic command units. This, it has be argued, reflects the Government's frustration in its continuing attempts to improve the efficiency of the police service (Baldwin and Ford, 2000). It is unlikely that ACPO supported this particular proposal.

Conclusion

This chapter has attempted to examine the role of the police representative associations in relation to the police and criminal justice policy-making process. It has sought to articulate the 'internal' and 'external' policy-networks of policing: *internal* in terms of the relationships between the police staff associations; *external* in terms of relationship between the police associations (and here most specifically ACPO) and other parties (competing groups, strategic allies and so on). Those networks have worked variously to *resist* policies, to *shape* policies and to *initiative* and *drive* policies in the policing and criminal justice sphere. We would argue that the police associations in general, and ACPO in particular, have over a number of years, become more assertive, proactive and effective as players within the policing and criminal justice policy network; to an extent this has been at the expense of the relative influence of other lobbying groups in the field. This greater influence over the policy process does, however, comes loaded with risk and surrounded by danger. It courts with risk in the sense that it inevitably undermines the rhetoric articulated by the police associations that 'policing' should be kept distinct from 'politics'. Indeed, one ACPO member interviewed for our research seemed fully aware of this when he argued that:

> I have concerns about our lobbying role. The one thing about us compared to a lot of other organisations is our political independence. I worry that if we are seen as an overtly lobbying body, as we were with Sheehy to an extent, we will very quickly lose that independence . . . I think in the long term we will lose more than we gain. (M23)

We would re-state this to say that what might be 'lost' would be less 'political independence' per se but the *capacity to claim* 'political independence' as a core feature of British policing. Beyond this the serious danger with the enhanced lobbying activities and effectiveness of the police staff associations witnessed in recent years lies with distortions it can create within the criminal justice system. Researchers have long argued that the police and police actions dominate the criminal justice process in terms of governing outcomes in the pre-trail and trial stages of the justice system (Sanders, 1997). This will be made only more problematic if the police, (through their associations) also dominate the *policy-process* which defines that justice system.

Note

1. The research focused on the changing role of ACPO and involved interviews with over 60 ACPO members past and present and over 30 interviews with representatives of organisations associated with the police service. Where quotations have been taken from interviews, interviewees have been code accordingly.

Bibliography

ACPO (1994) *Your Police: A Service to Value*, Fact Sheet No. 1 (London: Association of Chief Police Officers).
ACPO (1995) *In Search of Criminal Justice* (London: Association of Chief Police Officers).
ACPO (1998) *In Search of Criminal Justice: Three Years On* (London: Association of Chief Police Officers).
Baldwin, T. and Ford, R. (2000) "'Ofcop" Launched in War on Crime', *The Times*, 14 February.
Brogden, M. (1982) *The Police: Autonomy and Consent* (London: Academic Press).

Charman, S. and Savage, S. P. (1999) 'The new politics of law and order: labour, crime, and justice', in Powell M. (ed.), *New Labour, New Welfare State*? (London: Polity Press).

Charman, S., Savage, S. P. and Cope, S. (1998) 'Singing from the same hymn sheet: the professionalisation of the Association of Chief Police Officers', *International Journal of Police Science and Management*, 1(1).

Donovan, P. (1997) 'Tough on liberty: has Labour changed sides on law and order?', *The Independent*, 26 February.

Grant, W. (1984) 'The role and power of pressure groups', in Borthwick, R. and Spence, J. (eds), *British Politics in Perspective* (Leicester: Leicester University Press).

Grant, W. (1989) *Pressure Groups, Politics and Democracy in Britain* (London: Philip Allan).

Holliday, I. (1993) 'Organised interests after Thatcher', in Dunleavy, P. Gamble, A. Holliday I, and Peele, G. (eds), *Developments in British Politics 4* (Basingstoke: Macmillan, Press – Now Palgrave).

Home Office (1993a) *Inquiry into Police Responsibilities and Rewards* (London: HMSO).

Home Office (1993b) *Police Reform: A Police Service for the Twenty-First Century* (London: HMSO).

Home Office (1995) *Review of Police Core and Ancillary Tasks: Final Report* (London: HMSO).

Jefferson, T. and Grimshaw, R. (1984) *Controlling the Constable: Police Accountabilty in England and Wales* (London: Muller/Cobden Trust).

Jordan, A. and Richardson, J. (1987) *British Politics and the Policy Process* (Hemel Hempstead: Unwin Hyman).

Judge, T. (1994) *The Forces of Persuasion* (Surbiton: Police Federation).

Kettle, M. (1980) 'The politics of policing and the policing of politics', in P. Hain (ed.), *Policing the Police Vol. 2*, (London: John Calder).

Leishman, F., Cope, S. and Stanie, P. (1996) 'Reinventing and restructuring: towards a new "policing order", in Leishman, F., Loveday, B. and Savage, S. P. (eds), *Core Issues in Policing* (Harlow: Longman).

Loveday, B. (1995) 'Reforming the police: from local service to State Police?', *Political Quarterly*, 66,(2).

Lustgarten, L. (1986) *The Governance of Police* (London: Sweet & Maxwell).

Maloney, W., Jordan, G. and McLaughlin, A. (1994) 'Interest groups and public policy: the insider/outsider model revisited', *Journal of Public Policy*, 14, 1.

McLaughlin, E. and Murji, K. (1998) 'Resistance through representation: 'story lines', advertising and police federation campaigns', *Policing and Society*, 8(4).

McRobbie, A. (1994) 'Folk devils fight back', *New Left Review*, 203, January/February.

Olson, M. (1971) *The Logic of Collective Action* (Cambridge, Mass.: Harvard University Press).

RCCJ (1993) *Royal Commission on Criminal Justice: Report* (London: HMSO).

Reiner, R.(1985) *The Politics of the Police*, 1st edn, (Brighton: Wheatsheaf).

Richardson, J. and Jordan, A. (1979) *Governing Under Pressure* (Oxford: Martin Robertson).

Robertson, G. (1989) *The Individual and the Law* (London: Penguin).

Ryan, M. (1978) *The Acceptable Pressure Group* (Farnborough: Saxon House).

Salisbury, R. (1984) 'Interest representation: the dominance of institutions', *American Political Science Review*, 78, 1.

Sanders, A. (1997) 'From suspect to trial', in Maguire, M. Morgan, and Reiner, R. (eds), *The Oxford Handbook of Criminology* (Oxford: Oxford University Press).

Savage, S. (1998) 'The geography of police governance', *Criminal Justice Matters*, June.

Savage, S. and Charman, S. (1996) 'In favour of compliance', *Policing Today*, 2(1).

Savage, S. and Charman, S. (1997) *ACPO: The Views of the Membership*, report submitted to the Association of Chief Police Officers.

Savage, S. P. and Nash, M. (2001) 'Law and order under Blair: New Labour or old' conservatism, in Savage, S. P. and Atkinson, R. (eds), *Public Policy under Blair* (Basuigstoke: Palgrave).

Savage, S., Charman, S. and Cope, S. (1996) 'Police governance: the Association of Chief Police Officers and constitutional change', *Public Policy and Administration*, 11(2).

Savage, S. P., Charman, S. and Cope, S. (1997) 'ACPO: a force to be reckoned with?', *Criminal Lawyer*, April.

Savage, S., Charman, S. and Cope, S. (1998) 'ACPO: choosing the way ahead', *Policing Today*, 4(2), June.

Savage, S., Charman, S. and Cope, S. (1999) 'The state of independence: the discourse of constabulary independence', unpublished paper presented to the British Criminology Conference, Liverpool, July.

Savage, S., Cope, S. and Charman, S. (1997) 'Reform through regulation: transformation of the public police in Britain', *Review of Policy Issues*, 3(2).

Scraton, P. (1985) *The State of the Police* (London: Pluto).

Smith, M. (1990) 'Pluralism, reformed pluralism and neopluralism: the role of pressure groups in policy-making', *Political Studies*, 38: 302–22.

Smith, M. (1993) *Pressure, Power and Policy* (Hemel Hempstead: Harvester Wheatsheaf).

Straw, J. (1998) 'Crime and old labour's punishment', *The Times*, 8 April, p. 23.

3
Influencing or Influenced? – the Probation Service and Criminal Justice Policy

Mike Nash

Writing in 1976, King and Jarvis described the beginnings of the end of the probation service 'as it was'. What had been described was a small, personal service very much based on the individuality of probation officers, a characteristic also noted by McWilliams (1987). This service was not however without influence, despite its small size, and King and Jarvis (1976) record the strength of its 'moral authority'. They also note that probation officers were 'sought-after' witnesses, having 'special skills' and who were 'central to government penal policy' (74–5). Their relationships within the penal system in 1976 were described as having been forged with influential penal reform groups, such as the Howard League, philanthropic and influential sponsors and of course the magistracy. King and Jarvis felt able to describe a 'common front' between magistrates and probation officers against the growing importance of administrative decision-making. Over 30 years on it seems as if the battle against the 'administration' or managerialism (McWilliams, 1987) has been lost but the probation service remains important to the delivery of criminal justice policy – at times it is still even vital. This chapter will explore the changing nature of the world in which the probation service lives and in particular who it now lives with. The cause of penal reform is not what it was 30 years ago and the remarkable survival of the probation service under four successive Conservative Governments probably owed as much to its changing networks as it did to those Governments' needs to rein in public expenditure. Therefore, to understand why the probation service now interacts with whom it does it is important to understand the changing nature of its role and this will form the next section of the chapter.

55

From one to one to all for one

McWilliams (1987) described the individual probation officer as once representing the voice of the service. Through a series of personal contacts, the rehabilitative message was pushed out. Working relationships were characterised by personal knowledge of the probation officer by the Magistrate, through one to one sessions between offender and officer, increasingly based upon a casework relationship and indeed, one to one supervision between officer and supervisor (manager). There is not the space in this chapter to pursue a history of the probation service, this has been done elsewhere (for example, May, 1991), but it should be noted that the individual, personalised nature of the service has been dramatically abandoned during the past 30 years – at least theoretically – and replaced by a considerably enhanced management hierarchy, a sizeable bureaucracy and a constant stream of policy initiatives issued from the centre. As McWilliams (1987) would have it, the 'management' now speaks for the service from a policy perspective, rather than its officers from its professional side. Indeed, it is likely that even the managers will increasingly be less independent and able to challenge government policy in the future. Changes to the structure and organisation of the service, announced in April 1999 (Home Office Press Release, 13 April 1999), will see the number of Chief Probation Officers (CPOs) reduced in number from 54 to 42 and become directly appointed and employed by the Home Office (there will be further comment on these changes below). Parallel with the changing nature of the message which has to be conveyed by the probation service has come a change in the people and organisations needed to both support and facilitate that message.

The probation service is no longer a social casework-based court service. Since 1994 the requirement for probation officers to hold a professional qualification in social work has been abolished, replaced by a new qualification based on a combination of 'on the job' National vocational qualifications (NVQ), competency training and academic input from universities. A crucial part of the tender for organisations bidding to provide the new training was a requirement to sever links with previous social work providers. This development is perhaps only one of many which has seen a fundamental transformation in the role and responsibilities of the probation service, in particular since 1984 when the first national objectives for it were introduced (Home Office, 1984). Most notably, national standards have been introduced for just about every aspect of the service's work with the consequent reduction in professional autonomy and increase in central direction (Home Office, 1995). The probation service has had to sacrifice its 'local' nature to ensure survival on the national stage. As a result it has had to forge new alliances and those who claim to speak on behalf of the service have also changed (see below). From its early police court missionary zeal, through to 'advise assist and befriend' and more recently its emphasis on strict supervision, control and public protection, the 'friends' needed to support and further the aims of the service have changed. However, it is also fair to say that there is no longer one 'voice' of the probation service and therefore those who claim to speak on its behalf have developed independent networks and associations which they see as furthering their interests.

Professional associations

It is interesting to note that in 1976 King and Jarvis could write of the National Association of Probation Officers (NAPO):

> Until comparatively recently the Association could claim to speak for the Service as a whole.
>
> (77)

In their chapter they give prominence to NAPO over the Principal Probation Officers Conference (now Association of Chief Officers of Probation, ACOP) and make reference to close working relationships between the Association and members of the Home Office. NAPO was also described as forming a greater number of relationships with other organisations, ranging from the National Association for the Care and Resettlement of Offenders (NACRO) to Radical Alternatives to Prison and the Prison Officers' Association (POA), a group who might at first appear to be unlikely bedfellows. NAPO was developing its trade union voice and increasingly becoming involved in single issue pressure group politics. As it did so it began to move away from the other voice of the service, ACOP, leaving the probation service perhaps less united and able to consider resisting or influencing criminal justice initiatives as it had done in the past.

The roots of the probation service are deeply embedded in the history of individualised criminal justice policy, of humanitarian alternatives to custody and belief that people can change and re-establish themselves in society. This history predates a concern with either the 'dispersal of discipline' (Cohen, 1985), the 'carceral society' (Foucault, 1977), or alternatively a concern that 'welfare' is too soft and a more punitive approach to crime is needed. As such NAPO was able to work alongside governments which were broadly in line with its aims, the aims of the probation service and of the Home Office were not so far apart, indeed they were closely entwined (Rawlings, 1999).[1] Writing in 1958 Radzinowicz had commented:

> If I were asked what is the most significant contribution made by this country to the new penological theory and practice which struck root in the twentieth century... my answer would be probation.
>
> (Cited in May, 1991: 15)

Claiming that the probation service was 'important' in both delivering and shaping criminal justice policy in the period, perhaps until the 1960s, would appear to be reasonable. NAPO was seen as the organisation to consult with and to seek submissions from in terms of criminal justice policy development (King and Jarvis, 1976: 78). The importance of personal relationships, reflected throughout the work of the probation service, was seen in that between Home Secretary and the General Secretary of NAPO (ibid.) and this, rather than industrial muscle or wider support networks, perhaps reflected the influence of NAPO and the probation service in general. The probation service, and NAPO in particular, can be seen as having the ear of Ministers, it was an 'insider' organisation to a certain extent. It did this before the rise of a managerial bureaucracy and before chief probation officers increasingly saw themselves as speaking on behalf of the Service. More importantly perhaps for NAPO, governments were increasingly to listen to ACOP rather than NAPO, or perhaps more accurately, saw ACOP as the organisation which would oversee the implementation of new policy.

Undoubtedly, the expansion of the probation service, to cope with increased responsibilities such as working in prisons (1966), supervision of parole licences (1967), bail hostels, probation hostels, probation centres and community service orders (1972/73), increasingly moved it away from its localised, personalised service. At the same time, the move towards greater accountability was taking place, fuelling demand for a professional management hierarchy within the Service. May (1991: 18) noted that the ratio of supervisory to non-supervisory posts increased from 1:6 to 1:3 between 1960 and 1978 but interestingly notes that a 1966 NAPO working party report viewed this managerial expansion as 'positive', a line which has perhaps changed somewhat since then. It was to be the eventual difference in perception in probation task and direction which was to see the ending of the 'one voice' probation service and with it a change in the nature of the way in which it felt able to pursue its interests. Essentially NAPO was to move much more into a defensive position, reflecting for some time main grade concern that 'probation values' were being sacrificed by management, who were viewed as being too close to government policy which in itself was seen as the antithesis of good probation practice. The debate concerning 'values' is both extensive and ongoing and is too great to be included in this chapter (see, for example, Nellis, 1995 and Drakeford and Vanstone, 1996), but it is important to note that this debate has contributed to the fractured public image of the probation service, with NAPO seeing itself as a more vigorous defender of those values epitomised by the work of front-line practitioners, rather than senior managers who have sold out to government policies.[2]

In 1999 the then Chair of NAPO, Judy McKnight told me that:

> NAPO's campaigns over the last 20 years have been defensive. The most important influence has been to delay, to frustrate or to resist. Some press campaigns such as those on miscarriages of justice, women in prison, foreign nationals, discrimination within the criminal justice system and many more have had a cumulative effect.
> (McKnight, 1999, personal communication)[3]

These comments reflect a campaigning style of pressure group politics, more in line with other voluntary and charitable sector organisations. They also reflect a wider interest in criminal justice policy beyond simply the interests of the probation service. However, perhaps above all, the comments can be seen to reflect the 'outsider' nature of the role which NAPO now occupies. It no longer appears to have an automatic line to government ministers and the use of words such as resist, delay and frustrate are some way from influence and shape. Indeed Judy Mcknight recognised the changing nature of NAPO relationships with others in her comments, stating that organisations such as ACOP, Her Majesty's Inspectorate of Probation (HMIP) and even probation committees/boards, were all less important in helping it to influence policy in 1999 than they were in 1979. Interestingly, organisations recorded as being more significant were the POA, the Prison Governors Association (PGA) and the Penal Affairs Consortium (PAC).

Asked to identify areas where NAPO had managed to influence criminal justice policy in the past 20 years, Judy McKnight was again to take what might be termed a 'negative' stance of resistance rather than a positive stance of agenda setting:

> Again the key issue here is delay. The one campaign that dominates the last 15 years is electronic tagging. NAPO had been to the fore in resisting, but ultimately our main effect was delaying what was probably the inevitable (see ACOP comments below, *author comment*). NAPO has conducted dozens of campaigns over the period on pay and conditions, enlightening the criminal justice system, all of which have had a cumulative effect.

NAPO then emerges as a campaigning trade union, concerned not only with its members interests, but also wider criminal justice issues. Its involvement in the PAC, alongside ACOP is important as this organisation may carry sufficient weight to influence policy making in the future, although as will be noted below, there may not be huge differences between current government policy and what PAC are advocating. What Downes and Morgan (1997) describe as a previously 'unthinkable coalition' of interest and pressure groups may find their interests so varied that they become spokespersons for government policy rather than advocates of reform.[4] NAPO may in future have to settle for a role on the margins of policy making unless the government reverses recent attitudes to practitioner representative organisations (Downes and Morgan, 1997: 116), although this marginalisation is not that recent a phenomenon. In 1991 May reported on a survey conducted among probation staff in one area as to who exercised the most influence over policy formation. Top of the list of the 'very influential' category came probation (senior) management with 63 per cent – in this particular column NAPO polled 0 per cent. Indeed over 50 per cent felt that NAPO were 'not very influential'. It remains to be seen if NAPO's current stance of influence through resistance can be successful.

New friends – new coalitions?

This chapter began with an expression of surprise that the probation service had remained intact under four successive Conservative Governments. Its survival in an era which saw a major transformation of penal policy towards ever more punitive agendas is testament to its key position, a position described by Mair (1997) as a 'well kept secret'. However, to a great extent that secret is now out and, although the public may be little more aware of probation service tasks than it was; the probation service has undoubtedly been given a greater role in delivering the new penal policy, most notably punishment in the community (Home Office, 1988, 1990). Indeed more recently it has found its role in public protection, established by the Morrison Committee (Home Office, 1962), considerably enhanced to include the very public work it has in monitoring and supervising serious sexual and violent offenders. This high-profile and high-risk role has certainly placed the probation service much more onto the centre stage, although not necessarily in a way it would have chosen (see for example, Nash, 1999a).

However, the changing nature of probation service role cannot entirely be linked to government policy. During the 1970s and early 1980s considerable doubts arose as to the effectiveness of rehabilitation (Martinson, 1974; Brody, 1976). A new breed of 'radical' social workers increasingly subscribed to academic research which saw probation officers as agents of an oppressive state who did not tackle the real causes of crime but instead pathologised it. As a result, disenchantment set in with the notion of rehabilitation, both within and without the Service (see, for example, Bottoms and McWilliams, 1979; Walker and Beaumont, 1981). Concern with rising crime and the lack of power available to sentencers saw the growth of the 'justice' movement (von Hirsch, 1976), all of which would appear to have put the future of the probation service under severe threat. That it was able to ride out these storms and emerge in the early 1990s as a key component of Conservative criminal justice policy is undoubtedly a significant feat of organisational survival. However, the way in which this survival has been achieved is also very much a comment on the way in which the probation service has both been re-packaged and indeed re-packaged itself.

Part of that re-packaging involved not only responding to the increasing demands of central government but to a certain extent anticipating what was around the corner. For example, in 1988 ACOP produced a document, *More Demanding than Prison*, which aimed to both anticipate the new punishment in the community agenda as well as securing the future of the probation service to deliver it. In a sense ACOP might be seen as attempting to become more of an insider organisation, compared with NAPO, however there remains the question of the price to be paid for being allowed on the inside. For example, Downes and Morgan (1997) argue that the 1990s saw the Labour Party in opposition move closer to 'slighted' practitioner organisations and away from pressure groups with 'liberal and soft' credentials. Yet that process, which has undoubtedly continued with the Labour Party in office, has seen those organisations increasingly speak the government's words. The issue of electronic monitoring, fought so hard against by NAPO (see above), has found more support among ACOP members. This may of course be a result of the inevitability of the situation described by Judy McKnight, therefore ACOP pursue a more pragmatic line of securing the extra resources needed to deliver the policy:

> ACOP doesn't – by and large – have a huge impact on legislation. It does best nibbling at the edges – changes which don't thwart politicians main aims, but convert them into something more acceptable. Sometimes – electronic monitoring for instance – you do this by conceding the overall issue – accepting for instance that EM is inevitable whether we like it or not, but being prepared to contest the detail, line by line, until it is more workable.
>
> (CPO, personal communication)

Another CPO cited as a success of policy influence in recent years:

> The controlled and carefully monitored use of electronic tagging in pilot areas leading to the development of Home Detention Curfews.

Both of these CPOs indicate that ACOP has successfully constructed a role for itself in 'influencing' government policy, rather than lobbying for change or new developments. In other words it may not be in a position to *set* the agenda, or even to resist it, bit it can tinker at the edges and *shape* it. The first CPO mentioned above claims that ACOP are not good at being a pressure group but are effective by its increasingly 'insider' role. In support of this he cites ACOP secondments into the Probation Unit at the Home Office, at the Prison Service, and importantly onto the Comprehensive Spending Review team (which in fact secured increased resources for the probation service – with the caveat that this is to deliver a carefully prescribed range of activities). In summarising this role the CPO gave a hint of the continuing history of independence within the probation service:

> Pressure groups go for the jugular and for Ministers. ACOP sidles up to civil servants in the corridor and persuades them of the error of their ways. Less dramatic, but that's how it is ... ACOP is fatally weakened by the independence (or eccentricity, or bloody-mindedness) of CPOs I fear – but within limits it actually gets a lot changed.

Another CPO correspondent confirmed this view, perhaps in an even more upbeat summary:

> Over the past two decades ACOP has grown in confidence and assertiveness, finding its voice and using its network of influence in relation to Ministers, other Government departments, the Prison Service, the Police, the Judiciary etc.

This list reflects a series of relationships with other criminal justice professionals as well as government departments. It contains those whose importance to ACOP has undoubtedly increased over the years, such as prison and police services. The Judiciary have been, as we saw earlier, a traditional area of support for the probation service. Undoubtedly all the organisations represented in this list have faced considerable change and pressure to change further in recent years, so it might be represented as an alliance of self-interest in the face of challenging governments. It might equally be argued that little of the change has been successfully resisted and where it has, it has been at the cost of significant change to former working practices of each organisation. The probation service, not enjoying the public support or power of the police lobby, have perhaps been least able to resist change and perhaps sought to work in the way identified above. However, it might be argued that each change has been met by a request for more and one wonders what will be left of the probation service if this trend continues – no matter which government is in power. A sceptical view might be taken of this CPO's view of the measure of ACOP's recent success:

> Stage managed conferences in London and elsewhere are signs of ACOP's growing professionalism, as is the ability of the Association to pull in lead figures in criminal justice as well as secretaries of State. The contrast is telling by comparison to the early years when ACOP had its annual meetings in dingy university buildings with few outside speakers and a rather self congratulatory monolithic view of the world. It's become political, surer of its identity, more purposeful, lateral thinking in terms of building up significant alliances over the years.

That politicisation may however be viewed differently from that of NAPO. Political in the ACOP context could be taken to mean an awareness of the political game and making best use of access and positions of influence from within. Establishing networks with organisations which have long held a more significant insider role, such as the police and prison services, can only help that process. It is here that the potential for fragmentation of probation service policy, in terms of relationships between workforce and management, is most likely to occur. Increasingly statements made by HMIP, for example, are about the exercise of control over the probation workforce. Discussions on national standards at the Home Affairs Select Committee, suggested almost an 'us and them', attitude:

> (National Standards) have been first class for the probation service, giving HMIP a means of holding *them* to account which *we* never had before (emphasis added).

Although CPOs are responsible for the performance on national standards criteria, it is clear that their emphasis has to be viewed as an attempt to limit individual professional discretion. Announcements such as this by HMIP (with many ACOP secondees in its ranks) are unlikely to lose it a place on the inside of policy influence – and indeed it could be argued in certain areas, such as work with high risk and dangerous offenders, HMIP has actually taken the lead and set the agenda for other agencies (Home Office, 1995, 1998a; Nash, 1999a).[5]

New agendas – reinventing networks from the centre

The election of the Labour Government in 1997 did not see an immediate reversal of the punitive and populist policies of Michael Howard, indeed these continued, and to a certain extent increased, especially in the area of sex offenders. Clearly organisations such as the probation service may have seen a message of hope in Tony Blair's soundbite about being 'tough on the causes of crime' – especially when this was linked with measures to combat social exclusion and to provide more work, education and training opportunities. However, these are relatively long-term measures and the immediate agenda remains one of being 'tough on crime', the other part of Blair's statement. This ensures a continuation of the more controlling role that the probation service has been given in recent years and will indeed see it directed ever more from the centre and pushed into a series of associations with other agencies within the criminal justice system, most notably the police and prison services. It could be argued that Jack Straw has been prepared to go further than his predecessor in attempts to reshape the probation service. The prisons probation review (Home Office, 1988) was set up with the brief to consider the amalgamation of these two services with an aim of producing a 'seamless transition' from custodial to community corrections. Straw had been keen to see the probation service renamed, favourites had emerged such as 'community corrections officers', or 'public protection officers'. ACOP had fought a rearguard action around the title 'community justice officers' but the government then announced that the new name would be the Community Punishment and Rehabilitation Service. This announcement was met with hostility and derision. The initial letters of each word were quickly rearranged by critics to form the acronym CRAP and probation officers it was said would become CRAPOS. The reaction to the new name reawakened something of the probation service's old coalition networks, especially in Parliament. Some 110 MPs of all parties signed an early day motion calling on the Home Secretary to rethink the changes (*NAPO News*, April 2000) and there was a good deal of criticism in the Lords. In March 2000 that criticism was responded to by the Government in announcing that the probation service would become The National Probation Service for England and Wales. However to prove who was still the boss the Criminal Justice and Court Services Bill also announced that in future probation orders would be renamed community rehabilitation orders and community service orders would become community punishment orders.

However, for some while now, there has been a lack of a single probation 'voice' and as ACOP has moved towards greater harmony with the government's agenda for the probation service, so has it distanced itself from NAPO – and perhaps other members of and earlier probation policy network. For example, in 1987 ACOP, NAPO and the CCCP (Central Council of Probation Committees) had issued a joint paper entitled, *Probation – The Next Five Years*. May (1991) describes this as the first coherent statement of probation policy since the issue of the government's Statement of National Objectives and Priorities (SNOP) for the probation service in 1984. The document appeared to hold forth a unity of purpose, as follows:

It is important that developments build upon the established strengths of the probation service, utilise the skills of its professionals and other field work staff and work with the grain of the service. Any other approach risks disorientation, dislocation and inefficiency'.

(Cited in May, 1991: 46)

Yet within a year NAPO were complaining that neither it nor CCPC had been consulted about ACOP's paper *More Demanding than Prison* which both sought to anticipate and perhaps further the government agenda. A year after this NAPO was to reject the findings of the Audit Commission, which had called for greater targeting, a strengthened management and additional training. The probation voice was beginning to fracture.

Undoubtedly, senior managers of the probation service were, at least in part, in survival mode throughout the four successive Conservative Governments. Despite their periodically being placed 'centre stage' in the delivery of criminal justice targets, they remained vulnerable as a social work based, offender focused organisation. Therefore it might be argued that not only survival, but occasional expansion, such as that following the 1991 Criminal Justice Act (CJA) and more recently in 1998 with the publication of the Comprehensive Spending Review, is a tremendous achievement. The developing importance of ACOP and its new found policy partners is undoubtedly a feature in this. Yet, the insider role has been accompanied by a really quite substantial shift in role and function which not only causes periodic tension with the main grade but has significantly moved the service from its roots. There is an air of vulnerability about the service, as what have increasingly become deemed to be its core tasks are those which could be carried out by a range of organisations, including the private sector. Failure to deliver in these re-defined areas of practice leaves the door ajar for others to enter.

One good example of new work – new partners is that of public protection. Although, as stated above, this has long been a feature of probation service task and function, it is only in recent years that it has been given greater prominence in legislation. Even more recently have the probation service been linked in the public mind with a public protection role, especially in its dealing with serious sex offenders. A high profile task brings with it potential gain and loss. The gain could well be the establishment of the probation service in to the public consciousness as an organisation which serves a useful purpose, and indeed gives it a profile. Mair (1997: 1195) noted that in the early 1990s ACOP had been concerned about the image problem that the probation service had and commissioned research to investigate the issue – the results of which were not published. Public protection has undoubtedly given the service a profile but it is in a difficult area and one in which, by ACOP's admission, there is not a great deal that the service can actually do. An association with the police offers benefits in both sharing the potential problems and sharing the gains of being linked with an organisation traditionally seen as offering public protection and enjoying high levels of public satisfaction. The down side of this collaboration may well be a further dilution of the 'values' of the probation service and greater harmonisation with those of the police service. There is a well documented history in multi-agency work of one agency dominating, and the police have frequently taken on this role (Nash, 1999a). Therefore, in building new interest coalitions, the probation service must question if its interests will become subordinate to more powerful partners.

Forced agendas – forced partners?

Public protection is but one (albeit very high profile) agenda which has been set for criminal justice agencies by the government in recent years. These agendas have been highly politicised and have been set in terms that the organisations involved would have found hard to resist – for example any agenda which purports to protect vulnerable children cannot be resisted. Yet the Labour Government have pushed the agenda for collaboration much, much further and beyond specific issues or problems. There is now a clear agenda for harmonising the aims and objectives of all criminal justice agencies, but with special emphasis on the police, prison and probation services. The prisons probation review, established shortly after Labour was elected to office in 1997, did consider, as one its aims, the merger of these two organisations. The final report *Joining Forces to Protect the Public* (Home Office 1998b) rejected this idea but has called for not only reorganisation of the probation service into a Next Steps agency, but also a much greater harmonisation of its objectives with those of the prison service. Indeed the scene had already been set by the appointment of the first ever joint prisons probation Minister, Joyce Quinn. The review makes constant references to joint action plans, shared objectives and of course clearer national direction. There is mention of the creation of a 'national corrections policy framework' and the need work for work on agency boundaries to:

> develop common boundaries which enable agencies to become more familiar with each other's policies and practice and eliminates difficulties caused by overlaps.

It might also be seen as an attempt to eliminate 'difference'. The probation service will find its ethos developed even more along the corrections route, with a suggestion that it is this which will improve the public image of the service:

statutory duties will need to be to confront, challenge and change offending behaviour and to recognise punishment as a central part of that process. This should help the public to understand and value more highly the work which probation staff do on their behalf

The report identifies a range of potential hurdles to effective joint working delivery of aims, some of which are:

- the absence of adequate co-ordination, e.g. of correctional policy and joint strategy at Home Office level;
- differing aims and objectives;
- a conflict of cultures and preservation of separate identities;
- the absence of common training and cross postings;
- when making strategic plans, a lack of recognition of the other service's role, and the respective pressures on achieving strategic objectives.

To take this issue a stage further, the Home Secretary Jack Straw, speaking to the ACOP conference on 13 April 1999, announced that, in addition to the points mentioned above, the probation service would in future be 100 per cent Home Office funded (replacing the previous 80–20 split with local authorities). Probation Boards would be given a more strategic role and the Chair of the Board would be appointed and paid by the Home Office and significantly, 'The Home Secretary will take greater powers to direct – to require – necessary outcomes and standards of service delivery' (*NAPO News*, May 1999).

Therefore, the probation service will find itself working increasingly closely with the prison service, although it will not as yet become one with it! From being an organisation which not so long ago was pressured into keeping as many people out of prison as it could, and whose officers felt a natural antipathy towards prison, it now finds itself moving towards the seamless merger desired by the government. It could also be argued that the public protection role has brought about unprecedented sharing with the police service, and I have argued elsewhere that this collaboration predates that with the prison service and to a certain extent exceeds it – especially in cultural terms (Nash, 1999b).

The government has also gone much further than ever before in determining the membership of criminal justice networks by its extensive guidance on the measures included in the Crime and Disorder Act, 1998. These new partnerships will centrally include police, local authority, probation, social services and health authorities, crucially for crime reduction and community safety strategies. At a stroke the government creates a network of its own choosing who are working to its agenda. Barriers, such as the confidentiality of information held by individual agencies, are dealt with by the guidance notes and basically overridden by the need to maintain public safety and to enhance effective working.[6] For the probation service perhaps the newest partner organisation here is the local authority whose own history has been very much on the 'target hardening' and design side of crime prevention. The probation service has traditionally steered away from this area (Gilling, 1997) and it does represent a further retreat from its traditional role.[7]

In some senses, the new partnerships for the probation service take it back to its roots. It was a local organisation, known to local courts and with links in the local community – its job to rehabilitate offenders back into that community. On a national scale policy influence occurred through NAPO and its association with respected voluntary or charitable groups. Policy directives emanating from the centre were few and far between. The current recreation of the 'local' is quite different. It takes the form of a very specifically directed set of relations working to a pre set and determined agenda. Naturally the interpretation of this agenda will vary around the country, as will the speed of change and implementation. Nonetheless, any lingering hopes that the probation service might have held to maintain its independence appear to have been buried with the Labour government. The 'local' network will work towards a range of common interests which have been set for them. There will undoubtedly be strength in numbers and failure can be collectively shared. Success will undoubtedly be seen in the first instance in process terms, in other words simply the coming together of the range of agencies will be viewed as a successful outcome. Longer-term success indicators, such as the reduction of crime, increased effectiveness of crime prevention and, even more difficult, a reduction in the *fear* of crime, may be some way off, if achieved at all. Undoubtedly the way in which each agency has gone about its task in the past will be changed and the requirements to develop shared tasks and ways of working will increase, particularly for the prison and probation services.

The probation service has long faced change and competition for its share of the criminal justice market. In adapting to change requirements from the centre it has had to give up many of its traditional areas of practice. For example, the increased numbers of compulsorily supervised post-release cases arising from the 1991 Criminal Justice Act led to the reduction in the voluntary supervision of those serving less than 12 months in custody. However, this group form the vast majority of released prisoners and most of those likely to return to custody. New policy developments therefore have the effect of producing a gap in provision which should be filled in an effective 'joined-up' criminal justice sector. Resources will no longer allow probation services to fill the gap and it is likely that this task will be contracted out to the voluntary and independent sector – as has already been piloted in parts of the country. In this scenario former pressure group partners move into the mainstream and can be seen as competitors – although this is perhaps more acceptable than it was as the probation service faces a future guaranteed within the corrections sector. By this process, not only have the professional associations been drawn ever more closely into the government inner circle, it could be argued that an outer circle is created of those organisations who are given a greater share of the criminal justice cake. This leaves fully outside those who are not admitted to the decision-making inner circle and those opposed to many of the government's initiatives, and perhaps NAPO can now be seen in this light.

The power of the probation lobby?

That the probation service has survived a tumultuous 20 years is beyond question and perhaps speaks for the strength of its ability to mobilise support. Yet in surviving, it has made tremendous changes which, many might argue, have been greater than any other criminal justice organisation. It has never been a powerful organisation but it has had considerable influence over criminal justice policy. This influence coincided with the highpoint of its positivist origins within British criminal justice history, therefore perhaps it did not need to be powerful, it was a child of and for its times.

James and Raine (1998: 35) note the power of criminal justice elites to withstand market reforms of the 1980s and 1990s:

> strong opposition from powerful groups within criminal justice, notably the judiciary and chief constables, was a major factor in limiting the extent of the market-style reforms. Another constraint was the dearth of alternative providers in the market.

For the probation service this argument does not hold water. Alternative providers in the form of the independent sector and increasingly the private sector are available. Indeed, a feature of the *practice* reforms of the probation service is that other providers can more easily take on the task. More accurately, James and Raine say this of the probation service:

(It) for example, has experienced redrafting of professional and managerial training requirements, enhanced acknowledgement of ACOP in dialogue with Ministers, and separate identification and development of a central Inspectorate for Probation.

(1998: 114)

The increased importance and influence of the Inspectorate has been noted above and is perhaps emphasised in this comment from the Home Affairs Select Committee mentioned earlier:

We congratulate HMIP in its continuing efforts to ensure that all probation services follows 'What Works?' principles and urge the Home Office to join with the Inspectorate in putting pressure on all services to incorporate these principles into their work. Adherence to these principles should be a national standard.

It is evident that the centralised agenda will increasingly be set and monitored by HMIP. The incorporation of chief probation officers – and possibly assistant and deputy ranks – into the civil service, will undoubtedly increase the voice of the service at a national level, not least as it increasingly shares with the prison service. Yet that voice will, at the same time, quite likely lose the independent edge that it once held.

It is not possible to say that, had the probation service not done what it had been bid to do over the past 20 years, that it would have disappeared. The evidence suggests that this would have been unlikely but not impossible. However, it has faced a constant threat during this period and its senior management have responded, it might be argued, effectively, to ensure organisational survival. Atkinson and Coleman (1992: 155) can perhaps be viewed as summarising the situation shared by probation managers in common with others:

Public sector managers have discovered that in shouldering (this) responsibility, they cannot rely on traditional organisational forms styled on the Weberian model of bureaucracy. Accordingly state mangers have searched for new means to accomplish unfamiliar and often unwelcome tasks.

One of those means, pursued by ACOP, has been to regain 'insider' status for the probation service, a status lost from the 1960s until the 1990s. In so doing it has moved the service away from many of its old associations and lost much of its (public) campaigning edge – this now rests much more firmly on the shoulders of NAPO, although the CPOs noted in this chapter do indicate a certain campaigning 'behind the scenes'. However, it appears as if NAPO is increasingly not in the scene.

The probation service has worked with many organisations in the past and, like many campaigning groups, these partners have changed according to the 'issue'. It could therefore be argued that in the past it has been involved in 'issue networks' (Heclo, 1978) although it is difficult to say that it is that type of organisation today:

> a communications network of those interested in policy in some area, including government authorities, legislators, businessmen, lobbyists and even academics plus journalists. Obviously an issue network constantly communicates criticisms of policy and generates ideas for new policy initiatives.
>
> (Rhodes and Marsh, 1992: 7).

To a certain extent the probation service does now work in this way, but not in a loose coming-together of interested bodies to take on single issues and then reform for another. It works with others because it both needs to and has to – need because it helps the cause of survival, has to because in a sense the government has told it to. Our CPO correspondents indicate that there has been an increase in ACOP influence in recent years, but by their own admission, this has been more a slowing down or a resistance to the worst excesses of politicians. As Rhodes and Marsh (1992: 2) note, just because 'you're in', doesn't mean you will be listened to:

> While interest groups may make continuing representations to government, and such representations may even become institutionalised, the government remains independent of interest groups.

Indeed, it may be by allowing them a little voice government exerts much greater control over their activities.

As the probation service voice has fractured, so has the way in which it seeks to influence policy. Perhaps NAPO can now be viewed as continuing the issue network tradition, but ACOP has moved on from that. It may be that the probation service is entering a 'policy community' (see, for example, Rhodes and Marsh, 1992: 251) but one in which the policy interest is shaped by government rather than itself shaping the policy outcome. Entry into such a policy community would be a departure for the probation service. It has not enjoyed some of the characteristics of these groups in the same way as other members. For example, it has fewer resources and less influence – it has not therefore been an equal actor compared to say, the police service. However, the new policy community, underwritten by the Labour Government, sees the probation service perhaps sharing more of the features in common with its new partner organisations. According to Rhodes and Marsh (1992) these include the following; limited number, with some groups consciously excluded (NAPO?), professional interest dominate (substitute managerial?), frequent, high-quality interaction (now a government *requirement*) and participants sharing basic values). This last point is perhaps the most interesting and most contentious. As stated earlier, the recent history of the probation service is studded by debates on values. The increasingly shared nature of criminal justice values – especially when the probation service remains one of the lesser players? – is likely to lead to significant compromise to its traditional value base. The struggle for the heart and soul of the probation service may yet continue for a while, but the price for survival may well be the end of the process of 'ending' noted by King and Jarvis at the beginning of this chapter.

Notes

1. It should be noted that criminal justice policy before the 1970s was not a process of uninterrupted penal reform and liberal policy, nonetheless the ethos of the probation service was closely bound up with 'official' Home Office policy.
2. See the comments by Mair (1997: 1196) on what he terms the 'smug' nature of probation officers compared with other criminal justice professionals.
3. I am grateful for the comments of Judy Mcknight who responded to a questionnaire.
4. For example, see comments made by the Paul Cavadino of the PAC in evidence to the Select Committee on Home Affairs (Third Report, House of Commons, 28 July 1998) when, in talking of national standards he had said, 'it is important that they should be applied rigorously, both for public credibility but also so that the sentence itself can do its job of steering the offender away from crime or applying appropriate sanctions if the offender does not comply and is not steered away from crime'. These comments could equally have been made by a member of HMIP, ACOP or the government and are somewhat in contrast to NAPO's views which were more concerned with the quality issues of national standards.
5. However, despite the very influential work of HMIP and ACOP in this area, it can be viewed as another example of policy influence. Clearly the government intended public protection to become the major issue for criminal justice

agencies. The response of ACOP and HMIP ensured a continuing role for the probation service in this task and a stronger link with the police service and ACOP in particular have enhanced focus and credibility. However rather than respond in the way it did, ACOP (and the Opposition) may have been better placed to have spelt out the reality of serious and dangerous offending rather than almost collude with the crude populism which was prevalent at the time (Nash, 1999a).

6. Section 115 of the Crime and Disorder Act 1998, does not impose a requirement on agencies to disclose but removes any barrier to their ability to do so. However the inference is that there should be information exchange when it is in the public interest.

7. An interesting feature of the 'sharing' debate and the probation service was the traditional antipathy of probation officers to the police (and the opposite of course). In 1985 Laycock and Pease wrote suggesting that probation officers share information to other agencies which might support 'physical security measures' – a view rejected by NAPO at the time. In 1992 Sampson and Smith noted a police officer as saying 'we shouldn't have liaison with probation; it would make their job impossible' (108).

References

ACOP (1988) *More Demanding than Prison* (Wakefield: Association Of Chief Officers of Probation).

Atkinson, M. M. and Coleman, W. D. (1992) 'Policy networks, policy communities and the problems of governance', *Governance: An International Journal of Policy and Administration*, 5(2): 154–80.

Bottoms, A. E. and McWilliams, W. (1979) 'A non-treatment paradigm for probation practice', *British Journal of Social Work*, 9: 159–202.

Brody, S. (1976) *The Effectiveness of Sentencing: A Review of the Literature*, Home Office Research Study no. 35 (London: HMSO).

Cohen, S. (1985) *Visions of Social Control* (Oxford: Polity Press).

Downes, D. and Morgan, R. (1997) 'Dumping the "hostages to fortune"?: the politics of law and order in post-war Britain', in Maguire, M., Morgan, R. and Reiner, R. (eds) *The Oxford Handbook of Criminology*, 2nd edn (Oxford: Clarendon Press).

Drakeford, M. and Vanstone, M. (1996) 'Rescuing the social', *Probation Journal*, April: 16–19.

Foucault, M. (1977) *Discipline and Punish: The Birth of the Prison* (London: Allen Lane).

Gilling, D. (1997) *Crime Prevention: Theory, policy and politics* (London: UCL Press).

Heclo, H. (1978) 'Issue networks and the executive establishment', in King. A. (ed.), *The American Political System* (Washington: American Institute).

Home Office (1988) *Punishment, Custody and Community*, Cm 424 (London: HMSO).

Home Office (1984) *Probation Service in England and Wales: Statement of National Objectives and Priorities* (London: Home Office).

Home Office (1962) *Report of the Departmental Committee on the Probation Service (The Morrison Committee)*, Cmnd 1650 (London: Home Office).

Home Office (1990) *Crime, Justice and Protecting the Public: The Government's Proposals for Legislation*, Cm 965 (London: HMSO).

Home Office (1995b) *National Standards for the Supervision of Offenders in the Community* (London: Home Office).

Home Office (1995a) *Dealing with Dangerous People: The Probation Service and Public Protection*, Report of a Thematic Inspection (HMIP) (London: HMSO).

Home Office (1998a) *Exercising Constant Vigilance: The Role of the Probation Service in Protecting the Public from Sex Offenders*, Report of a Thematic Inspection (HMIP) (London: Home Office).

Home Office (1998b) *Prisons Probation: Joining Forces to Protect the Public* (London: Home Office).

James, A. and Raine, J. (1997) *The New Politics of Criminal Justice* (Harlow: Addison Wesley Longman).

King, J. F. S. and Jarvis, F. V. (1976) 'The influence of the probation and after-care Service', in Walker, N. and Giller, H. (eds), *Policy-Making in England*, Papers presented to the Cropwood Round-Table Conference, December Cambridge.

Laycock, G. and Pease, K. (1985) 'Crime prevention within the probation service', *Probation Journal*, 32: 43–7.

McWilliams, W. (1987) 'Probation, pragmatism and policy', *The Howard Journal*, 26, (2): 97–121.

Mair, G. (1997) 'Community penalties and the probation service', in Maguire, M. Morgan R. and Reiner, B. (1997) *The Oxford Handbook of Criminology*, 2nd edn (Oxford: Clarendon Press).

Martinson, R. (1974) 'What works? – questions and answers about prison reform', *The Public Interest*, 35: 22–54.

May, T. (1991) *Probation: Politics, Policy and Practice* (Buckingham: Open University Press).

Nash, M. (1999a) *Police, Probation and Protecting the Public* (London: Blackstone Press).

Nash, M. (1999b) 'Enter the Probation officer', *International Journal of Police Science and Management*, March 1(4): 360–8.

Nellis, M. (1995) 'Probation values for the 1990s', *The Howard Journal of Criminal Justice*, 34(1): 19–44.

Rawlings, OO (1999) *Crime and Power: a History of Criminal* Justice 1688–1998 (Harlow: Longman).

Rhodes, R. A. W. and Marsh, D. (1992) *Policy Networks in British Government* (Oxford: Oxford University Press).

Sampson, A. and Smith, D. (1992) 'Probation and community crime prevention', *Howard Journal*, 31: 105–19.

von Hirsch, A. (1976) *Doing Justice: The Choice of Punishment* (New York: Hill and Wang).

Walker, H. and Beaumont, B. (1981) *Probation Work: Critical Theory and Socialist Practice* (Oxford: Basil Blackwell).

4

The Legal Profession and Policy Networks: an 'Advocacy Coalition' in Crisis?

Peter Starie, Jane Creaton and David Wall

Introduction

The legal profession is undergoing its most profound transformation for many years. Traditionally, a powerful professional élite protected by the ideology of self-regulation, barristers and solicitors in the UK have, since the late 1970s, been simultaneously exposed to the forces of the market and the state (Brazier *et al.*, 1993; Hanlon, 1998). In this chapter we focus upon the impact of these changes.

We begin by situating the changing nature of the legal profession in terms of a wider crisis of professionalism that has engulfed capitalist societies (Hanlon and Jackson, 1999). This provides a broad context in which to examine the internal and external dynamics of change in respect of legal services in general and the legal profession in particular. This will be followed by a discussion of the respective professional bodies which represent the legal profession – the Law Society and the Bar Council – and the changing nature of their relationship as they have responded to various government initiatives.[1] We will contend that these pressure groups formed a relatively cohesive 'professional policy network' with parts of the state, especially the judiciary, until the 1980s.[2] However, as the context changed – liberalisation of markets, deregulation and re-regulation – the nature of the network changed. The legal profession is now fragmented and divided when compared with its traditional structure. We will argue, however, that these developments should *not* necessarily be interpreted as evidence of the decline of the power of the legal profession or its professionalism. Rather, they are a characteristic of the lawyers adapting to change by renegotiating both their professionalism (Paterson, 1996) and also their professional position within the policy making process.

The changing nature of 'professionalism'

There has long been a debate about the definition of a profession and the concept of 'professionalism' (Johnson, 1972; Dingwall and Lewis, 1983; Seneviratne, 1999). Traditionally, 'professions' have been viewed as somehow different from other forms of employment in the sense of being a distinct type of occupation based on specialised knowledge, education and training, and membership of a governing body – all of which conferred a certain status and prestige on its members. Moreover, 'professionalism' has also been associated with providing services to the wider community who did not possess this specialised knowledge and who had not made the sacrifice of long periods of education and training. Thus, to be a 'professional' was to have a vocation with the purpose of benefiting the clients of the profession. In return, a profession was to be granted autonomy in regulating its own affairs and controlling its members (Hanlon, 1998; Seneviratne, 1999: 6). This description of the traditional view of professionalism combines elements of the 'trait' and 'functionalist' approaches (Johnson, 1972; Seneviratne, 1999). The trait approach stresses that there are certain characteristics which define a profession while the functionalist approach emphasises the altruistic nature and beneficial functions to societies of the professions. However, both approaches have tended to ignore the self-interest of professions and the power relationships involved.

Increasingly, professions have come to be viewed as groups which attempt to exclude others in order to protect their monopolies and privileges. This was because they could control entry to the profession because in turn they provided specialised services that demanded a high degree of training and integrity (Seneviratne, 1999: 7–8). So, professionalism was seen as occupational control over a particular market (Brazier *et al.*, 1993: 197; Abel, 1995). However, this did not happen in a social and political vacuum. For professions to achieve autonomy and self-regulation, they needed to strike a bargain with the state (Brazier *et al.*, 1993: 198). As Seneviratne argues:

> In return for the licence from the state to carry out some of the dangerous and important tasks for society, the professions have

claimed a mandate to define and control their own work, and to influence its content and delivery.

(Seneviratne, 1999: 8)

This means that professionalism should not be viewed in terms of a neutral set of characteristics solely defined by the professions themselves, but as a 'socially constructed, contingent and dynamic concept that is capable of evolution' (Seneviratne, 1999: 19). Moreover, it is crucially contingent on the changing nature of society and the state.

Many commentators, therefore, have situated the changing nature of professionalism in terms of wider social and political forces (Perkin, 1989, 1996; Brazier *et al.*, 1993; Hanlon, 1998; Hanlon and Jackson, 1999). Perkin has gone as far as arguing that the current stage of civilisation is characterised by the 'rise of professional society' (1989) and that we have been witnessing a struggle between public sector and private sector professionals with the latter coming out on top in the last 20 years (1989: 518). Hanlon has commented that while this thesis is persuasive, it does not tell the whole story (Hanlon, 1998: 46). Hanlon concurs that there has been a 'struggle for the soul of professionalism' but argues that it transcends the public–private split. He contends that there has been a battle between the established professions, previously less important professions, and newly emerging professions. He argues that:

> This struggle revolves around whose definition of professionalism emerges as hegemonic.... This contest reflects wider socio-economic forces and represents a structural fragmentation of the service class based on different forms of economic sustenance.
>
> (Hanlon, 1998: 50)

Thus Hanlon argues that we are living in an era of transition defined by a shift from a 'social service professionalism' to a 'commercialised professionalism' which broadly corresponds to the changing nature of capitalist production and a related transformation of the state (Hanlon, 1998). In broader terms, the changing nature of the professions reflects the shift from the Keynesian welfare state to the neo-liberal competition state (Cerny, 1990; Jessop, 1990). Thus, Hanlon squarely situates the redefinition of professionalism in the context of the New Right's ascendancy since the 1970s. Professions have come to be seen much in the same way as trade unions: defending the privileges and monopolies of their members. Hanlon and Jackson comment that:

In short, the right wanted to destroy social democracy and because it saw the professions as a bulwark for this democracy it attacked many of the privileges the professions had taken for granted.

(1999: 560)

While this analysis is also persuasive, it is too sweeping to explain the complexity of the changes that have faced individual professions. For instance, with regard to the legal profession, lawyers cannot simply be classed in the same category as other social service professionals. First, they have been allowed by the state to exercise much more self-regulation. Secondly, they have not been as closely identified with the social democratic welfare state. Moreover, the changing nature of professions is part of a much wider trend than simply a right-wing ideological onslaught. In hindsight, the neo-liberal revolution, while initially propagated by right-wing parties, has proven to be a much more enduring and world-wide phenomenon (as proven by centre-left governments). Thus, our analysis follows that of Brazier *et al.* (1993) in terms of their broad analysis but also in terms of its application to the legal profession.

Brazier *et al.* argue that the deregulation and re-regulation of the 1980s has its origin in the watershed of the mid-1970s. The economic crises that affected both Conservative and Labour governments 'produced a reform-minded coalition in the state élite' (Brazier *et al.*, 1993: 199; see also Middlemas, 1991). This meant that certain professions and other interest groups were vulnerable. Brazier *et al.* rightly comment that professions such as medicine and the law were particularly exposed to the winds of change because they were 'trying to defend regulatory arrangements created during a pre-democratic era in a society with democratic institutions and declining deference' (Brazier *et al.*, 1993: 199). However, they also correctly point out that the winds of change did not hit all of the professions at the same time. First, this would have been tactically naive. But, secondly, and more importantly, some groups were more successful than others in holding off the forces of change because of the 'quality of the alliances' (ibid.) they forged. In a passage strikingly reminiscent of much policy network analysis (but not utilising the terminology), they argue that the encroachment of the state has depended on the 'character of the historical links between an occupation and the state machinery' (ibid.). It is here that we can see why one part of the legal professional policy network was so successful in resisting change. The Bar has had very close links not only with key government departments such as the Lord Chancellor's Department but more broadly with a crucial part of the state, the judiciary.

Thus, several conclusions can be drawn in terms of contextual analysis. First, broad trends can be discerned in terms of the changing nature of society and the state. But, the manner in which these have affected the professions cannot be simply 'read off' from these structural trends. Quite clearly, there has been a shift of power from the public to the private sector (Perkin, 1989) and equally clearly, professionalism has become more commercialised (Hanlon, 1998). However, if there has been a general trend affecting all professions, it is more likely to be that of the 'new managerialism' which is closely linked to private sector commercialism but is not necessarily exactly the same. Nevertheless, the nature of these changes has not been uniform: some professions have been able to resist the tentacles of both the market and the state for a considerable time. The legal profession managed to resist many of these changes because of its close connections to the judiciary and because of the quality of its alliances (a close-knit 'policy community' in the policy networks terminology). However, by the mid-1980s, even the legal profession came into the firing line. In order to understand why this happened, it is not enough to be able to depict the networks resisting the tides of change. A fuller analysis must also briefly examine the socio-legal context.

The changing socio-legal context

The following key trends can be identified which, during recent years, have been responsible for shaping public demand for legal services and, thus, the socio-legal context in which the legal professions are located.

There has been a *marked rise in public demand for legal advice*. By recalculating Smith's (1996: 53) statistics, Wall (1996: 559) illustrated that during the past three decades there has been almost a five-fold increase in the numbers of people seeking legal advice or one sort or another. The impact of this 'advice culture' has two significant impacts. On the one hand, the increased use of lawyers follows an upward trend in the numbers of people who are reaching out for help for 'both the material and psychological aspects of their problems' (Smith, 1996: 52). On the other hand many consumers/clients are now more knowledgeable and reflexive than they used to be which has led to a growing strength of consumer movements. Not surprisingly, this trend translated into to a steep increase in the number of practising lawyers. Since 1969 the total number of solicitors holding practising certificates has grown by 237 per cent at an annual average rate of 4.1 per cent. As of July 1999, there are 79,503 practising solicitors (The Law Society Research and

Policy Planning Unit, 2000). The number of barristers in independent practice is 9,932 (October 1999) having increased at an annual average rate of 5.1 per cent over the last ten years (BDO Stoy Hayward, 1999). There has been a dramatic *increase in the volume and complexity of law.* Although the annual number of laws, in the form of acts of Parliament and statutory instruments, have more or less remained unchanged for the past half century at about 65 and 2,500 respectively, the number of pages covered by those acts tripled from 675 pages in 1951, to 2,222 in 1991. Also, during this period the number of sections and schedules more than doubled from 803 to 1985, as did the number of pages covered by the statutory instruments (from 3,500 to over 6,000) (*Hansard Society,* 1992; Wall, 1996: 557).

There has been a 'qualitative' increase *in the pervasiveness of law.* Galanter (1992: 1) and others (Barton, 1975; MacNeil, 1985), have referred in their work to the 'legal explosion', excessive litigation and the liability crisis. In comparing the legal world of the late 1980s with that of the 1960s Galanter concluded that the law itself is now more plural and decentralised, and it now comes from multiple sources with more rules and standards being applied by more participants to more varied situations, which means that legal outcomes are contingent and changing. Because law is contingent, flexible and technically sophisticated, he argues that legal work has become increasingly costly, yet desired (op. cit.). Consequently, more outcomes are being negotiated rather than being decreed. It is therefore no surprise that there are more lawyers, more claims, more legal players and more expenditure on law (op. cit.).

The trends listed above have impacted upon the legal profession in the following ways:

(1) The relationship between lawyer and client has changed. The traditional 'trustee' relationship between the lawyer and client (Johnson, 1972) has been superseded by a relationship in which lawyers are no longer seen to provide a legal *service* in the traditional sense but are now perceived as conducting legal *business* with the client. As the legal services market has become more varied, clients more diverse and lawyers more specialised then consumers are more ready to complain (op. cit.: 32). Peele comments that '[t]he demands for greater formal regulation and for more effective instruments of accountability reflected wider cultural changes as well as greater exposure to the practices of other political systems' (Peele, 2000: 71). These factors, when combined with the general socio-economic

factors of the last 30 years, to a large extent explain why the legal profession has not remained immune from the winds of competition and regulation. As Seneviratne comments:

> In the past, a deference to professionals probably protected lawyers from too much adverse criticism, and from too much investigation into their work. This is no longer the case. Consumer organisations, departments of Government, and academics are becoming concerned to know what lawyers do, what they charge for doing it, and what accountability and redress mechanisms are available to consumers.
>
> (Seneviratne, 1999: 1)

(2) There has been a change in the nature of the relationships between lawyers themselves. The development of a specialised division of labour within the practice of law has brought about a marked decline in the general practitioner model of legal practice. Lawyers are now generally expected to specialise in an area of law.

(3) There is an increasing polarisation between legal practices which have engaged in the use of information technology and those which have not (Wall and Johnstone, 1997).

(4) As Seneviratne has observed, the composition of the profession has changed: it is younger, has more women members and is more diverse in terms of race and class (Sommerlad and Sanderson, 1998; Seneviratne, 1999: 214).

In summary, the changing socio-legal context has shaped the nature of professionalism in general and the legal profession in particular, and it has redefined traditional legal relationships and it has diversified the legal professions. We now turn our attention to the nature of the professional bodies representing lawyers and outline the changes that have taken place since the late 1970s and early 1980s.

The professional bodies of the legal profession

The above discussions have located the legal profession in the context of the changing nature of professionalism and in the social and economic restructuring of the state in the 1980s and 1990s. However, we need to disaggregate the 'legal profession' into its two key component parts. In fact, the legal profession is two distinct professions, each with a separate professional body and regulatory framework. Although the two professions have had a common interest in maintaining self-regulation and resisting competition from external providers of legal services, their competing interests in the market for legal services have led to bitter jurisdictional disputes. An understanding of this complex and shifting relationship between the two professions is crucial to an analysis of the legal professional policy network and its influence on policy making in criminal justice.

As explained above, the traditional analysis of the relationship between the professions and the state has seen a profession being granted self regulatory and monopoly powers in return for ensuring that members maintain high standards of competence and conduct in the interests of the public. By the 1980s solicitors and barristers had established extensive controls both over entry to the professions and the supply of legal services.

The Law Society, which is the professional body responsible for solicitors, was granted statutory authority by the Solicitors Act 1843 to maintain the roll of qualified practitioners, and in a series of subsequent acts of parliament culminating in the Solicitors Act of 1974, was given regulatory powers over education and training, professional standards and discipline. Solicitors enjoyed the benefit of statutory monopolies over conveyancing, probate and the right to commence or conduct litigation on behalf of another.

Barristers have been regulated by the four Inns of Court for most of their history. The Inns controlled access to the profession by admitting students to the Inn and subsequently calling them to the Bar; provided social and educational facilities for members and exercised disciplinary functions. The Bar Council came into existence in 1895, when it was established to supervise matters relating to professional conduct and etiquette, and slowly wrested regulatory powers and authority over the profession from the Inns. Although the Inns continue to call students to the Bar, the Bar Council has assumed regulatory powers in relation to education and training, professional standards and complaints and discipline.

Barristers had a monopoly over higher court rights of audience, that is, they had an exclusive right to appear as advocates on behalf of clients in the High Court, the Crown Court, the Court of Appeal and the House of Lords. However, the Bar's monopoly derived not from statutory authority, but from the judiciary's common law powers over their courts. The judiciary were drawn from the Bar and close links between the two were maintained through the Inns of Court. Brazier *et al.* observe that the power of a group to maintain its professional privilege 'is closely connected to the historical connections between a group and the state machinery, and therefore to the quality of the alliances the group can forge in resisting reform' (1993: 199). The relationship between the Bar and the judiciary and between the Bar and the Lord Chancellor was an alliance of the highest quality.

Solicitors were also linked into the alliance through complementary monopolies and interlocking restrictive practices that bound the professions together in their common interest. Solicitors were required to instruct barristers to appear on behalf of clients in the higher courts, and the Bar was exclusively a referral profession, accepting instructions solely through solicitors. Although the Law Society consistently challenged the Bar's monopoly over higher court rights of audience, its own monopolies over conveyancing, probate and right to conduct litigation maintained a consistent market share for solicitors.

The legal professions were remarkably successful in maintaining their monopolies and restrictive practices up until the 1980s. The Royal Commission on Legal Services had been established in 1976 'to inquire into the law and practice relating to the provision of legal services, and to consider whether any, and if so what, changes are desirable in the public interest in the structure, organisation, training, regulation of and entry to the legal profession' (Benson Report, 1979). The legal professions argued vigorously against any changes to the status quo and the Commission's Report in 1979 rejected arguments for abolishing the solicitors monopolies, believing that they were essential to the maintenance of high standards of legal advice and services. It also rejected any widening of higher court rights of audience. The Commission accepted evidence from the Bar and the judiciary that the skills required in the higher court rights were of a different order to those exercised by solicitors in the lower courts and also that the nature of solicitors' practices did not permit them sufficient opportunity to exercise advocacy skills regularly. The Commission also resisted change on the explicit grounds of protecting the Bar from competition. A sufficient number of solicitor advocates would have a 'serious and disproportionate impact on the income and capacity of barristers to practice' (Benson Report, 1979, vol. 1: 216).

However, this convenient accommodation between the legal professions as to the division of the legal services market was under increasing pressure. As has been explained earlier in the chapter, external shifts in the political agenda and in the professions would inevitably impact on the market for and delivery of legal services. Glasser argues that this period saw a paradigm shift towards the new managerialism and the perception of the recipients of legal services as customers (cited in Sommerlad, 1996: 292). The consensus between the two professions was finally broken in 1985 as the Administration of Justice Act abolished the solicitors' conveyancing monopoly and permitted licensed conveyancers to undertake this area of work. Looking to protect its members from the potential loss of income from the loss of the monopoly, the Law Society renewed its attack on the Bar's exclusive rights of audience in the higher courts.

The Marre Committee on the Future of the Legal Profession was established by the Law Society and the Bar Council in 1986 in an attempt to reach a new accommodation within the two branches so as to hold off government imposed reform and to preserve it from competition from other providers of legal services. The Committee proposed a limited extension of higher court rights of audience to appropriately qualified solicitors and to balance this proposal, agreed that the Bar should be able to receive instructions directly from a limited number of non-solicitor professional clients. However, this compromise was unacceptable to the barrister members of the panel who issued a dissenting report. It was this paralysis within the legal profession over the rights of advocacy (a not very effective 'advocacy coalition' to use Sabatier's, 1988, terminology) that, according to Brazier *et al.*, precipitated the intervention of the state in the form of the Courts and Legal Services Act (1993). As Thomas argues, '[c]learly, the efforts of the legal profession during the decade of the 80s to put their house in order had been deemed insufficient' (Thomas, 1992: 6).

As we have seen the Bar relied heavily on its links with the judiciary to defend its interests and the Lord Chancellor as a former barrister and a senior judge was the Bar's foremost protector of their interests in the Cabinet. Lord Hailsham vigorously protected the Bar's interests as did his successor, Sir Michael Havers. However, his successor was Lord Mackay of Clashfern. This was a highly astute appointment. Lord Mackay was a Scottish advocate and not a member of the small and tightly knit English Bar. Moreover, he was a 'semi-detached Thatcherite . . . a figure representative of the efficiency-minded élite who so influenced British government after the great crisis of the mid-1970s' (Brazier *et al.*, 1993: 212).

The Lord Chancellor's Department produced three Green Papers in 1989, one of which, *The Work and Organisation of the Legal Profession*, proposed a transformation both in the regulation of the market for legal services and in the market itself. As Thomas has argued:

The documents were worded in the language of the market. Consumerism, choice, and value for money replaced the notions of altruism and self-regulation which for so long had justified the protected status of the legal profession.

(Thomas, 1992: 5)

The Green Paper proposed the removal of the solicitors' monopoly on the right to conduct litigation, conveyancing or probate but the granting of full rights of audience to solicitors and to lawyers in the Crown Prosecution Service. The Lord Chancellor would determine the appropriate qualifications and training required to appear as an advocate in each of the courts.

Whilst the Law Society welcomed the general principle that the Bar's monopoly on higher court rights should be removed, both professions were united in their condemnation of the overall thrust of the proposals for undermining the independence of the legal profession and the judiciary. The legal profession successfully lobbied for a watering down of the proposals. The Bar Council raised a 'fighting fund' of £1 million and used the services of Saatchi and Saatchi (Thomas, 1992: 5). Moreover, the Bar had significant links with the House of Commons as the MPs were exempt from the Bar Council's rule that a barrister's practice must be his or her primary occupation. Senior judges were members of the House of Lords and could lobby effectively. The former Lord Chancellor, Lord Hailsham believed some aspects of the Green Papers were 'definitely sinister' and argued that 'the legal profession could not be regulated like a grocer's shop in Grantham' (cited in Thomas, 1992: 6). Furthermore, sitting judges considered a one-day strike and the Lord Chief Justice attacked the Green Papers as 'one of the most sinister documents ever to emanate from Government' (ibid.).

The subsequent Courts and Legal Services Act 1990 was significantly less radical than the Green Papers. The proposal that the Lord Chancellor could determine the appropriate qualifications and experience for advocates had disappeared. Changes to the professional bodies' rules and regulations still had to be approved by the Lord Chancellor but he was required to consult with four designated senior judges, any of whom could veto the proposed changes.

Despite the compromises forced on the Lord Chancellor, the 1990 Act was a watershed. As Brazier *et al.* comment, 'the very fact of legislation [for barristers] is momentous' (Brazier *et al.*, 1993: 207). Significant inroads had been made into the principle of self-regulation. For the first time in both their histories, the Bar Council and the Law Society had to seek the approval of the Lord Chancellor for any changes to their training regulations and codes of conduct. As part of the approval process, he was also to be advised by the Advisory Committee on Legal Education and Conduct (ACLEC) and the Director General of Fair Trading where the amendments would have or be likely to have, the effect of restricting, distorting or preventing competition to any significant effect. The Act removed the Bar's monopoly on higher court rights of audience, but more significantly permitted applications from other organisations to become authorised bodies, thus removing the legal profession's monopoly on litigation.

As a result of the Courts and Legal Services Act 1990, the Law Society put forward proposals for a Higher Court rights qualification which was eventually approved by the Lord Chancellor and the designated judges. The Institute of Legal Executives and the Institute of Patent Agents were approved as authorised bodies and they gained limited rights to conduct litigation and advocacy. However, there was no radical transformation in the delivery of advocacy services. Ten years after the Act had been passed, less than 1,000 solicitors had qualified as advocates.

The Labour Government was elected in 1997 with a clear agenda for reform of the civil and criminal justice systems. The twin aims of the White Paper *Modernising Justice* (1998) were to bring about a significant increase in access to justice and to obtain the best value for taxpayers' money spent on legal services and the courts. The government proposed to abolish restrictive practices in order to increase competition between lawyers and ensure legal services were delivered at lower cost. As the Lord Chancellor argued in his speech to the Bar in 1999: 'I have far too great a respect for the quality of my own profession to believe that, to flourish, it needs the protection of any restrictive practices' (Lord Irvine, 1999). The prime targets were rules which prevented employed barristers and most solicitors from appearing in the higher courts. The 1998 White Paper also proposed a radical overhaul of the civil legal aid system, replacing the existing system with a mixture of contracting for legal services, conditional fees and legal insurance. The Government also proposed replacing the current criminal legal aid scheme with a new Criminal Defence Service.

The legal professions adopted quite different tactics in responding to the proposals in the Bill. The Law Society has a Parliamentary Unit which targets legislation relating to the interests of the legal profession or delivery of legal services and provides briefings to press and politicians. Other lobbying activities included briefing backbench MPs and submitting evidence to committees and in response to government proposals. This time, however, it opted for a more confrontational approach, running a £600,000 press campaign, directly attacking government proposals to replace legal aid in personal injury claims with conditional fee agreements. It was presented as a campaign to protect the most vulnerable in society but as Young and Wall argue '[t]he legal profession has always been adept, however, at invoking the interests of clients in advancing its own case' (Young and Wall, 1996: 12). Certainly, a large number of solicitors firms specialising in criminal defence became dependent on criminal legal aid (Kerner, 1996) and the threat to remove it had huge implications for individual firms and the profession. Although other organisations supported the campaign, the Lord Chancellor concentrated his attack on the Law Society, accusing them of 'irresponsible scaremongering' and misrepresenting his proposals. One outside commentator described the campaign as political suicide, and this seemed to be borne out when the government amended the Bill to prevent the Law Society spending practising certificate income on 'trade union activities'.

The response of many individual members of the Bar to the 1998 White Paper was as forceful as it had been almost a decade previously in relation to the proposed reforms in the 1989 Green Paper on *The Work and Organisation of the Legal Profession*. High profile opposition came from retired Law Lords, Tory barristers and Labour Queens Counsel (QC) peers. This approach could be characterised as 'agenda resistance' (see Savage and Charman, this volume). However, the Bar Council itself, led by Dan Brennan QC as Chairman, adopted an agenda reshaping approach. The new Lord Chancellor, Lord Irvine of Lairg, had remained in practice until the date of appointment and many senior members of the Bar had New Labour credentials (for example, Helena Kennedy QC and Peter Goldsmith QC) and two obtained key roles in the new government (Lord Williams of Mostyn and Lord Falconer). The use by the Bar Council of external public relations consultants exemplified the new approach. The Bar Council spokesman was Jon McLeod who had previously worked for the Law Society and other members of the team had worked at Millbank.

The Bar Council publicly accepted that the profession could no longer defend its monopoly on historical grounds and took the position that barristers had nothing to fear from competition. It concentrated its lobbying efforts on ensuring the high quality of advocacy services and on the independence of the advocate being in the public interest. It sponsored amendments to the clauses which established the fundamental principles on which the Community Legal Service and the Criminal Defence Service will operate and to the clauses on conditional fee agreements and to the clause extending full rights of audience to employed advocates working for their employer. It persuaded the government that only barristers employed by a firm of solicitors should be entitled to appear as an advocate on behalf of the employers' clients and also to include a clause which gave statutory recognition to the principle that an employed advocate must place the interests of his client and the Court before those of his employer.

In return, the Lord Chancellor met the Bar Council's request for statutory authority to issue compulsory practising certificates, thus confirming the Bar Council as the pre-eminent regulatory authority over the Bar and ensuring a secure source of income for its activities. It also enabled the Bar Council to exploit the Law Society's attempt to defend the ability to use its fees to pay for 'trade union' activities in the result of its legal aid campaign, arguing that it had no desire to use practising certificate income for functions other than regulatory activities and education and training. The Lord Chancellor acknowledged the Bar Council's contribution in his speech at the Bar Conference in 1999:

> Let me pay tribute to the positive approach the Bar Council took while the Access to Justice Act was before Parliament. The Bar, of course, opposed some parts of the Bill, and opposed them vigorously, not the least the proposals for some salaried defenders; but at all times there was constructive dialogue.
>
> (Lord Irvine, 1999)

Dan Brennan QC, Chairman of the Bar in 1999 and subsequently ennobled as a Labour peer commented that:

> The bar developed a successful working relationship with the Government that allowed it to influence the content of the Access to Justice Bill.
>
> (*The Lawyer*, 24 April 2000)

The Access to Justice Act 1999 implements the main proposals of the 1998 White Paper. All solicitors and barristers are deemed to have rights of audience in all courts subject only to the education and training requirements set down by the authorised bodies. While the Lord Chancellor must still consult the designated judges over proposed rule changes, their power of veto has been removed. The Act also gives the Lord Chancellor the power to 'call in' rules of the professional body which do not appear to be in the public interest.

The reforms to the market for legal services set out in the Access to Justice Act have prompted another realignment and renegotiation of the relationship between the professions and between the professions and the government. It seemed as if the power relationship in the legal professional policy network was moving in favour of solicitors and the Law Society. However, the Law Society's lobbying activities were, in 2000, overshadowed by the bitter and protracted dispute over the Deputy Vice President's alleged bullying and intimidation of Law Society staff, which culminated in her resignation. The Society's complaints and discipline body, the Office for the Supervision of Solicitors, continued to grapple with a backlog of 13,000 complaints under the shadow of the Government's threat to remove self-regulation. Concerns were raised in the press that these episodes would 'damage the public's confidence in the profession and the legal system, and stultify our influence with Government and the Bar'. There are suggestions that some of the City law firms may be pushing to set up their own professional body. The City firms were instrumental in pressurising the Law Society to disband the Law Society's compulsory mutual indemnity insurance scheme and enable law firms to get their insurance on the open market, but not before a group of City and commercial firms had threatened to take it to court.

The legal professions also have to contend with a forthcoming Office of Fair Trading (OFT) investigation into restrictive practices in the legal and accountancy professions. This Treasury-led initiative seems out of place coming so soon after major legislation on competitiveness in the legal profession and may have more to do with tensions within government rather than a concerted attack. However, the Bar's status as a referral profession is likely to be at issue. The Bar Council permits certain legally qualified companies and institutions to instruct the Bar directly under a scheme called BarDirect, but individual barristers are not required to participate. It is thought by many that the target of the OFT's investigation was more likely to be the market dominance of a few very large firms of accountants and solicitors in the lucrative commercial market.

It is unclear to what extent the Bar will be able to retain its status as a referral profession in an environment where solicitors, its main source of work, are potentially in direct competition. One barrister commented that 'a profession which depends for its survival on a profession in direct competition is bound to come to a sticky end' (*Guardian*, 26 October 1999). While BarDirect allows for limited access from other professions and organisations with appropriately qualified personnel, this may be counterproductive in the long term. Solicitors may be reluctant to brief barristers who are taking work away from them by accepting instructions directly from the client. On the other hand, by lessening reliance on solicitors and exploring new ways of securing work, this may strengthen the Bar.

The reconfiguration of the legal professional policy network?

The profession is currently engaged in 'a fundamental restructuring whose outcome is indeterminate' (Abel, quoted in Seneviratne, 1999: 219). One option is that the Bar will adapt and survive, and certainly previous predictions about its demise have been premature and wide of the mark. It is still far from clear what impact the Access to Justice Act will have on the market for legal services. The latter half of 1999 and the beginning of 2000 saw a significant number of chambers disband, merge or reform as they attempted to restructure and rationalise in the new legal environment. Research undertaken in relation to Solicitor-Advocates in Scotland suggests that unless the Bar becomes more market driven and responsive to solicitor demands, solicitor advocates will increasingly encroach on the work of the junior Bar (Hanlon and Jackson, 1999).

The professional bodies – the Bar Council and the Law Society – also face the need for strategic realignment (Watkins *et al.*, 1996) in order to respond to the marketisation of the legal environment. Other professional bodies have found that the traditional committee model, reliant on voluntary participation by members, may not be sufficiently responsive to adapt to changes. Other professions are collaborating or merging, and at the Law Society Conference in 1999, the President of the Law Society, Robert Sayers, said that the Bar was an 'anachronism', and that the professions should merge within five years under the regulation of the Law Society. The Bar Council dismissed the suggestion saying that 'the Law Society's track record on self-regulation is at best mediocre and at worst alarming'. Certainly, unless and until the Law Society can demonstrate satisfactory regulation of its complaints and disciplinary procedures, any expansion of its regulatory powers seems a remote prospect. Indeed, the Law Society is already suffering a crisis in confidence of its membership with some commentators predicting that some of the larger city firms will break away from the regulatory authority of the society. There is an increasing divide between the large, internationalised law firms and the smaller firms.

Despite the deregulation of the market for legal services, the regulatory bodies retain a large measure of self-regulation. Indeed to some extent the mechanisms of self regulation have been increased in that the statutory framework places clear responsibilities on both the Law Society and the Bar Council to supervise and maintain education and training, professional standards, etc. However, this puts pressure on the dual functions of the professional bodies to both regulate and represent their members. As Seneviratne rightly comments:

> There is some doubt about whether professional bodies can both represent their members, and at the same time regulate their conduct. . . . The two roles can only be reconciled if professional bodies no longer see themselves as protectors of particular monopolies or privileges. This involves a change in the culture of the profession.
>
> (Seneviratne, 1999: 213)

While the professional associations are clearly being challenged by the market forces which have driven lawyers to increasingly protect their own (local) monopolies and privileges, this fragmentation should not necessarily be viewed as a symptom of the decline of legal professionalism. As lawyers and legal practice become more specialised, then it is no surprise that the (monolithic) professional bodies will fail to represent adequately their members increasingly diverse interests in a policy making environment which has become less hierarchical. To cope with these changes, there has been a marked increase in the number of legal interest groups which each represent specific interests and engage with policy-makers in terms of the issues relating to those interests. In addition to the main professional associations, such as the Law Society and Bar Council, there are many groups which are constituted by a range of characteristics. These characteristics are listed below along with some selected examples of the constituent groups.

- *jurisdiction*: Law Society of Scotland, The Law Society of Northern Ireland, The Law Society of Ireland, Scottish Bar, Northern Irish Bar;
- *specific characteristics shared by lawyers*: African Caribbean & Asian Lawyers' Group, Association of Women Barristers, Association of Women Solicitors, Society of Black Lawyers, Society of Blind Lawyers, Trainee Solicitors Group;
- *common interests in areas of substantive law*: Criminal Bar Association, Criminal Law Practitioners' Group, Criminal Law Solicitors' Association, Employment Law Bar Association, Employment Lawyers' Association, Family Law Bar Association, Environmental Law Foundation, Forum of Insurance Lawyers, Housing Law Practitioners

Association, London Criminal Courts Solicitors Association, Public Law Project, Solicitors' Family Law Association, Solicitors' Property Centres, Society for Computers and Law, Society of Trust and Estate Practitioners;

• *common interests in particular forms of legal service delivery*: The Sole Practitioners' Group, Family Mediators' Association, Centre for Dispute Resolution, Solicitors for Independent Financial Advice, Solicitors' Pro-Bono Group, Legal Aid Practitioners' Group, Mediation UK;

• *socio-political issues or interests*: Legal Action Group, Solicitors' Human Rights Group, The Haldane Society, Law Centres' Federation, National Association of Citizens' Advice Bureaux, Howard League for Penal Reform, NACRO, Justice, Liberty, Prison Reform Trust, Society of Labour Lawyers;

Of key importance, with regard to many of these groups, is the fact that they are affiliated or linked to one or other of the main professional bodies, which adds considerable weight to the argument stated earlier in this chapter that the professional bodies, as well as the legal professionals, are in the process of adapting to occupational changes and are acting reflexively. Also of key importance is the way that each of these groups has the tendency to develop strategic alliances with one or other on some issues, but not necessarily on others.

Conclusion: the legal profession and policy networks

This chapter has sought to examine the changing nature of the legal profession and its relationship to the state. Clearly, the legal professions have not simply been the victim of neo-liberal ideologues in the Conservative and New Labour parties. Rather, the change in the legal profession has reflected much wider attempts by successive governments to modernise aspects of the socio-economic structure of the UK in order to bring it into line with the leading forces of the global economy. While the Conservative's project was one of *regressive modernisation*, New Labour's is, at least in intention, a project of *progressive modernisation*. In the midst of these tensions and the changes that they have effected, legal professionals and their representative bodies have striven to adapt and survive.

By exploring the internal relationship between the legal policy network's two key professional bodies and illustrating the changing nature of its relationship with the state, we have demonstrated that the legal policy network was particularly vulnerable to the winds of change. This was because of its pre-democratic regulatory bargain with the state which meant that it had clung on for far too long to an 'outdated ideology of professionalism' (Brazier *et al.*, 1993; Seneviratne, 1999: 18) which basically allowed self-regulation and autonomy. This link was so close that the legal professions openly acknowledged that they believed they had a 'special relationship' with government. Michael Mears, a former President of the Law Society, stated that 'until 1989, we had been able to deceive ourselves that we were an accredited appendage of government enjoying, almost, a "special relationship"'. A relationship that remained until 'the Thatcher government ... served formal notice of our expulsion from the establishment. It amounted also to a more or less frank declaration of hostility or (worse) contempt' (Wall, 1996: 564). The Labour government's reform proposals and the responses of the legal profession were set out in detail in order to compare the changing nature of the policy network's strategy and tactics in dealing with the reform-minded political élite.

In terms of policy network analysis, the legal profession, although divided into two distinct professions with separate governing bodies, has traditionally formed a close working relationship over a number of years whereby both participants played by the rules of the game. Moreover, one part of this intra-policy network, the Bar, had very close personal and structural connections with one part of the state, the judiciary. This meant that the issue of reforming the legal profession was often kept off the agenda. In terms of Rhodes's typology of policy networks (1990), the legal profession, therefore, was a 'professional policy network' on the 'policy community' end of the continuum (see Cope, Chapter 1, this volume). However, this changed in the 1990s due to the advance of the market and the state. The Green Papers of 1989 marked the first move on behalf of the state in setting a new agenda. As Brazier *et al.* comment, this:

> represented a major 'bid' by the state to change the terms of the regulatory bargain governing its relations with solicitors and barristers.
>
> (Brazier *et al.*, 1993: 207)

As we have seen, this initial attempt at reform was greeted with howls of protest by the Bar, the judiciary, Conservative peers, Labour QCs and the Law Society as a concerted campaign of agenda resistance took shape. This meant that the initial proposals were watered down. However, the tide could not be turned back forever and the Courts and Legal Services

Act represented a major watershed in terms of the reform of the professions. While the Bar Council and the Law Society have drawn several important lessons from this episode about how to shape policy, there has, nevertheless, been an important recognition that certain reforms could not be held off forever. The changing nature of legal services, and the greater heterogeneity of the legal profession and its consumers, means that the old, cosy 'policy community' is probably at an end, the profession now coming to resemble a looser 'issue network' (see Cope, Chapter 1, this volume). This does not necessarily imply, as some commentators have argued, that the legal profession and, indeed the ethos of legal 'professionalism' is in decline (see Seneviratne, 1999: 14–21). Rather, it means that the nature of the profession has been undergoing fundamental changes, some of them internal to the profession, some due to the changing nature of legal services and some due to wider socio-economic and political factors. The legal professions and their representative bodies are renegotiating their position within society and in relation to the state. Whether this means that there will be an 'internal re-ordering of the power relationship within the profession' (Seneviratne, 1999: 18), and a restructuring of the legal policy network, it is probably too early to tell. But the indications are that loose affiliations and strategic alliances will become an integral part of all future policy making processes.

Notes

1. While focusing on the Bar Council and the Law Society, we do recognise that the legal professional policy network is a wider entity composed of many more organisations and pressure groups. We concentrate on these two organisations as the key groups within the legal professional policy network; however there is a discussion of the impact of the many legal interest and pressure groups immediately prior to the conclusion. This chapter does not discuss the role and position of para-legals.
2. We are using the concept of 'policy networks' in terms of describing and analysing a) the internal relationship between pressure groups and b) the relationships between these groups and government. Thus, in terms of policy networks analysis, this chapter is concerned with 'interest intermediation'. We are not using the term policy networks, as some European scholars do, to denote a new mode of governance in the widest sense, i.e. that societies are now being governed by networks. However, it is clear that the governance of the legal profession is also changing. For a discussion of the different types of policy network analysis see Borzel (1998).

References

Abel, R. (1995) 'England and Wales: a comparison of the professional projects of barristers and solicitors' in Abel, R. and Lewis, P. (eds), *Lawyers in Society: An Overview* (University of California Press, LA).

Barton, K. (1975) 'Beyond the legal explosion', *Stanford Law Review*, 47: 57.

BDO Stow Hayward (1999) *Report on the 1999 Survey of Barristers' Chambers*, (London: BDO Stow Hayward).

Benson Report (1979) *Report of the Royal Commission on Legal Services in England and Wales*, Cmnd. 7648.

Borzel, T. (1998) 'Organizing Babylon – on the different conceptions of policy networks' *Public Administration*, 76, Summer: 253–73.

Brazier, M., Lovecy, J., Moran, M. and Potton, M. (1993) 'Falling from a tightrope: doctors and lawyers between the market and the State', *Political Studies*, XLI: 197–213.

Cerny, P. (1990) *The Changing Architecture of Politics*, (Sage: London).

Dingwall, R. and Lewis, P. (eds) (1983) *The Sociology of the Professions: Lawyers, Doctors and Others*, (London: Macmillan Press – now Palgrave).

Dyer, C. (1999) 'Trouble at the Bar', *Guardian*, 26 October.

Galanter, M. (1992) 'Law abounding: legalisation around the North Atlantic', *Modern Law Review*, 55(1): 47–61.

Green Papers (1989) *The Work and Organisation of the Legal Profession* (Cm. 570), *Contingency Fees* (Cm. 571), *Conveyancing by Authorised Practitioners* (Cm. 572).

Hanlon, G. (1998) 'Professionalism as enterprise: service class politics and the redefinition of professionalism' *Sociology*, 32(1): 556–82.

Hanlon, G. and Jackson, J. (1999) 'Last orders at the bar?: competition, choice and justice for all – the impact of solicitor-advocacy', *Oxford Journal of Legal Studies*, vol. 19: 556–82.

Hansard Society (1992) *Making the Law: The Report of the Hansard Society Commission on the Legislative Process* (London: The Hansard Society for Parliamentary Government).

Lord Irvine (1999) 'Keynote address to the Annual Conference at the Bar', <www.open.gov.uk/lcd/speeches>.

Jessop, B. (1990) *State Theory* (Cambridge: Polity).

Johnson, T. (1972) *Professions and Power* (Basingstoke: Macmillan Press – now Palgrave).

Kerner, K. (1996) 'Legal firms, lawyer's attitudes and criminal legal aid in Scotland' in Young, R. and Wall, D. (1996b).

MacNeil, I. R. (1985) 'Bureaucracy, liberalism and community – American style', *North Western Law Review*: 111–19.

Middlemas, K. (1991) *Power, Competition and the State: volume 3 – The End of the Post-war Era* (London: Macmillan Press – now Palgrave).

Paterson, A. (1996) 'Professionalism and the legal services market', *International Journal of the Legal Profession*, 3(1): 327–40.

Peele, G. (2000) 'The law and the constitution' in P. Dunleavy *et al.* (eds), *Developments in British Politics 6* (Basingstoke: Macmillan Press – now Palgrave).

Perkin, H. (1989) *The Rise of Professional Society: England Since 1880* (London: Routledge).

Perkin, H. (1996) *The Third Revolution: Professional Elites in the Modern World* (London: Routledge).

Rhodes, R. (1990) 'Policy networks – a british perspective', *Journal of Theoretical Politics*, 2(3): 291–317.

Seneviratne, M. (1999) *The Legal Profession: Regulation and the Consumer* (London: Sweet and Maxwell).

Smith, R. (1996) 'Legal aid and justice', in Bean, D. (ed.), *Law Reform for All* (London: Blackstone Press).

Sommerlad, H. (1996) 'Criminal legal aid reforms and the restructuring of legal professionalism' in Young, R. and Wall, D. (1996b).

Sommerlad, H. and Sanderson, P. (1998) *Gender, Choice and Commitment: Women Solicitors in England and Wales and the Struggle for Equal Rights* (Brookfield, VT: Ashgate).

The Law Society Research and Policy Planning Unit (2000) *Trends in the Solicitors Profession, Annual Statistical Report 1999* (London: The Law Society).

Thomas, P. (1992) 'Thatcher's will', *Journal of Law and Society*, vol. 19: 1–2.

Wall, D. S. (1996) 'Legal aid, social policy and the architecture of criminal justice: the supplier induced demand thesis and legal aid policy', *Journal of Law and Society*, vol. 23,00.

Wall, D. S. and Johnstone, J. (1997) 'The industrialisation of legal practice and the rise of the new electric lawyer: the impact of information technology upon legal practice', *International Journal of the Sociology of Law*, vol. 25,00.

Watkins, J., Drury, L. and Bray, S. (1996) *The Future of the UK Professional Associations* (Cheltenham: Cheltenham Strategic Publication).

White Paper (1998) *Modernising Justice: The Government's Plans for Reforming Legal Services and the Courts*, Cm 4155 (London: HMSO).

Young, R. and Wall, D. (1996a) 'Criminal justice, legal aid, and the defence of liberty', in Young and Wall.

Young, R. and Wall, D. (eds) (1996b) *Access to Criminal Justice: Legal Aid, Lawyers and the Defence of Liberty*, Blackstone Press Ltd, London.

5
The Courts: New Court Management and Old Court Ideologies

Ben Fitzpatrick, Peter Seago, Clive Walker and David Wall

The development of the courts in England and Wales during the past decade has taken place within a changing environment of political administration and has been particularly affected by the ethos that has become known as the 'new public management'. This ethos includes: the functional separation of administration from policy; an emphasis upon the 'holy trinity' of economy, efficiency and effectiveness; the desire to satisfy 'consumer' needs; the measurement and audit of performance; the comparison of performance between different service-deliverers; inter-agency working; and the involvement of the private sector.[1]

In this chapter we shall explore the impacts of the agenda of new public management upon criminal justice policy as it relates to the criminal courts in the UK. For two reasons, the focus of this essay will be upon the magistrates' courts in England and Wales. Firstly, it is these summary courts which handle the vast majority (over 95 per cent) of the criminal proceedings in England and Wales (*Criminal Statistics for England and Wales*, 1997: 123). Secondly, many of the most dramatic changes in the criminal legal system have taken place in this tier. We shall argue that while new public management, or 'new court management' as we shall label it, has clearly had a considerable impact upon the structure of the courts, its overall impact has, nevertheless, been considerably tempered by the persistence of discourses of localism and laity and also by the principle of judicial independence, all of which we shall call here the 'old court ideologies'. Notwithstanding that the concept of new public management is itself contestable, it still can provide a heuristic device against which to contrast the old court ideologies. It is the nature of this contrast which will provide the overall theme of the chapter.

The first section of this chapter will look briefly at the historical development of the court structure to map out the terrain that was the organisational basis for old court ideologies. The second section will examine more specifically the impact of new court management upon the magistrates' courts. The third section will discuss the contrast between old and new court ideologies. The fourth section will identify the various professional associations and representative organisations within the court sector constellation and their role in shaping the policies and practices of the courts. The final section will offer some conclusions.

The historical development of the court structure

In this section we shall try to give a brief overview of the history behind the present day structures and ideological conflicts surrounding the criminal courts of first instance.[2] It will briefly describe the major themes relating to the historical development of the court structure and will contrast the past with the present.

The courts of criminal jurisdiction

Until 1971, three courts dealt with first instance criminal cases, all with localised jurisdictions and administrative structures. These were the Assizes, Quarter Sessions and Petty Sessions. The Assizes were the senior courts and dealt with the most serious offences.[3] They grew up out of the practice of the Norman Kings to send royal officials on a tour of inspection of the country. When they arrived in a particular town, arrested criminals were handed over for trial. These travelling officials held the commissions of 'oyer and terminer' (the power to try all cases presented to the assize by the Grand Jury) and 'gaol delivery' (the power to try the cases of anyone in prison when the justices came into a town).

Quarter Sessions arose from the practice of appointing local lay dignitaries, originally called Keepers of the Peace, to carry out local government tasks; they took this function away from the sheriffs who had become mistrusted. They were obliged to sit four times a year; hence the name Quarter Sessions. Gradually, they acquired the right to deal with serious criminal cases (felonies), and they began to deal with less serious offences out of sessions, and these sessions became known as the petty sessions (now called magistrates' courts) (Dawson, 1960; Milton, 1967; Page, 1967; Moir, 1969; Harrison and Maddox, 1975; Skyrme,

1979; 1991; Landau 1984; Pain, 1988; Raine, 1989). In some areas (especially London), it became difficult to find reliable and willing locals, so the practice was adopted of appointing lawyers as stipendiary (paid) magistrates.[4]

There was for many years a distinction between the County and the Borough Quarter Sessions. Under the Municipal Corporations Act 1882, the Borough Quarter Sessions had a sole lawyer-judge called a recorder, who was a practising barrister of at least five years standing and who was appointed by the Crown on the advice of the Lord Chancellor. The recorder would sit alone with a jury to hear pleas of not guilty. In the remaining courts of Quarter Sessions the bench would comprise lay magistrates with a jury, but the practice grew up of appointing legally qualified chairmen in which case the jurisdiction of the court was increased. In contrast to the boroughs, the counties retained lay magistrates until 1938, when the Administration of Justice (Miscellaneous Provisions) Act of that year, allowed for the appointment of lawyers – thereafter, lay magistrates began to decline in the county quarter sessions.

This structure continued until the Courts Act 1971, which, following the Beeching Royal Commission, abolished the Assizes and Quarter Sessions and replaced them with the Crown Court. The Crown Court is a single national court with a unified administrative structure (now placed in the hands of an executive agency of the Lord Chancellor's Department, the Courts Service)[5] but with the power to sit in any of its locations (*Royal Commission on Assizes and Quarter Sessions*, 1969).[6] It hears the indictable offences not suitable for summary trial by reason of the seriousness of the potential penalty. Its judges are professional High Court Judges, circuit judges and recorders. A lay jury is still used to try issues of guilt, but the link with the local community is far less close than before 1972. There are now only 78 court centres (as compared to 64 Assize and 157 Quarter Sessions venues in 1969), and the Beeching Report conceded that the problem of balancing physical convenience and economic loading for these higher courts was intractable (iop. at.: 118–20, 275, 283). The distribution of cases between Crown Court and the magistrates' courts has been modified several times since 1971, with the pressure always to make greater use of the cheaper summary courts (Interdepartmental Committee, 1975; Home Office, 1995, 1999).

The organisation of the magistrates' courts

The administration of the magistrates' courts has gradually evolved throughout the twentieth century. It will suffice for present purposes if we try to outline the picture in the period around about 1980, since when the pace of change has arguably been most marked.

Up to around 1980, the basic unit was the Petty Sessional Division which may have comprised one court or, particularly in rural areas, a group of courts. In the Leeds area, for example, Leeds City Court was a single court Petty Sessional Division. Outer Leeds comprised three Petty Sessional Divisions, of which Wetherby and Morley were single court Petty Sessional Divisions and Pudsey and Otley a two court Petty Sessional Division. The day-to-day administration of these courts was in the hands of the justices' clerk, and other support staff. The justices' clerk also acted as legal adviser in the courtroom to the lay magistrates. A justices' clerk could be responsible for just one Petty Sessional Division or for a group of Petty Sessional Divisions. In the Leeds area, there was one justices' clerk for Leeds City and one justices' clerk for the three outer Petty Sessional Divisions. At that time a justices' clerk, even in a large Petty Sessional Division such as Manchester, would expect to act as a court clerk in the courtroom once or twice a week, in order to emphasise the judicial as opposed to the administrative side of his or her office. However, during the 1950s the workload in some Petty Sessional Divisions was so light that the post was filled only part time, the justices' clerk splitting the week between work as a private sector solicitor and work as a justices' clerk.

Under the Justices of the Peace Act 1949 and following the recommendations of the Roche Report (1944: para. 99), magistrates' courts committees were established primarily to deal with the appointment of the justices' clerks and their staff. The Act provided that there should be a magistrates' courts committee for each county, each county borough and for each non-county borough with its own Commission of the Peace and a population of over 65,000. Consequently, a magistrates' courts committee might be responsible for a single Petty Sessional Division with its justices' clerk, or a group of Petty Sessional Divisions under a single justices' clerk or even a group of Petty Sessional Divisions under two justices' clerks.[7] The magistrates' courts committee would comprise around 24 or so of magistrates elected by their colleagues to represent their Petty Sessional Division. The committees were an extremely unwieldy tool of strategic planning, given their size and the local rivalries on display.

There was at this time a great variation in the efficiency and professionalism of the magistrates' courts. The training of lay magistrates was scarce and to a large extent optional. Though training for lay justices was introduced in 1966 (Training of Justices, 1995), only those magistrates appointed after 1980 have had to give a commitment to undertake it.[8] Throughout this period local authorities were responsible for one fifth of the financing of the magistrates' courts in their area,[9] and their reluctance to spend money on the administration of justice was a serious impediment to the efficient running of the system.

The position to date

The picture presented in 1980 was of a large number of courts, each with its own administration and with considerable variations in sentencing policy from one court to another. The defects were fragmentation, inefficiencies and lack of professionalism and consistency. The remedy was new court management.

Several proposals were advanced for consolidating control of the magistrates' courts system entirely into the hands of one central government and more particularly into the control of the Lord Chancellor's Department. Despite the fact that virtually the whole court system was under the control of the Lord Chancellor's Department, as was the appointment of magistrates, responsibility for the administration of magistrates' courts was for historical reasons (broadly relating to the policing functions of justices of the peace), in the hands of the Home Office. Accordingly, overall responsibility for the magistrates' courts service was transferred to the Lord Chancellor's Department in 1992.[10]

In the meantime, the Magistrates' Courts Committee were responding to central government exhortations to reduce the number of petty sessional divisions, usually facing down opposition from Petty Sessional Divisions which would lose their separate status and eventually their court-houses. There was also an increasing focus on the cost-effective and expeditious transaction of administrative work. As in all walks of public life during the 1980s and early 1990s, efficiency and cost effectiveness became the yardsticks against which the courts were measured. Magistrates' courts committees began to achieve efficiency and financial gains, *inter alia*, by increasing use of information technology and by reducing the number of clerks. Thus, in Leeds for example, where there had been two justices' clerks, one to manage the Petty Sessional Division of Inner Leeds and one to manage the three outer division Petty Sessional Divisions, the magistrates' courts committee which controlled both divisions, decided to merge the management and to dispense with one of the justices' clerks. This type of cost saving meant an increase in administrative duties for the justices' clerks, who found it increasingly difficult to sit as a clerk in court.

In 1989 the Le Vay Report (1989) concluded that there was no coherent management structure in the magistrates' courts system as a whole. The Report focused on the resourcing and management systems for magistrates' courts and sought to leave to one side their judicial function. It recommended that the system should be consolidated and be brought under central control via an executive agency, subject to as much local delegation of administration as possible. The justices' clerks should concentrate more on their legal work, while day-to-day administration should be in the hands of court managers who would be responsible to the new agency.

In response, the Police and Magistrates' Courts Act 1994[11] provided for powers to impose the merger of magistrates' courts committees. It also established a new justices' chief executive. The intended pattern was to be a group of Petty Sessional Divisions each with a justices' clerk in charge of the legal side with a justices' chief executive in charge of the overall administration.[12] The basic idea is that the justices' clerks should be freed from much of the administration to enable them to concentrate on the judicial side of their duties. A common pattern under the new scheme is for an administrative officer to work alongside each justices' clerk. The administrative officer is responsible for the day to day administration of that clerkship, and their line manager is the justices' chief executive. The 1994 Act further provided for a magistrates' Courts Service Inspectorate, which can carry out surveys and disseminate good practice.[13]

The Act did not adopt the ultimate centralising proposal of the Le Vay Report – that the whole system should be managed by a central agency – local interests proved either too alluring or too obstinate to allow that change. The result is to leave magistrates' courts committees as the key nodes in the administrative system. Consequently, they were also the subject of substantial reform in the 1994 Act. A major change was that the number of magistrates serving on the new magistrates' courts committees was reduced, to a maximum of 12 and often to 10.[14] Members were no longer to be elected by their bench colleagues but chosen by a panel of selectors who were elected (admittedly often on Petty Sessional Division lines) at the Bench Annual General Meetings. The idea is that those selected to the magistrates' courts committees should no longer consider themselves as representing their own Petty Sessional Division but as serving the interests of the whole area.

The post-1997 Labour Government has now returned to the issue and has forced further mergers to ensure that there should be co-terminocity among the Crown Prosecution Service, police and probation services and magistrates' courts committee areas (Lord Chancellor's Department, 1998a: ch. 5). Further, those areas which managed to persuade the previous government that the same person should hold the office of justices' clerk and justices' chief executive (for example at Leeds, Halifax, Rotherham and Hillingdon) now face an ultimatum from the Lord Chancellor. While magistrates' courts have been considerably streamlined, questions continue to emerge as to whether the efficient running of a multi-million pound system can, in this age of rational bureaucracy, be left to any significant extent in the hands of willing volunteers from amongst the 30,000 or so lay magistrates. It is anticipated that an agency system will return to haunt the local laity, but, if it does, it will increase simmering concerns about the impact of all of these changes on the fundamental nature of the judicial function at this level, for the boundaries between judicial and administrative duties are far from distinct.

New court management and the magistrates' courts

This section describes the doctrines around new public management and some of the post-new public management variants, especially 'new court management'. It will seek to explain how these ideas have affected the magistrates' courts since the late 1970s.

New public management is a *post hoc* label, which, as we have outlined above, can be used as a generic heading for the process of infiltration of a variety of administrative techniques and strategies, commonly associated with the private sector, into arenas more readily described as 'public'. It is difficult to pinpoint the exact genesis of new public management in the UK, but it arose out of financial management initiatives in central government in the early 1980s (Treasury and Civil Service Select Committee, 1982; Baldwin, 1988; Drewry, 1988; Ibbs Report, 1988; Lewis, 1994; Greer, 1994). It is subsequently possible to observe the encroachment of new public management into a variety of fields, those attracting the majority of media attention being health and education. It was inevitable that criminal justice, as a significant arena of public 'consumption' and also a metwand of political popularity, should be affected by new public management. Naturally, some aspects of the delivery of criminal justice, as impinged upon by new public management, have proven more newsworthy than others (Cope, 1996; Crawford, 1997; Raine and Wilson, 1997). The contracting out of increasingly significant services in the prison sector, from the conveyance of prisoners to the management of prisons themselves, has been towards the top of the media's agenda. One can also point to the performance of the police, no longer as 'force' but as 'service' in new public management speak, as exciting even more attention. By contrast, it is perhaps unsurprising that the manner in which the magistrates' courts have been affected by new public management has been the subject of little comment.[15] But, given their centrality to the ascription of criminal guilt, added to the proliferation of civil, family and ancillary matters which the magistrates' courts must handle, the case for insouciance is considerably undermined. In reality, the consideration of new public management is especially pertinent to magistrates' courts; by contrast to the Crown Court, they are conventionally conceived as being rooted in locality and as being possessed of an ability to respond sensitively to the needs of the community they serve. However, new public management presents a potential challenge, through its tendency towards centralisation and uniformity, not just to the functioning of the magistrates' courts, but also to their very *raison d'être*. So, to what extent has new public management in fact affected the manner in which the magistrates' courts deliver their 'product'?

Managerialism has been brought to bear cumulatively on magistrates' courts, following the Le Vay Report in 1989,[16] the White Paper (1992), *A New Framework for Local Justice*, in 1992 and the Narey Report in 1997. It was most marked in legislative terms by Part IV of the Police and Magistrates' Courts Act 1994. The following are some identifiable 'manifestations' of new public management.

The post of Justices' Chief Executive

As already indicated, the post of Justices' Chief Executive was created by the Police and Magistrates' Courts Act 1994.[17] The original intention of the Government had been to accord to the office the title 'chief justices' clerk' and to require the postholder to act as both head of service and in a judicial or quasi-judicial capacity. Unsurprisingly perhaps, this raised considerable fears within the justice community that the independence of the judiciary might be compromised and that the constitutional doctrine of the separation of powers might be infringed.[18] The archetypal concern was of the chief justices' clerk using their executive capacity to influence judicial decision-making in order to meet efficiency targets. The name of the post was changed on its passage through Parliament, and it became, in theory, an office charged with exclusively administrative functions. This distinction between administrative and legal tasks is acutely problematic. Problem functions, in the 'grey area' at the intersection of legal and administrative, include: listing of cases; the magistrates' rota; the granting of legal aid; and fine enforcement. The lack of clear classification of a task as legal or administrative can make it difficult to determine which officer, justices' clerk or justices' chief executive, is ultimately responsible. Attempts have later been made to clarify the distinction, and Schedule 13 to the Access to Justice Act 1999 transfers a number of administrative functions to justices' chief executives which previous statutes had imposed on justices' clerks.

Through the separation within the Magistrates' Courts Service of legal/judicial from administrative functions, the Clerks to the Justices have been relieved of the burden of operational administrative management, which (it appears to be relatively common ground among those concerned), were hindering the effective discharge of their primary legal duties. The justices' chief executive acts as a day to day manager of the courts service within the magistrates' courts committee area, and with the magistrates' courts committee itself in the latter's discharge of its function of strategic management of the service.

At the time of the passage of the Police and Magistrates' Courts Act 1994, opinion was divided as to whether the justices' chief executive should be a qualified lawyer. In the event, the Act provided that a justices' chief executive had to be eligible for appointment as a justices' clerk[19] – that is, a qualified barrister or solicitor, but this remained a vexed issue. Now the requirement of legal qualification has been removed by section 87 of the Access to Justice Act 1999. Nonetheless, we can expect the debate to continue as to the optimal characteristics for an effective justices' chief executive. Should they be a former justices' clerk (as most have been hitherto), possibly sensitive to the nuances of inter-personnel relationships in the Magistrates' Courts Service, but with the potential perhaps to overstep their administrative remit to their legal background? Should they be a non-justices' clerk lawyer, with experience of participating in the processes of the Magistrates' Courts Service, but not necessarily with appropriate managerial experience? Should they be explicitly non-lawyers, with proven success in administration and management in other fields, and able to bring a fresh eye to the arena of the magistrates' courts? Clearly, the impetus in the 1999 Act is towards the latter model, though experience elsewhere in the public sector of such outside appointments has not always been a happy one – the case of Derek Lewis' dismissal in 1995 as head of prison service may be instructive. Time will tell whether, and under what circumstances, the sustained efficiency and effectiveness gains which form the rationale for the creation of the post are realised in practice.

The amalgamation of Magistrates' Courts Committee Areas

As we observed earlier, the magistrates' courts committee is a localised body, comprising almost exclusively of lay magistrates selected by their fellow magistrates, and responsible for the effective and efficient administration of courts within its area.[20] The committees have been streamlined[21] to emerge as local management boards which are responsible for the 'efficient and effective administration' of their courts.[22] However, the extent to which the magistrates' courts committees have taken on this core management task was questioned by the Lord Chancellor in his statement to the House of Lords on 29 October 1997:[23]

> The provisions of the 1994 Act have yet to be implemented in a way which achieves significant improvement in the organisation and management of the magistrates' courts throughout England and Wales.

It was felt that, despite all the reforms, effectiveness and efficiency were being compromised by a number of deficiencies, including: the configuration of magistrates' courts committees, which meant that they were serving not merely geographical areas of differing sizes, but were responsible for the administration of differing numbers of staff, court buildings, and, of course, magistrates; excessive bureaucracy through an over-proliferation of sub-committees and a lack of clear terms of reference for the various levels to which responsibilities might be delegated; duplication of tasks by staff in different magistrates' courts committees, which could be obviated by unifying and standardising those tasks through amalgamation; a lack of strategic planning with relation to magistrates, staff, and buildings, caused in some cases by an insufficiency of estate resources to enable meaningful planning to take place; insufficient monitoring and networking of performance targets and achievements, with the correlative difficulty of developing universal good practice; and the difficulties faced when attempting to liaise with other criminal justice agencies, caused by a lack of geographical alignment with the boundaries of those other agencies, most notably, police, probation and Crown Prosecution Service. The Lord Chancellor suggested that where amalgamations of magistrates' courts committees had taken place on a voluntary basis, effectiveness and efficiency gains were notable. The aim was therefore to condense by about half the then 96 magistrates' courts committees (the figure is 84 at the end of 1999). The process of amalgamation is ongoing and is now enshrined in various policy documents and default statutory powers[24] and is likely to occupy the Lord Chancellor's Department, and various magistrates' courts committees into the new millennium. In the meantime, Lord Chancellor's Department has commissioned research (Fitzpatrick *et al.*, forthcoming),[25] to be conducted along qualitative, as well as quantitative lines, into the changing 'courtscape'. This research will shed some light on the methods used at the local level to implement centrally dictated strategies, and on the manner in which the key personnel at magistrates' courts committee level, most particularly, the justices' chief executive, the clerks to the justices, the magistrates' courts committee members, and those personnel involved in training staff and magistrates towards the realisation of effectiveness and efficiency, affect the way in which those strategies are implemented.

The Magistrates' Courts Service Inspectorate

The 1994 Act provided for a new national audit system, the Magistrates' Courts Service Inspectorate (MCSI).[26] This mechanism can again readily be seen as a threat to localism and laity which are distinctive of magistrates' courts, especially as it is based within, and funded by, the Lord Chancellor's department, though the MCSI itself claims independence.[27] Neither is the MCSI barred from visits to courts in open session, raising concerns about the distinction between judicial and administrative functions (Baker and English, 1994: 124).

The usual panoply of management-speak has followed all of these reforms, with an extensive management information system (MIS), performance indicators, aims, objectives and mission statements. For example, the Leeds MCC states that it is committed to 'achieving the highest standards of local justice and service through a system which, within financial constraints, is efficient, expeditious and commands public confidence'. This change in culture has perhaps been one of the main achievements of the MCSI, though it has not, of course, been secured by its efforts alone. In contrast to this rather intangible objective, much more specific reforms are canvassed in its inspection reports – including boundary changes, good practice in regard to court business, and the best use of building and information technology. These recommendations can now be enforced: the Access to Justice Act 1999, section 85 grants the Lord Chancellor a power to direct the implementation of recommendations.

Old court ideologies versus new court management

Though the new public management remains an important determinant of developments in the magisterial sector, it is by no means the only influential discourse. Indeed, new public management challenges much older and more firmly established discourses. The interplay between the new public management and the older discourses should now be considered.

The old court ideologies include the attachment to the values of localism and laity. The concept of geographically sensitive justice is troublingly vague, but such a lay 'bench ethos' can be constructed from what Carlen calls a 'mass of situationally evolved knowledge' (Carlen, 1976: 75). Lay magistrates do seem to view themselves as 'the custodians of the community', representing and understanding the locality and its customs and values, so that 'a threat to the community becomes a threat to the magistracy and *vice versa*' (Brown, 1991: 111–12). In addition, the rules of appointment expressly state that magistrates must live within 15 miles of the boundary of the commission area.[28] So, these are values which are seen to be important in criminal justice as a way of making the courts accessible, in tune with the public interest and even democratic. But they cut across the standardisation and professionalisation of new public management which therefore challenges the claims of lay localism. There are, for example, far fewer magistrates' courts sites than in the past, so that any local attachments will be less strong for all justices, whether lay or professional. This trend was given a boost by a Home Office Consultation Paper on *The Size of Benches* (1986) (Raine and Wilson, 1993: 106) which pressed for both the abolition of benches with fewer than 12 magistrates and also a reduction in the number of petty sessional areas. Consequently, the number of benches has been reduced from nearly 650 to under 400 as a result. The administrative squeeze has also been backed by cash limits from 1992 onwards, all of which prompted the closure of smaller court-houses in favour of larger inner-city court buildings. This combination of changes could be said to remove the physical and symbolic link between localities and magisterial justice.[29] The logical next step would be to rationalise further in terms of the provision of judicial services. In this way, as justice becomes less localised, why should magistrates' courts buildings be distinct from Crown Court buildings, and most controversial of all, in the absence of any practical need for, as opposed to abstract ideology of, localism, why is there a need for lay justices to reflect local connections?

Another established old court ideology is that judicial independence remains a sacrosanct principle. The meanings of judicial independence are also malleable, but whatever they turn out to be, the discourses of new public managerialism can easily be viewed as 'at odds with the conventions and expectations of the justice system' (Raine and Wilson, 1993: 2) by skewing the values and objectives within the institution (Power, 1997). This fear was voiced as long ago as 1988 by Sir Nicholas Browne-Wilkinson (as he was then), who warned of the insidious threat from the application of disciplines such as value for money and efficiency and called for judges to decide the allocation of monies within global budgets set by Parliament.[30] More specifically, this concern arises since judicial decision-making and judicial administration may no longer be severable (Woolf, Rt Hon. Lord Justice, 1996):

> the judge of today cannot retain his earlier passive judicial role. The extraordinary complexity of modern litigation requires him, if his cases are not to linger for years, to exercise a crucial management function.

> (Kaufman, 1979: 686)

This means that concerns about standardisation and even efficiency and economy must be moderated, as ultimately judges (magistrates) must be allowed to be unbiddable and even quirky.

It would be a mistake to view these competing values as simply a counterpart 'old public management', for they are concepts which are both substantive as well as processual. Nor were they suddenly fashioned as a coherent programme in response to the circumstances or prevailing ideology of a particular era. But they certainly cut across the aims of new public management and have served to both obstruct and interact with it in ways which have sometimes been unpredictable. For example:

The functional separation of administration from policy

This aspect of new public management is seen in the appointment of chief executives under the Police and Magistrates' Courts Act, but many have been reconstituted justices' clerks and the further calls of the Le Vay Report for an umbrella agency have not been pursued.

An emphasis upon economy, efficiency and effectiveness

This aspect of new public management is reflected in the closure of court-houses and the consolidation of magistrates' courts committees. It is also reflected in a continuing agenda of reform in the institutional and procedural aspects of magistrates' court business. Among the waypoints of the policy are the Narey Report and the various policy developments in relation to stipendiary magistrates (Seago *et al.*, 2000). But the core of the system remains the lay magistrate who is over 30 times less efficient than an equivalent professional magistrate but to whom the government remains committed for (old) ideological reasons. Lord Chancellor Irvine adverted to some of the dilemmas in a speech in 1999:[31]

> Local diversity is your unique strength – the factor which can take into account the idiosyncrasies of local culture and behaviour. But society can be hard in its judgement on what it perceives as inconsistency. The public, and the media, look critically at the decisions of bench against bench. They can interpret differences as proof that the magistrates are uncertain amongst themselves, and that nature of justice that you get depends on where you live.

Nevertheless, the principle seems to one of support for lay justices, and this has been reaffirmed from time to time by the Lord Chancellor's Department:[32]

> The Lord Chancellor has no plans to work toward the appointment of stipendiary magistrates in every town with a population exceeding 70,000. Stipendiary magistrates appointments are to commission areas and the Lord Chancellor will consider such appointments normally when he receives requests from those areas and he considers that the workload warrants that course. The Lord Chancellor has full confidence in the ability of the lay magistracy to cope with the bulk of work. The purpose of stipendiary appointments is to support the lay magistracy.

The measurement and audit of performance

This is taken up by the MCSI, but as already described, its role has been hitherto mainly advisory and hortatory. Only in 1999 (under the Access to Justice Act, section 85) has the power been granted to the Lord Chancellor to give a direction requiring the MCC to take the recommended action within a period specified in the direction.

Inter-agency working and private sector involvement

Inter-agency working may for the future be achieved through the harmonisation of jurisdictional boundaries, and the post-Woolf Criminal

Justice Consultative Councils demand such co-operation (Woolf and Tumin, 1991). But because of judicial independence, the degree of inter-activity is likely to be extremely limited and will mainly concentrate upon the exchange of information. Tooling up the courts with the necessary information technology equipment has been the main function of the private sector (Bellamy and Taylor, 1998; Walker, 2000), and it is notable that no attempt has been made to 'privatise' the judicial function whether through arbitration, diversion or otherwise. In addition, though there is a power under section 28 of the Justices of the Peace Act 1997 to co-opt two non-justices of the peace to the MCC, this power was conceived with the higher judiciary and (in rural areas) Lord Lieutenants in mind; there is no equivalent to the representation of business acumen as with the reconstituted Police Authorities.[33]

The conflicts between new public management and old court ideology can also be related to the different interest groups within the magistrates' courts.

Professional associations and representative organisations

This section will identify the various professional associations that exist within the sector. An attempt will be made to map their stances in general and reactions to sample policy initiatives. Of course, there are many others professionals – legal representatives, the police and Crown prosecutors – whose work brings them into contact with the courts and who may well pressure the courts in various ways, but it is sufficient here to concentrate on the 'insiders'.

Lay magistrates

The vast majority of the 30,000 or so magistrates in England and Wales belong to the Magistrates' Association.[34] Through its representative council and specialist committees, it will form a response to all matters affecting the summary courts. It has taken the initiative to provide magistrates with national sentencing guidelines, initially for road traffic offences, but more recently for all types of commonly occurring offences. In policy terms, it serves as a champion of old court ideologies. One example concerns its views on the appointment of stipendiary magistrates, an issue which has been of great concern to lay magistrates who see the increasing cohort as a threat to their own position. It has sought to persuade the Lord Chancellor's Department that it is unhappy about one of the three criteria used to determine whether a stipendiary was needed by a particular court; the Association alleged that the criterion that a bench of 150 magistrates was likely to be unwieldy and therefore in need of stipendiary support was too low and a figure of 250 should be substituted. Likewise, when the Lord Chancellor's Department was minded to increase long-standing ceilings on the total number of provincial stipendiary appointments, it was recognised that this would be a sensitive issue and a committee was established to examine the arguments (Venne Report, 1996). The Association was represented on this committee.

For most lay magistrates, the local bench is the forum at which policy may be made. The Annual Meeting may well adopt views on sentencing policy. It may take a position different from that expressed in the magistrates' associations guidelines and in that way exert an even stronger sense of localism. The bench will take a view on the desirability of appointing a stipendiary magistrate, though at the end of the day the decision is taken by the Advisory Committee.

The Central Council of Magistrates' Courts Committees is the body which represents the views of local committees in policy processes. It is not a well-known body among magistrates in general, and it is difficult to assess its influence though it has clearly been powerless to hold back the far-reaching amalgamations which have taken place over the past decade.

Stipendiary magistrates

Given their relatively small number (around 100 in total) compared to lay magistrates, stipendiary magistrates outside London have tended not to have a major impact on policy debates. At present, the provincial stipendiary magistrates can join the Stipendiary Magistrates' Association for England and Wales which holds meetings, often of an educative nature, on a regional basis. The Metropolitan stipendiary magistrates have their own mandatory meetings. Overall, there exists a Council of Stipendiary Magistrates upon which both provincial and Metropolitan stipendiary magistrates are represented. A legal committee of this council will consider and form views on any legal matters that are likely to have an effect upon their work. For example, this committee has in the past expressed strong views on the delegation of some of their powers to court clerks.

For the future, the stipendiaries are likely to become more prominent. Not only are their numbers set to grow[35] but also they are to have a chief – 'a senior judicial figure at their head who would have a "presidential" role, similar in some respects to that currently performed in London by the Chief Metropolitan Stipendiary Magistrate' (Lord Chancellor's Department, 1998c: para. 20).[36] So, there will be a Senior District Judge (Chief Magistrate), and it is expected that this office will be filled by the Chief Stipendiary Magistrate and that a provincial deputy will be appointed (op. at.: para. 22)[37] Alongside the signal of authority, the appointment is also seen as being beneficial in terms of standardisation (and thereby professionalisation). According to Lord Chancellor Irvine in a speech in March 1999:

> [Unification] will help to improve consistency in sentencing. At present, with the separate Metropolitan and Provincial Benches, there is no one central figure of authority. I know that stipendiary magistrates take into account the Magistrates' Association sentencing guidelines. The unification of the two stipendiary benches will enable the future head of the unified bench to issue additional guidelines to all stipendiaries where needed.

In this way, it can be seen that stipendiary magistrates inherently represent, and provide pressure for, professionalisation to some extent. But their outlooks are often similar to lay magistrates – common sense and local experience (Seago, *et al.*, 1995: paras 4.5.13, 4.6.12), values which are inherent rather than the product of training or professionalisation, comprise a dominant ideology shared by magistrates in both camps.

Court clerks

The Justices Clerks' Society is perhaps the most influential of all the potential pressure groups in the lower courts.[38] As its name suggests, it is an association which represents the clerks to the justices.[39] More recently it has admitted justices' chief executives, most of whom will have been justices' clerks or joint post holders. There are moves afoot to convert it into an institute with membership open to all who are qualified to take courts. The Society will almost certainly be asked for its views on any issues relating to the magistrates' courts. At present this may include administrative as well as judicial matters, but with the recent changes which have restricted justices clerks to the judicial area, this may well change. The Society made various comments on what was to become the Police and Magistrates' Courts Act 1994. More recently the Society has encouraged the Lord Chancellor's Department to give the courts a clear indication of the way in which the courts would be expected to develop. Furthermore, it would even accept an agency approach as long as the structures of accountability were clearly stated.

Under section 41(3) of the Justices of the Peace Act 1997, the justices' chief executive is under a duty to make arrangements for the justices' clerks in the MCC area to hold meetings to discuss legal issues. These have become known colloquially as Legal Forums. In West Yorkshire, for example, it was noticed that there had not been the take-up of curfew orders as might have been expected. The Legal Forum concluded that this might be because the local magistrates and probation officers had not properly understood the system. It was decided to prepare a document to set out the position more clearly.

The Council of the Justices' Clerks Society has become a sort of National Forum. It hears local problems on a national basis. For example, in some areas it was reported that the police were refusing to place on the Sex Offenders' Register[40] those defendants who had been awarded a conditional discharge on the basis that this was not a conviction. The Council has now advised all Justices' Clerks to insist that the police should place such offenders on the Register.

One of the Society's committees, the Standing Conference of Training Officers, has a considerable input into the training of magistrates.

In these ways, the emphasis is upon professional standards, while localism is a less important value.

Judicial studies board

Obviously those involved in training the judiciary are in a strong position to influence attitudes. Most of the groups mentioned above will have some input into training as part of their professional credentials, but it is the Judicial Studies Board which undertakes training of the judiciary on behalf of the Lord Chancellor's Department (Heaton-Armstrong, 1993: 27; Partington, 1994: 319).[41] This comprises a main Board together with a series of committees to look after specific areas. These are (a) The Civil and Family Committee; (b) The Criminal Committee; (c) the Magisterial Committee (d) the Tribunals Committee and (e) the Ethnic Minorities Advisory Committee (to which has been added Human Awareness Training to take account of gender issues (Reeves, 1994: 55).[42] While the Magisterial Committee provides training for stipendiary magistrates, it merely exercises a supervisory jurisdiction over the training of lay magistrates; the numbers make any greater involvement impossible. Nevertheless it does produce core training materials which it expects to see adopted in the local training programmes. To date is has produced packages for the Children Act 1989 and for the Criminal Justice Act 1991. Most recently it has introduced the Magistrates' New Training Initiative which seeks to introduce com-

petence-referenced training throughout the magistrates' training programme. It has also issued core training materials relating to the Human
Rights Act 1998. In this way the Board could exercise considerable
influence upon magistrates' attitudes to particular initiatives or legislation and thereby diminish localism. The result is also an uneasy compromise between laity and professional training – 'sound legal learning'
(Home Affairs Committee, 1996) is seen in this light as a threat to
independence rather than pillars of it – and the absence of this feature
in lay justices is conversely a strength not a weakness.

These insider interest groups have each taken distinct stances as
between the new and the old discourses, with the Magistrates' Association perhaps most resistant to new public management. Similarly, the
Justices Clerks' Society and stipendiaries have opposed many of the
centralising tendencies of new public management but are perhaps
more open to professional values. The result has been to mediate the
government inspired policy thrusts and to encourage intra-court policy
contra-networks which produce singular compromises around the
country. A fragmentation of judicial administration therefore remains.
The magistrates' courts are not as standardised or as efficient as the Lord
Chancellor's Department would wish. But its favouring of those sectors
within the magistrates' courts which are most reflective of new public
management, namely the professional clerks and stipendiary magistrates, as well as the empowering of the Magistrates' Courts Service
Inspectorate, can be expected to shift the balance gradually.

Conclusions

The governance of the courts, especially the lower courts, has developed
in recent years from what were essentially pragmatic local arrangements, based on hierarchical authority, towards a more professionalised
bureaucracy. New public management has provided an important vector
in the movement towards change. Nevertheless, the old court ideologies
such as the principles of localism and laity have acted to temper the
thrust of new public management and have bolstered the traditional
hierarchical values. This intervention could be interpreted in one of two
ways. On the one hand, such an outcome could be viewed as a failure
within the management and audit culture which new public management seeks to engender. At best, there is conceded a sort of new local
managerialism where the desired outcomes of managerialism must be
achieved on local terms. On the other hand, it could be interpreted as an
example of the continuing adaptation of justice to meet the encroach-

ing demands of modernity. The latter would perhaps be the interpretation of most of the players in the court policy network. While accepting new court management values such as efficiency, effectiveness and service delivery as important performance indicators for the management of works and estates, they seek to differentiate those values from those seen as valid for the core court 'business' of judging, which relate to fair (but not necessarily cheap or quick) process and outcomes, independence, localism and lay common sense. In this way, the legal system provides a difficult setting for new public management as it can generally make claims to ideologies which are even more powerful and sacrosanct than those of the Treasury. At the same time, while the reliance may be upon old court ideologies, these court players have become some of the most effective moral entrepreneurs in the business – able to play upon the value of representation of the local community without actually rendering any effective accountability to it and without having been chosen or endorsed by it in the first place.

Notes

Parts of this chapter were previously published as Fitzpatrick *et al.* (2000); they are included with the kind permission of Kluwer Academic Publishers.

1. See for general accounts: Osborne and Gaebler (1992); Stewart and Walsh (1992); Zifcaf (1994); Rhodes (1997, 2000); and Smith (1999).
2. Also see further: Manchester (1980: ch. 7) and Skyrme (1991).
3. Certain cases could only be tried at Assize, the most important of which were any offences which could be punished on first conviction by death or life imprisonment and also offences such as bigamy which might raise difficult issues of law. It follows that most indictable offences were tried at Quarter Sessions: in 1961, 23,500 out of the 31,000 defendants found guilty on indictment.
4. The early history is fully recounted by Jackson (1946); Browne (1956: chs 2, 3); Milton (1967); Page (1967); Babbington (1969); Skyrme (1979; 1991: Vol. 2); and Bartle (1995).
5. See <http://www.open.gov.uk/courts/court/cs_home.htm>.
6. The provisions relating to the Crown Court have been incorporated into the Supreme Court Act 1981.
7. For example in West Yorkshire there were the following magistrates' courts committees: (a) Inner and Outer Leeds; (b) Bradford, Bingley and Keighley; (c) Halifax; (d) Huddersfield and Dewsbury; (e) Wakefield, Pontefract and Castleford.
8. By September 1999 all courts must have adopted the Magistrates New Training Initiative (MNTI or Minti as it is called) which seeks to identify the competencies needed at various stages of a magistrates' career and to back the training up with ongoing appraisal.

9. The remaining 80 per cent comes from central funds (largely financed by the fines and other penalties imposed by the courts).
10. H L Debates, vol. 533, col. 83wa, 19 December 1991, Lord Mackay.
11. s.69(3). See now Justices of the Peace Act 1997 s.32(3).
12. Once a merger has been effected and a new magistrates' courts committee selected and a justices' chief executive appointed, it will be possible for the Committee to review the question of how many justices' clerks will be needed for the region as a whole. Petty Sessional Divisions which in the past have had their own justices' clerk might find in future they are sharing one with another Petty Sessional Division.
13. See now Justices of the Peace Act 1997 Pt.VII.
14. See s.70 of the Police and Magistrates' Courts Act 1994 (now Justices of the Peace Act 1997 s.28).
15. There has been long-standing criticism of the neglect of magistrates' courts as objects of research, probably attributable to the fact that they act as fora for the resolution of essentially trivial matters; see further McBarnet (1981).
16. See further Raine and Wilson (1993; 1997: 80); James and Raine (1998: ch. 3).
17. Section 75. See now Justices of the Peace Act 1997 s.40.
18. See for example the concerns voiced by Lord Peyton (*Hansard*, H. L. Vol. 552, col. 561), and the Lord Chief Justice (ibid., col. 564).
19. Section 75. See now Justices of the Peace Act 1997 s.40(5).
20. Section 73. See now Justices of the Peace Act 1997 s.31.
21. Police and Magistrates' Courts Act 1994 s.75 (see now Justices of the Peace Act 1997 s.40) and Lord Chancellor's Department (1998b). There are currently 84 MCCs, but the number is projected to fall.
22. Police and Magistrates' Courts Act 1994 s.69(4) (see now Justices of the Peace Act 1997 s.31).
23. HL Debs. vol. 582 col. 1058.
24. Access to Justice Act 1999 ss.81, 83. The Access to Justice Act 1999 ss 74, 75 makes it easier to change territorial boundaries within MCCs. See Lord Chancellor's Department (1998a: para. 5.19; 1999).
25. 'New public management and the administration of justice in magistrates' courts: a report to the Lord Chancellor's department'.
26. Police and Magistrates' Courts Act 1994 s.86 (see now Justices of the Peace Act 1997 s.62). The Police and Magistrates' Courts Act 1994 s.89 (see now Justices of the Peace Act 1997 s.39) also provides for the possibility of studies by the Audit Commission with a view to improving economy, efficiency and effectiveness in the performance of the MCC's functions.
27. Compare Annual Report of Her Majesty's Chief Inspector of the Magistrates' Courts Service 1993–94 (1994), p. 2.
28. Justices of the Peace Act 1997 s.6. The Lord Chancellor requires that candidates should have a reasonable degree of knowledge of the area to which they wish to be appointed and generally expects them to have lived in that area for a minimum of 12 months.
29. Concern on this ground is expressed by the Home Affairs Committee, *Judicial Appointments* (1995–96 H.C. 52–I), para. 198.
30. 'The independence of the judiciary in the 1980s' [1988] *Public Law* 44. But note that, for example, the courts service categorise the court-listing function as a judicial, rather than an administrative issue.

31. Speech to the Council of the Magistrates' Association (1999) <http://www.open.gov.uk/lcd/speeches/1999/25-3-99.htm>.
32. House of Commons Debates, Vol. 220, col.376 wa, 8 March 1993, Mr John M Taylor.
33. See Police and Magistrates' Courts Act 1994 s.3 as consolidated by s.4 and sch.3 of the Police Act 1996.
34. See <http://www.magistrates-association.org.uk/>.
35. Following the Venne Report, the maximum number of permitted full time provincial stipendiaries was increased from 40 to 50: The Maximum Number of Stipendiary Magistrates Order 1996 SI No. 1924. There were proposals to raise this figure to 60 (Lord Chancellor's Department Circular to Advisory Committees (9)99, 24 June 1999), but the ceiling has been pegged back to 56 (*The Times*, 11 November, 1999, p. 5).
36. See Access to Justice Act 1999 s.78.
37. See Justices of the Peace Act 1997 s.10A(2).
38. The Association of Magisterial Officers is the Trade Union representing clerks who work in the magisterial service.
39. Its views can be seen in the journal, *Justice of the Peace*.
40. Sex Offenders Act 1997.
41. Also see: Judicial Studies Board, *Reports*, 1979–82 (1983), 1983–87 (1988), 1987–91 (1992), 1991–95 (1995), 1995–97 (1997).
42. Judicial Studies Board, *Report* 1991–95 (1995) para. 2.23.

References

Babbington, A. (1969) *A House in Bow Street* (London: Macdonald).
Baker, S and English, J. (1994) *A Guide to the Police and Magistrates' Courts Act 1994* (London: Butterworths).
Baldwin, R. (1988) 'The Next Steps', *Modern Law Review*, 51: 622.
Bartle, R. (1995) 'Historical origin of the stipendiary magistrate', *Justice of the Peace*, 159(8): 126.
Bellamy, C. and Taylor, J. (1998) *Governing in the Information Age* (Buckingham: Open University Press).
Brown S. (1991) *Magistrates at Work* (Buckingham: Open University Press).
Browne, D. G. (1956) *The Rise of Scotland Yard* (London: Harrap).
Carlen, P. (1976) *Magistrates' Justice* (London: Martin Robertson).
Cope, S (1996) 'New Police Management' in Leishman, F., Loveday, B. and Savage, S. (eds), *Core Issues in Policing* (London: Longman).
Crawford, A. (1997) *The Local Governance of Crime* (Oxford: Clarendon Press).
Criminal Statistics for England and Wales 1997 (1998) Cm. 4162 (London: HMSO).
Dawson, J. P. (1960) *A History of Lay Judges* (Cambridge: Harvard University Press).
Drewry, G. (1988) 'Forward from F.M.I.', *Public Law*, p. 503.
Fitzpatrick, B., Seago, P. and Wall, D. (forthcoming), 'New public management and the administration of justice in magistrates' courts: a Report to the Lord Chancellor's department'.
Fitzpatrick, B., Seago, P., Walker, C. and Wall, D. (2000) 'New courts management and the professionalisation of summary justice in England and Wales', *Criminal Law Forum*, 11/1: 1–11.

120 *Policy Networks in Criminal Justice*

Greer, P. (1994) *Transforming Central Government: The Next Steps Initiative* (Buckingham: Open University Press).

Harrison, B. F. and Maddox, A. J. (1975) *The Work of the Magistrate* (London: Shaw and Shaw).

Heaton-Armstrong, A. (1993) 'Judges should go back to school', *New Law Journal*, 143: 27.

Home Affairs Committee (1996), *Judicial Appointments*, HC 1995–96, 52–I.

Home Office (1995), *Mode of Trial*, Cm. 2908 (London: HMSO).

Home Office (1999) *Determining Mode of Trial in Either-Way Cases*, <http://www.homeoffice.gov.uk/cpd/pvu/contrial.htm>.

Ibbs Report (1988) *Improving Management in Government*, Prime Minister's Efficiency Unit, H. C. Debs., Vol. 127, col. 1149, 18 February.

Interdepartmental Committee (1975) *Report of the Interdepartmental Committee on the Distribution of Criminal Business between the Crown Court and the Magistrates' Court*, Cmnd. 6323 (London: HMSO).

Irvine, Lord Chancellor (1999) Speech to the Council of the Magistrates' Association <http://www.open.gov.uk/lcd/speeches/1999/25–3–99.htm>.

Jackson, P. (1946) 'Stipendiary magistrates and lay justices', *Modern Law Review*, 9: 1.

James, A. and Raine, J. (1998) *The New Politics of Criminal Justice* (London: Longman).

Judicial Studies Board (1995), *Report of the Judicial Studies Board 1991–95*, para. 2.23.

Kaufman, I. R. (1979) 'Chilling judicial independence', *Yale Law Journal*, 88: 681.

Landau, N. (1984) *The Justices of the Peace 1679–1760* (Berkeley: University of California Press).

Le Vay Report (1989) *Magistrates' Courts: Report of a Scrutiny* (London: HMSO).

Lewis, N. (1994) 'Reviewing change in Government', *Public Law*, p. 105.

Lord Chancellor's Department (1998a), *Modernising Justice*, Cm. 4155 (London: HMSO).

Lord Chancellor's Department (1998b), *The Future Role of the Justices' Clerks*, <http://www.open.gov.uk/lcd/consult/general/jc-role.htm>.

Lord Chancellor's Department (1998c) *Creation of a Unified Stipendiary Branch*, <http://www.open.gov.uk/lcd/consult/general/stipecon.htm> ('*LCD Consultation Paper*').

Lord Chancellor's Department (1999) *The Greater London Magistrates' Courts Authority Implementation Issues*, <http://www.open.gov.uk/lcd/consult/general/mags1.htm>.

Manchester, A. H. (1980) *A Modern Legal History of England and Wales 1750–1950* (London: Butterworths).

McBarnet, D (1981) 'Magistrates' courts and the ideology of justice', *British Journal of Law and Society*, 8: 181.

Milton, F. (1967) *The English Magistracy* (Buckingham: Oxford University Press).

Moir, E. (1969) *The Justice of the Peace* (London: Penguin).

Narey, M. (1997) *Review of Delay in the Criminal Justice System*, <http://www.homeoffice.gov.uk/cpd/pvu/crimrev.htm>.

Osborne, D. and Gaebler, T. (1992) *Reinventing Government* (Cambridge, mass.: Addison-Wesley).

Page, L. (1967) *Justices of the Peace* (London: Faber).

Pain, K. (1988) *The Lay Magistrate* (Chichester: Barry Rose).

Partington, M. (1994) 'Training the judiciary in England and Wales: the work of the Judicial Studies Board', *Civil Justice Quarterly*, 13: 319.

Power, M. (1997) *Audit Society* (Oxford: Oxford University Press).

Raine, J. W. (1989) *Local Justice* (Edinburgh: T & T Clark).

Raine, J. W., and Wilson, M. J. (1993) *Managing Criminal Justice* (Hemel Hempstead: Harvester Wheatsheaf).

Raine, J., and Wilson, M. (1997) 'Beyond managerialism in criminal justice', *Howard Journal of Criminal Justice*, 36: 80.

Reeves, P. (1994) 'Racial awareness – training for the legal profession', *Justice of the Peace*, 158: 55.

Rhodes, R. A. W. (1997) *Understanding Governance: Policy Networks, Governance, Reflexivity and Accountability* (Buckingham: Open University Press).

Rhodes, R. A. W. (ed.) (2000) *Transforming British Government* (London: Macmillan).

Roche Report (1944) *Report of the Departmental Committee on Justices' Clerks*, Cmd. 6507 (London: HMSO).

Royal Commission on Assizes and Quarter Sessions (1969) *Report of the Royal Commission on Assizes and Quarter Sessions*, Cmnd.4153 (London: HMSO).

Seago, P., Walker, C. and Wall, D. (1995) *The Role and Appointment of Stipendiary Magistrates* (Leeds: Centre for Criminal Justice Studies/Lord Chancellor's Department).

Seago, P., Walker, C. P. and Wall, D. S. (2000) 'The development of the professional magistracy in England and Wales', *Criminal Law Review*.

Skyrme, Sir T. (1979) *The Changing Image of the Magistracy* (London: Macmillan).

Skyrme, Sir T. (1991) *History of Justices of the Peace*, vols 142 (Chichester: Barry Rose).

Smith, M. (1999) *The Core Executive in Britain* (London: Macmillan).

Stewart, J., and Walsh, K. (1992) 'Change in the management of public services', *Public Administration*, 70: 499.

Training of Justices (1995) *The Training of Justices of the Peace in England and Wales*, Cmnd. 2856 (London: HMSO).

Treasury and Civil Service Select Committee (1982), *Efficiency and Effectiveness in the Civil Service*, Cmnd. 8616 (London HMSO).

Venne Report (1996) *The Role of the Stipendiary Magistrate*, Lord Chancellor's Department Working Party (London) *Lord Chancellor's Department*.

Walker, C. (2000) 'Criminal justice processes and the Internet', in Akdeniz, Y., Walker, C. and Wall, D. (eds), *The Internet, Law and Society* (London: Longman).

White Paper (1992) *New Framework for Local Justice* (1992), Cm. 1829 (London: HMSO).

Woolf, Rt Hon. Lord Justice (1996) *Report on Access to Justice: Final Report*, <http://www.open.gov.uk/lcd/civil/final/sec3c.htm>.

Woolf, Rt. Hon. Lord Justice, and Tumin, S. (1991) *Prison Disturbances April 1990: Report of an Inquiry by the Rt. Hon. Lord Justice Woolf and His Honour Judge Stephen Tumin*, Cm.1456 (London: HMSO).

Zifcaf, S. (1994) *New Managerialism* (Buckingham: Open University Press).

6
Networking and the Lobby for Penal Reform: Conflict and Consensus

Chas Wilson

Introduction

> The United Kingdom is perhaps unique in the strength and vigour of its penal reform lobby.
>
> (Flynn, 1998: 146)

This chapter will examine the nature, development and, as far as can be ascertained, the impact of the lobby for penal reform from 1979 to the present day. It will focus primarily on the views of those most involved in the process: the reformers themselves, in the three major penal reform organisations in Britain today – the so-called 'campaigning charities': the Howard League for Penal Reform (HL); the National Association for the Care and Resettlement of Offenders (NACRO) and the Prison Reform Trust (PRT). It will go on to consider competing accounts of the development of one of the most important vehicles for lobbying and networking in the field of penal policy in the 1990s: the Penal Affairs Consortium (PAC). Following a consideration of issues of achievements and effectiveness, it will then conclude with brief comments about the usefulness and limitations of some recent work by political scientists with an interest in policy networks in making sense of developments in the lobby for penal reform.

Four preliminary points must be made:

(1) For both legal and political reasons the scope of this chapter is largely limited to England and Wales, although it should be noted that while being legally distinctive, the reach of penal policy-making typically also encompasses Scotland[1]. The penal situation in Northern Ireland is clearly quite different. Furthermore, politically Britain

is, or more accurately, has been until now, a highly centralised state, with legislative and associated lobbying activity being located almost entirely in London, where not surprisingly, the three above-mentioned organisations are based.

(2) The focus of the chapter is on penal policy more broadly defined, going beyond prisons and the prison system to include all the agencies involved in the punishment or treatment of offenders. This reflects the changing emphasis of government policy in recent years away from dealing with the prisons in isolation towards a more integrated focus on the penal system as a whole, to include crime and crime prevention as well, and it may well be that the campaigning activities of the reform organisations themselves are partially responsible for such a development. Today only one of the groups campaigns solely around prison-related issues, the PRT, which was set up in 1981 specifically for this purpose. The HL actually dropped 'penal reform' from its official title in the early 1980s to signify the broadening of its remit to cover the criminal justice system as a whole and NACRO has always emphasised the importance of crime prevention in becoming a major provider of largely government funded services for ex-offenders in the community (employment, housing, education, etc.).

(3) Little has been written specifically about activities and relationships within the penal reform lobby. While each of the major organisations produces an annual report and regular briefing papers and reports on current issues of concern, little material is available on the changing relationships between the organisations, the nature of their lobbying and campaigning activities and the extent of their possible influence over penal policy making. Mick Ryan's (1978) comparison of the Howard League, characterised as 'the acceptable pressure group', with Radical Alternatives to Prison (RAP), the 'radical outsider', and his later *The Politics of Penal Reform*, which sketched out the contours of the penal reform lobby up to the early 1980s (in chapter 6), are interesting but now of less value in analysing the contemporary situation. Similarly Ryan's later study of *Inquest* (1998) is necessarily restricted to the specific question of deaths in custody, although there is a useful discussion of whether the penal reform lobby can be characterised as a 'policy community' or an 'issue network' (168–73) which is here examined in the conclusion.

(4) As a result of this dearth of published material it was felt that it was essential to provide some empirical grounding for the discussion in the views of the penal reformers themselves. So a noteworthy feature

of this chapter is the fact that it is informed by interviews with a number of 'key players' in the penal reform lobby: Andrew Rutherford, Chair, and Frances Crook, Director of the HL; Paul Cavadino, Director of Policy and Information, Helen Edwards, Chief Executive, and Vivien Stern, ex-Director of NACRO, and Stephen Shaw, Director of the PRT, with, in addition, Lord Hurd, Chair of the PRT, answering some questions by letter, to all of whom the author is extremely grateful for their invaluable help and cooperation[2].

Background: penal policy in the 1980s and 1990s

It hardly needs to be pointed out that the 1980s and 1990s have been periods of virtually unprecedented activity in the field of criminal justice and penal policy-making. The 1979 General Election can be seen as marking 'the end of the post-War consensus approach to law and order' (Dunbar and Langdon, 1997: 100). The increasing politicisation of law and order that has characterised this period, fuelled by a rapidly increasing crime rate, saw the evolution of a right-wing policy agenda which swept away the old reformist and rehabilitationist approaches and instituted a new focus on just deserts, the need to toughen up punishments (both in prison and in the community) and, latterly, a commitment to the belief that 'prison works'.

In such a climate the prison scene became dominated by concern about rising populations, increasing prison overcrowding, impoverished conditions and regimes, deteriorating industrial relations and recurrent outbreaks of disorder and rioting (the overall number of disturbances increased from 38 in 1985/86 to 146 in 1993/94, according to Parliamentary Answers, 18 January 1995). This culminated in the riots at Strangeways and other prisons in 1990, which seemed to vindicate the recurrent claim made by many commentators that the prison system was in a serious state of crisis. The following Inquiry into the prison system under the Chairmanship of Lord Woolf (1990) was seen by penal reformers as marking the climax of their influence over the penal policy-making process, with a total of 65 groups catalogued as having given evidence. Thereafter, under Michael Howard, things could be seen as rapidly going downhill. Today, New Labour holds out the promise of a brighter future for the pressure groups, although the nature of the relationship is not viewed with unbridled optimism. As Frances Crook pointed out, despite the good relationship with Labour while in opposition: 'Our relationship with government is different today, but not that different' (interview 8 January 1999).

Another factor is that arguably the pace of change has accelerated over this period. Criminal Justice Acts, which were once single landmark legislative reforms for a government, carefully prepared and discussed over a long gestation period, have become almost annual events. Green papers are followed by white papers, criminal justice bills and then criminal justice acts with bewildering speed. Policies come and go, for example, the 'short, sharp, shock' for juvenile offenders was introduced with the Criminal Justice Act of 1982 and abolished with the Criminal Justice Act of 1988. Core provisions of the Criminal Justice Act 1991, seen by the penal reform groups as a major success story in the pursuit of a humane penal system, were controversially reversed in the Criminal Justice Act 1993. Electronic tagging came, went and has come back again under New Labour in the guise of the Home Detention Curfew. The rapid introduction of privately managed prisons, in the teeth of the united opposition of the whole penal lobby, is another example: The Green Paper, *Private Sector Involvement in the Remand System* (HMSO 1988) first raised the possibility of the contracting out of remand prisons to the private sector; by the end of 1998 there were six privately operated prisons, with a further five being in the pipeline. The Prison Officers' Association (POA) now actively campaigns with the reform groups against privatisation, with other professional groups (probation officers, prison governors, etc.) increasingly being drawn into the penal reform lobby. All this activity has generated a fertile range of pressing and serious problems for possible take-up by the groups within the penal reform lobby.

The Labour Party has also significantly repositioned itself on law and order issues during this period. During an interview on BBC Radio's 'The World This Weekend' on 10 January 1993, Tony Blair memorably produced his famous soundbite that we should be 'tough on crime and tough on the causes of crime' in response to John Major's announcement of 'a crusade against crime' in the *Mail on Sunday* (21 February 1993, following the murder of James Bulger). Furthermore, during the notorious Michael Howard period at the Home Office, representing nothing less than a 'law and order counter-reformation' according to Cavadino and Dignan (1997), both Tony Blair, Labour Party leader, and Jack Straw, shadow Home Secretary, proved themselves only too willing to be drawn into a highly public debate over the severity of punishments in the run-up to the 1997 General Election which shifted Labour Party law and order policy even further to the right. In office New Labour has made several controversial policy 'U' turns (over prison privatisation, secure training centres for young offenders and the electronic tagging of offenders) and has seen the prison population rise to record levels with little public expression of concern (to the dismay of the penal reform groups).

How has the penal lobby responded to the challenges posed by such dramatic changes in the terrain of penal policy-making? What is the penal lobby and how can we describe and explain the changes that have occurred within it over this period? These are difficult questions and at this stage only a tentative beginning can be made providing possible answers. However, a useful starting point is provided by someone with direct experience of trying to reform 'from below', Geoff Coggan, the Director of PROP (Preservation of the Rights of Prisoners) – the National Prisoners Movement. Coggan points out that prior to 1972, when PROP was formed:

> it would have been difficult to describe the penal reform lobby as a movement at all, because movement in any form was the least noticeable of its virtues.
>
> (1998: 10)

According to Coggan grass-roots organisations like PROP, together with Radical Alternatives to Prison (RAP), which was set up in 1970, 'effectively sidelined the (then) stuffy and conservative Howard League and introduced a completely new agenda to the movement' (op. cit.). While it is beyond the remit of this chapter to evaluate the influence of this new radical agenda, clearly it is significant, with the Woolf Inquiry seen by Coggan as 'taking on board much of the penal reform agenda from two decades of campaigning' (op. cit.: 11), a comment which generally coincides with the views of the penal reformers interviewed here.[3]

However, into the 1980s and 1990s, with the shift to the right in politics, this radical 'abolitionist' agenda became a waning force: today RAP has disappeared and, with apologies to Geoff Coggan, PROP really only exists on paper – it's impact on policy-making is negligible. A range of new groups and organisations have appeared on the scene. NACRO was formed in 1966 and, especially since 1979, has expanded tremendously. Inquest and the PRT appeared in 1981, with other more focused and radical groups like Women in Prison (WIP), Women in Special Hospitals (WISH) and Prison Watch coming along later.

Today an increasing number of groups and organisations, voluntary, charitable, statutory and professional, have developed an interest in penal affairs and become involved in a number of overlapping and shifting networks, which vary over time and according to the issue of concern and, increasingly, reach beyond the domestic into the international context[5]. This picture of rising complexity is reflected in both the number and range of organisations that became involved in a key development in the lobby for penal reform in the 1990s – the PAC (see later). It is further complicated by the fact that under the Conservatives, groups like the Magistrates' Association, which effectively campaigned against key provisions of the 1991 Criminal Justice Act, and right-wing think-tanks like the Adam Smith Institute, which lobbied hard and effectively for prison privatisation, became increasingly influential (see Ryan, 1989: 170).[6]

The next section provides a more detailed examination of the nature and development of the lobby for penal reform since 1979.

Networking for penal reform: evolution and change

The main focus of this chapter is on the three largest organisations in the penal reform lobby which, despite the apparently unpropitious political climate, have experienced significant growth in this period. As Andrew Rutherford pointed out:

> This period has been very conducive to the penal reform groups ...successful fundraising has allowed them to grow considerably and increase their operations substantially.
>
> (Interview, 19 November 1998)

Into the new millennium we are certainly witnessing the development of a penal reform lobby which is better organised, financially sound and highly professional in approach. Whether it is likely to be any more effective is another matter (see the later discussion).

Beginning with the Howard League, which is the oldest and probably internationally best known of the groups: founded in 1866 as the Howard Association after John Howard, the first penal reformer, it merged with the Penal Reform League in 1922 largely through the efforts of Margery Fry[7] to become the Howard League for Penal Reform. The HL is an independent charity (described as 'fiercely independent' by Andrew Rutherford in the 1997/98 Chair's Report) which is financed mainly by donations from charitable trusts and membership subscriptions. It had a total income of £420,000 in 1997/98 (see the Annual Report): this had been only £90,000 when Frances Crook became Director in 1986 with the aim of eliminating the recurrent financial crises that had threatened the survival of the organisation. This seems to have been at least partially achieved. The HL now owns its rather cramped and dowdy offices in Holloway Road, North London (albeit with a mortgage), has a complement of ten staff members, and is currently fundraising to set up a Centre for Penal Reform as both a new headquarters and a 'focus for penal reform work for the future' (Frances Crook). The HL publishes the prestigious *Howard Journal of Criminal Justice* and also the *Howard League Magazine*, recently relaunched with a trendy new title: *HLM*.

A major focus of the work of the HL is on the setting up of 'demonstration' projects, the policy of the HL being to initiate such projects and then pass them on to another organisation for longer-term development. An example is the Troubleshooter Project which aimed to 'rescue' and take out of the penal system 15- and 16-year-olds. This took up the issue of children remanded to prison and found a 28 per cent increase in numbers between 1994 and 1996 and helped over 650 children before being handed over to The Children's Society[8]. Another notable recent HL campaign concerned the use of prison custody for teenage girls. A report was published in 1997 (*Lost Inside: the Imprisonment of Teenage Girls*) based on an inquiry chaired by Lady Masham which interviewed over 80% of the 74 girls held in prison; an amendment to the Crime and Disorder Bill was tabled but defeated, despite cross-party support (from Lord Hurd and Barbara Castle), and, following the Flood case, supported by the HL, it became unlawful to hold sentenced teenagers in adult jails. The latest project, on 'Citizenship and Crime', with a budget of over £300,000, is seen as very much setting the agenda for future approaches to crime prevention[9].

The networking activities of the HL have undergone something of a transformation in recent years, with, as Frances Crook explained, the development of a deliberate strategy of drawing more groups into the penal lobby:

> The links are much wider than just in the prison or penal system. The HL is also part of other networks. We also work very closely with other voluntary, statutory or semi-statutory organisations.... All sorts of groups have been brought in. All the children's organisations... which has motivated them in a extremely effective way.
>
> (Interview, 8 January 1999)[10]

A mark of this is the fact that The Children's Society now seems to be becoming more politicised than hitherto, recently placing prominent full page advertisements in the newspapers announcing 'We are the only national charity working with youngsters on remand in prison' (contained in the *Independent* of 17 February 1999 and 25 February 1999).

This suggests that there are now far more groups to network with, extending far out beyond what were once seen as the traditional boundaries of the penal system.

Concerning ideological approach, in the past the HL has been characterised as being close (some would say too close) to the reins of power and as benefiting from 'the inside track enjoyed by the more Establishment academic liberal reformers' (Downes and Morgan, 1997: 114). Certainly a feature of the HL has been the fact that many of its governing members were 'political figures with well-established contacts with those in Whitehall and at Westminster' (Ryan, 1983: 106), and these close informal contacts and unforced access, which at times amounted to a 'virtual partnership' (op. cit.), were seen as allowing the HL to enjoy a certain amount of influence over penal policy-making in the period up to the 1960s and 1970s. However, undoubtedly, this analysis is much less true today. Although informal contacts with decision makers can still be an effective means of making your views known, and penal reformers are frequently bumping into important politicians and officials in their busy round of conferences and meetings, no single organisation now enjoys the inside track. Seeking to influence policy by a well-informed word in the ministerial ear has now given way to much more confrontational modes of pressure-group activity, at least in the period up to the 1997 General Election.

NACRO was founded more recently and has become by far the largest of the groups in the penal reform lobby. NACRO was established in 1966 out of the National Association of Discharged Prisoners' Aid Societies, which became redundant when the probation service took over prison after-care. There was an initial grant of £10,000 from the Home Office (the 'midwife' of NACRO according to Stephen Shaw) to fund an office in South London, which it shared with the probation service. Over a period of time there were debates over whether NACRO would be an academic 'think tank' or a practical 'social service' organisation and although NACRO still does both, and has developed a reputation for the excellence of its information service on the criminal justice system,[11] the emphasis on helping people through housing, education and training schemes has become the central defining feature of the organisation. In 1969 regional councils were established and NACRO started to work through a regional network in the early 1970s to develop new initiatives, particularly in the housing of ex-offenders.

In 1977 Vivien Stern took over as Director and the decision was made to involve NACRO in the training schemes that were becoming a key part of the expanding 'unemployment industry', to the extent that by

1978 NACRO had set up 126 schemes and was handling a budget of over £40 million. By 1987/88 this budget had shot up to £79 million, with NACRO providing 16,188 places for long-term unemployed people via the Manpower Services Commission (MSC) funded Community Programme schemes. In addition, NACRO's New Careers Training Agency was running 35 MSC funded Youth Training Schemes directed at young offenders (see *Annual Report*, 1987/88). However, during 1988 the bubble burst: the Manpower Services Commission (MSC) was first renamed the Training Commission and then abolished. Vivien Stern herself describes the process of change that NACRO went through during this period:

> In 1977 NACRO was small, amateurish and young and over the next twenty years it became more professional and grew enormously in terms of turnover and the number of activities. It became a major service provider...and became influential in setting some of the terms of the debate about how we should treat prisoners.
>
> (Interview, 7 January 1999)

Today NACRO is both a registered charity and a limited company, with offices in Clapham Road, South London and numerous regional outposts. It has a complicated organisational structure: NACRO Community Enterprises Ltd (NCE) runs the housing projects; NACRO New Careers Training (NCT) administers the training contracts, and NACRO Trading Ltd (incorporated in 1995) carries out commercial activities to raise funds (70% of its profits are covenanted to NACRO which, in 1996, amounted to over £200,000). At the top is the Council (the governing body) which, until recently, was supported by an Executive Committee and a series of Advisory Committees. However, in 1996 'a process of organisational change was initiated to ecourage more active involvement from our trustees' (*Annual Report*, 1997/98: 20) and the Executive Committee was abolished, the Council now meeting more frequently[12].

The scope of NACRO's activities are much reduced compared with the 1980s. Although it currently manages housing projects which accommodate over 3,000 ex-offenders and homeless people; employment projects which cater for over 10,000 people; youth projects which provide structured activities for over 5,000 young people, and numerous additional projects for families and communities, resettlement services and consultancy services, particularly around the 1998 Crime and Disorder Act, by 1997/98 its turnover had plummeted to £34.2 million (less than half the 1987/88 total). This was itself significantly down on the £35.3 million in the previous year (see the Annual Reports for 1996/97 and 1997/98), which suggests a worsening financial crisis reaching a climax in the 1990s. This point is acknowledged by Helen Edwards (Chief Executive of NACRO):

> It has not been the easiest time for NACRO in that its campaigning and lobbying work has not always endeared it to all politicians, particularly some (!)...Michael Howard was the first Home Secretary for whom it had been an issue and...he was instrumental in our funding being reduced, which was not helpful to us.
>
> (Interview, 3 December 98)

Tony Christopher, Chairman of NACRO,[13] emphasises the problems in the 1995/96 *Annual Report*:

> finding resources to do the work is increasingly difficult...it is hard to understand why the Home Office should choose this moment to reduce financial support so significantly.
>
> (2–3)

The situation was no better a year later:

> a serious reduction in Government support for our core activities over the last two years has added to the difficulties.
>
> (Chairman's Introduction, Annual Report 1996/97: 2)

These 'difficulties', which are likely to be a feature of any organisation which seeks to both provide government-funded services and also campaign as a reforming pressure group,[14] quite probably had serious consequences for NACRO's activities during the 1990s (see later). As Vivien Stern pointed out:

> NACRO is clearly not a campaigning organisation in the sense that many prisons organisations are.
>
> (Interview, 7 January 99)

In what sense NACRO can be seen as a campaigning organisation is an important question, but one which, unfortunately, cannot be explored here[15].

According to Stephen Shaw (who was in at virtually the start), the PRT, the most recent arrival on the penal scene, was not a grass-roots initiative but:

very much the creature of the liberal establishment. It was the last of the great causes to see a new modern pressure group founded to promote it.

(Interview, 3 December 98)

Shaw describes a series of meetings (which took place before his own involvement commenced) involving journalists, politicians, officials, and 'members of the liberal establishment', hosted by David Astor (former editor of the *Observer*), which addressed the question 'what could be done?' about the fact that the prison system was the one area of social policy where the least progress had been made: prison numbers were increasing; the prison estate remained in a deplorable state. From this emerged the idea of a new, high profile, but strictly short-term, campaigning body, the PRT, which was launched at a very well reported press conference in London in September 1981.[16] The first (founder) Chairman was Sir Monty Finniston (a well-known industrialist), deliberately chosen for not being a 'bleeding heart liberal', with the other founder-trustees being very much establishment figures. Shaw reports that from the start there was a concern not to compete with the HL ('they were very sensitive about that') and that 'NACRO was then and has always been very supportive throughout our career'. However:

Our relationships with the HL have necessarily always been more 'edgy' ... we are about the same size as the HL and there must be an element of competition for funds, column inches and for the ear of ministers.

(Interview, 3 December 1998)

Today the PRT owns smart open-plan offices in Clerkenwell, with a full-time staff of seven and an income of £350,000 in 1997/98, slightly less than the HL, but from similar sources (i.e. subscriptions, donations, covenants and grants). With Lord Hurd newly installed as Chair[17] over 600 people attended the 1998 Annual Lecture given by the Home Secretary, Jack Straw, who concluded that: 'I approach my task with a realisation that the Trust's work continues to be essential' (*Annual Report*, 1997/98: 37).[18] The PRT publishes its own magazine, *Prison Report*, and intends 'to break new ground next year by holding meetings on prison matters outside London' (op. cit.: 2). Its main achievements in recent years have been the production from January 1993, jointly with the Prison Service, of the *Prisoners' Information Book*, to be presented to every new inmate; the monitoring of private sector involvement in prisons through Prison Privatisation Report International, which now has a global readership, and the publication of the book *Introduction to Prisons and Imprisonment* by Nick Flynn (Deputy Director), jointly with Waterside Press (1999).

Although all three organisations exist in an increasingly competitive environment for both resources and media attention, the penal reformers report, perhaps not surprisingly, that good cooperative relationships are maintained between them. According to Andrew Rutherford:

> The general picture is that the relationships between the groups are quite good, constructive and helpful, and that allowed something like the Penal Affairs Consortium to flourish.
>
> (Interview, 19 November 1998)

This is confirmed by Paul Cavadino (Director of Policy and Information for NACRO):

> There have always been close relationships between the penal organisations. For many years the HL shared offices with NACRO. We work quite closely together... We try to liaise... In other areas you often find reform organisations attacking each other, but not in the penal lobby.
>
> (Interview, 3 December 1998)

According to Stephen Shaw this is because 'the ideology of the groups has tended to coalesce' with the result that 'there really is very little difference between ourselves, NACRO and the HL, or, indeed, the old radical lobby' (interview). Helen Edwards (Chief Executive of NACRO) reinforces this point:

> There is a broad consensus about lots of things and certainly during Michael Howard's period at the Home Office that coalesced even more...
>
> (Interview, 3 December 1998)

However, despite these increasing ideological similarities and close working relationships, there were sources of tension that developed in the 1990s over the major recent cooperative venture, the Penal Affairs Consortium, which will be discussed in the next section.

The PAC

A major vehicle for lobbying and campaigning activities in the 1990s was the PAC,[19] an organisation whose development has excited extraordinarily little attention or generated much apparent interest on the penal scene. Its formation is merely mentioned in passing in the second volume of Windlesham's excellent analysis of 'penal policy in the making' (1993: 406–7);[20] Downes and Morgan only see fit to comment on the 'previously unthinkable combination' of groups involved in the PAC in their analysis of pressure-group politics (1997: 114), and Cavadino and Dignan (1997), while simply noting its formation (chapter 3 note 3), make extensive reference to its (excellent) briefing papers. Talking to penal reformers about the origins and development of the PAC reveals an interesting difference of opinion about perceived changes in the role of the PAC which has broader implications for an understanding of the influence and impact of the penal lobby in the 1990s and beyond.

There is general agreement about the origins of the PAC. According to Paul Cavadino (who was elected permanent Chair following a brief period when the position 'floated' between members):

> The PAC was set up initially specifically to coordinate Parliamentary lobbying by organisations with an interest in penal reform.
>
> (Interview, 3 December 1998)

He later interestingly elaborated:

> In the course of the 1988 Criminal Justice Act MPs and peers . . . found themselves bombarded with a whole series of possible amendments. . . . from a wide range of organisations and found it quite confusing. . . . Things had moved on since the 1970s when relatively few organisations were geared up to Parliamentary lobbying to a situation in which a lot of organisations have become conscious of the fact that this is something they might do . . . and they sent a flood of communications to MPs and peers.
>
> (Interview, 7 January 1999)

There is also agreement that the moving force behind the setting up of the PAC was Lady Jane Ewart Biggs,[21] a Labour peer with an interest in penal reform, who felt that 'the penal lobby was not having the impact it should have on Parliamentarians' (Stephen Shaw). According to Frances Crook:

Jane Ewart Biggs was getting fed up with getting lots of briefings from different organisations and said why don't you coordinate it; why don't we have a meeting to set it up? That's what the PAC grew out of.
(Interview, 8 January 1999)

More information is provided about this first meeting by Stephen Shaw :

The PAC was started as the result of a meeting at the Palace of Westminster at which I spoke, Paul Cavadino from NACRO spoke and Frances Crook from the HL spoke. We were all there at the beginning.
(Interview, 3 December 1998)

In fact, there was an initial series of meetings leading up to the publication of the first Joint Manifesto for Penal Reform in February 1989,[22] with 13 organisations participating, representing 'a very wide-ranging alliance, from the POA to radical pressure groups' (Paul Cavadino, 3 December 1998). This included the PGA, the ACOP and Justice, the campaigning organisation of jurists. Stephen Shaw noted that the PAC 'was able to talk with more authority with the backing of bodies like the PGA and the POA as well as the pressure groups' (interview 3 December 1998). By 1992 this had increased to 24 organisations, reaching 31 by 1996, with the current total standing at 39, which must be seen as some measure of its perceived effectiveness (see the Appendix for the full membership list, which can be taken to represent a fairly comprehensive taxonomy of the penal reform lobby today).

The first priority was to establish the issues on which there was agreement among the 13 organisations. According to Paul Cavadino, this proved to be surprisingly easy, which he felt was 'remarkable' bearing in mind the range of organisations involved:

We found a lot of common ground. There was a large number of issues on which there was a consensus, related to reducing the use of prison and promoting positive and constructive prison regimes.
(Interview, 7 January 1999)

Cavadino goes on to describe the methods used by the Consortium as fourfold:

(a) Having regular meetings with MPs and peers sympathetic to penal reform; (b) lobbying on relevant legislation which was going through Parliament . . . deciding on amendments to legislation . . . and persuad-

ing sympathetic MPs and peers to put these down; (c) producing briefing papers that make the case for reform in more detail, and (d) giving
evidence to Parliamentary enquiries on issues relevant to penal affairs.
(Interview, 7 January 1999)

However, it is clear that from about 1993/94 both the approach and the
public profile of the PAC underwent a significant change and that this
was seen as controversial to at least some of its members. Paul Cavadino
puts it thus:

> the original purpose was to coordinate Parliamentary lobbying ... but
> subsequently we developed additional aims. ... We decided that we
> would specifically seek media publicity for the Consortium's views,
> which wasn't the initial main aim.
>
> (Interview, 7 January 99)

The effect of this was that during the period 1994–97 (which almost
exactly coincided with Michael Howard's tenure at the Home Office) the
public profile of the PAC increased dramatically, and, correspondingly,
decreased thereafter, following the 1997 General Election and the vic-
tory of Tony Blair and the Labour Party.[23]

This change of emphasis is insightfully observed by others. For example, according to Stephen Shaw, during this period 'you would find
very few references to NACRO in the press and a massive number for the
PAC, (3 December 1998), with Frances Crook pointing out that:

> There was a shift in emphasis from the original objectives ... towards
> becoming another lobbying, research based organisation very similar
> to the PRT and the HL.
>
> (8 January 1999)

She went on to criticise this development as 'pointless and irritating and
a spoiler in the very good relationships that had existed. It was not the
point of the Consortium' (interview, 8 January 1999).

Paul Cavadino explained this development as reflecting two factors.
First, a deliberate policy decision:

> In the course of the Howard era the PAC made a conscious decision to
> put a higher proportion of its work into public profile work with the
> media ... and adopted a particularly high profile at that time.
>
> (Interview, 7 January 1999)

and, secondly, because he was seconded full-time to work on the Consortium during this period and so 'was able to generate much more activity'. However, these factors do not fully account for the nature of the change, the nature of the activity and resulting increasing public profile of the PAC, or the apparent reversal of the PAC to its original aim in 1997 (when the secondment ceased and Paul Cavadino returned to NACRO).

Clues to a fuller and more accurate explanation of the changing public profile of the PAC between 1994 and 1997 might well be found in the increasing problems being experienced by NACRO during this period (see earlier section). It seems that this change in the public profile of the PAC coincided almost exactly with the decline in NACRO's public profile that resulted from a funding crisis that came to a head with Michael Howard's tenure at the Home Office. As an anonymous commentator explained:

> It was made clear to NACRO that if it continued to be critical of Home Office policy it would find that not only was its core grant removed, but it would find it more and more difficult to get any projects. In other words: shut up or you will be closing up!

It seems highly likely that one response to this funding crisis, to which NACRO was extremely vulnerable as a largely government funded organisation, and to which financial cut-backs led to the issuing of redundancy notices to NACRO staff, might well have been not only to 'shut up', but also to seek ways of diverting critical activity elsewhere, to which the less vulnerable PAC was admirably suited. There is indeed some evidence that this happened, although further research would be needed to provide confirmation and certainly other interpretations are possible.[24] Paul Cavadino was seconded to the PAC, NACRO muted its criticisms of the government and finally managed to get its money, resulting in the withdrawal of redundancy notices. After this the PAC became more strident in its campaigning and media work (as documented above), at least until the election of New Labour in 1997 with a contract with the voluntary organisations that made it clear that government-funded bodies would not be put at financial risk if they criticised government policy.[25] So, today the PAC remains in place, but has reverted back to its original role as an important and highly effective channel for Parliamentary lobbying. Little direct campaigning activity is apparent, with Briefing papers being less frequent and more factual in content.

To conclude this section, it is not easy at this stage to provide an accurate assessment of the impact and influence of the PAC. It was formed in response to a difficult and challenging political situation and is still evolving. However, the achievements of the PAC, as outlined by Paul Cavadino, are undoubtedly significant and only time will tell whether they will become even more so in the future:

> (a) It has provided a mechanism for much better coordination of Parliamentary lobbying; (b) it has demonstrated to Parliamentarians the existence of a wide consensus on penal issues; (c) it has also over the last few years, and particularly during 1994–97, made a very considerable impact . . . as a major voice in the media debate.
>
> (Interview, 7 January 1999)

The next section examines the issue of the achievements and effectiveness of the penal reform lobby, again through the views of the key players.

The effectiveness of the penal reform lobby: away from agenda resistance?

> We are trying in our small way to change the world for the better.
> (Stephen Shaw, interview with Holly McLaren, 1998)

While the aim of many pressure groups is to change the world in some way, in the case of the penal reform lobby the basic aims are relatively straightforward and agreed by all of the groups: a reduction in the use of prison; a greater use of alternatives to custody, and the development of more constructive prison regimes (creating a 'better, more humane and more effective penal system', according to a PRT brochure).[26] In principle, therefore, the effectivenes of the penal lobby might be evaluated by examining just these factors: trends in the prison population, the use of alternatives to prison and the nature of prison regimes. However, in practice the situation is clearly much more complex. Whether the system has indeed changed for the 'better' (or got worse) and the role of the penal lobby in the process are both highly contested issues. With such diffuse aims (including that of influencing public opinion) and a rapidly changing political context (a general shift to the right), the question of effectiveness becomes much more difficult to estimate. This section offers a different approach by examining the views of the penal reformers themselves on the question of the effectiveness of the penal reform lobby using, where appropriate, notions of agenda resistance, agenda re-shaping and agenda setting as an organising framework, focusing mainly on the HL (Andrew Rutherford and Frances Crook) and the PRT (Stephen Shaw).

Beginning with the HL, Andrew Rutherford (Chair) provides the following analysis of recent developments, the bare bones of which all the penal reformers would undoubtedly agree:

> The HL was resisting in the early 1980s, particularly around prison system growth, nearer to supporting or shaping in the late 1980s... with Douglas Hurd as Home Secretary... and, since the early 1990s, particularly with the advent of Michael Howard and Jack Straw, the HL has reverted back to more of a resisting role.
>
> (Interview, 19 November 1998)

According to Rutherford, during the Hurd era:

> shaping isn't really the right word, but what the HL was saying in public discussions and speeches helped to provide a framework for government... we were largely singing from the same song sheet.
>
> (Interview, 19 November 1998)

He particularly highlights the fact that the HL 'helped shape the ideas that went into the Green Paper of 1988' which was 'consistent with the sorts of things that the HL had been saying for a long time'. However, since then 'the HL has found itself more and more at odds with New Labour', particularly over, for example, the U turn on Secure Training Centres, which the HL has consistently opposed:

> We have had a very busy time recently with the rush of legislation from the Labour government, particularly the Crime and Disorder Act.
>
> (Interview, 19 November 1998)

Frances Crook (Director of the HL) elaborated the difficulties experienced during the Howard era:

> We had formal but quite open relationships with Douglas Hurd, Waddington and Kenneth Baker. It became more difficult with Kenneth Clark, but Michael Howard refused to see us... he just didn't

reply to letters, even from our President.... It was quite difficult. ... All we were going to do was put a different viewpoint before the public... and try to stop things from getting any worse.

(Interview, 8 January 1999)

Crook went on to point out that 'We have had significant successes', highlighting particularly the announcement by David Waddington at the HL Annual Conference in 1990 that he was agreeing to the abolition of the imprisonment of 14 year olds. She saw this was a 'fantastic concession to work that we had done over many years'. However, 'under Howard it changed' and it became 'just a question of holding the line'. So, agenda resistance increased under Michael Howard and:

we are still doing that to a certain extent, for example, the secure training centre, we are still resisting that like mad, and campaigning against it by putting forward more constructive options.

(Interview, 8 January 1999)

But, according to Crook, under New Labour 'agenda reshaping has probably become more important' with the Crime and Disorder Act a major example:

We are now trying to work with government to try and shape, re-model and set a framework for the practicalities within the very broad framework of the legislation.

(Interview, 8 January 1999)

Crook feels that agenda setting also takes place, currently through the Citizenship and Crime project, working with school children through-out London (see note 7), but also through the HL taking up issues that hitherto had not been seen as important, with women and community service being another current example. Crook finally claims that:

We set the agenda on girls and imprisonment.... Nobody had ever done a national survey of juvenile girls in prison.... As a result of that the prison service is setting up special units for juvenile girls and in Scotland the government has given an assurance that they will get juvenile girls out of the prison system completely. I would see that as a significant success and an example of agenda setting.

(Interview, 8 January 1999)

Stephen Shaw (Director of the PRT) saw the influence of the prisons lobby as being in 'headlong descent' under Michael Howard (interview, 3 December 1998), although he did immediately suggest that this should be softened slightly to 'marked decline'. Adopting a longer time span, he pointed out that:

There was a period between 1979 and 1981, with Willie Whitelaw as Home Secretary with an agenda of opening up the prison system, when there was a feeling that one could achieve something.[27] However, the high point of the lobbies influence was from the late 80s ... when Douglas Hurd went to the Home Office, through Strangeways, the Woolf Report, the 1991 White Paper, up to Kenneth Clark. When Michael Howard was Home Secretary he would have happily towed the prisons lobby out to sea and sunk us, if he thought we were important enough to sink ... which he didn't.

(Interview, 3 December 1998)

Concerning achievements, Shaw was prepared to take at least some of the credit, albeit shared with the penal lobby as a whole, for the fact that:

Compared with a decade ago, notwithstanding the increase in the prison population, prisons are immeasurably better in terms of physical conditions, regimes and activities.

(Interview, 3 December 1998)

and felt that this was in no small amount due to the Woolf Report (regarded as a 'historic document') and the important role played by the penal lobby in Woolf's deliberations ('the Report is peppered with references to our evidence'). However, Shaw regards 'our inability to protect the gains that had been made under Douglas Hurd and which followed from Woolf, the White Paper and the 1991 Act' as 'our greatest failure', with Woolf being seen as 'our greatest success':

We had strategies for **demanding** things, but failed to develop strategies for **defending** things. There our performance was woeful.

(Interview, 3 December 1998)

Shaw saw prison privatisation, a policy which the whole penal lobby (including the POA and the PGA) had consistently opposed, but which has now become 'mainstream' and 'unlikely to be reversed', as a prime example of failed agenda resistance. However, more positively, there was also evidence of successful agenda resistance from a broader perspective:

> The fact that I can now look forward to the next few years as being ones in which there will be significant advances in the prison system suggests that.... we did keep alive values and ideas during the dark days of Michael Howard.
>
> (Interview, 3 December 1998)

Concerning agenda reshaping, Shaw provided two examples of areas in which the lobby was seen to have exerted some influence: (a) in developing ideas of reparation and restitution (the restorative approach), seen as 'the most significant "new idea" of the last 25 years',[28] and (b) in promoting and supporting a mood of penal optimism which has contributed to the movement away from a 'nothing works' philosophy:

> Compared with 25 years ago there's a much greater optimism now with people working in prison and probation that their efforts can make a difference to the individuals in their charge.
>
> (Interview, 3 December 1998)

Shaw sees agenda setting as 'the life blood of the pressure group', saying 'that's what pressure groups do through their manifesto', but admits that 'We have been better at agenda setting in terms of what happens in prison than about the appropriate **use** of prison':

> I don't see us as having achieved much in terms of agenda setting with the public or the politicians on the size of the prison population.
>
> (Interview, 3 December 1998)

However, he provides many examples of successful agenda setting in terms of 'how you run prisons, what you do within them', mentioning specifically the treatment of sex offenders; dealing with HIV and AIDs; pressure to introduce the Prisons Ombudsman; work on prison discipline; work on race issues in prison, and providing information for prisoners (the Prisoners' Information Pack), all of which he feels adds up to 'quite a respectable record of achievements'.

Concerning the impact of New Labour, Shaw appears to be more optimistic than some of the other penal reformers:

There is absolutely no question as to the extent of the cultural change which has come about with the Labour Government . . . the ideas that we promote were suddenly allowed out to see the light of day, remarkably quickly. Our closeness to the levers of power and methods of working have changed markedly since 1997.

(Interview, 3 December 1998)

However, he went on to admit realistically that:

It's very early days for us to assess what influence we are having now. . . . Today you have really excellent access to ministers and officials, and every suggestion that they are listening to what we say: but access, of course, is not the same thing as influence.

(Interview, 3 December 1998)

It remains to be seen whether the impact of New Labour will lead to any fundamental changes in the relationship between government and the penal reform lobby.

Conclusions: political science, policy networks and penal policy-making

This chapter concludes with some brief comments on the usefulness of recent developments in the political science of policy networks for understanding the nature and impact of the penal reform lobby on the penal policy-making process. The limitations of these comments are readily acknowledged. As indicated above (in the first section), little systematic research has been carried out on the nature of penal policy making in this country and changes therein, and this chapter is itself based on an extremely limited amount of empirical research (just six interviews with key penal reformers).

Other contributors to this volume (see, for example, Ryan, Chapter 8, writing on Liberty) have indicated some of the problems in applying the policy networks approach to criminal justice and most of these apply equally to penal policy-making. For example, while much of the recent empirical work by political scientists seems to be based on the study of single-issue pressure groups in lobbies with a relatively narrow policy focus and few players (like sea defences and nuclear power: see Sabatier and Jenkins-Smith 1993), none of the groups in the penal reform lobby is a single issue pressure group.[29] They all operate across an increasingly diverse range of networks, involving a number of different issues and a variety of government departments. A great deal of further research would be needed to even make a start at establishing the networks of just one group in the penal reform lobby at one point in time.

Similarly, the policy networks approach seems to assume a relatively close and cooperative working relationship between pressure groups, government officials and politicians, a situation which has rarely, if ever, been the case with the penal lobby. Admittedly, working relationships were probably closer in the 1980s than during the Michael Howard era, with Downes and Morgan (1997) documenting the 'myriad links between the Home Office and the pressure groups' that developed, producing a situation where 'opportunities abounded for pressure groups to inform penal policymaking processes' (1997: 114). However, even then 'a huge imbalance of power' remained, with the Home Office able to 'brush aside any protest' (op. cit.: 116), notably over issues like prison privatisation.

Another feature of the work of political scientists is the attempt to categorise different types of lobbies or policy networks (Rhodes and Marsh 1992, as summarised by Cope, Chapter 1, this volume, see Table 2). This typically involves distinguishing between *policy communities*, characterised by a single or, at most, two or three pressure groups, operating directly to a single government department in a relatively stable framework of shared assumptions, with the pressure groups having regular access to decision-makers and settling differences behind closed doors, and *issue networks*, involving many groups with competing policies, little consensus and uneven and frequently acrimonious contact with government officials. How useful is this (admittedly, ideal) typology or continuum? Ryan suggests that in the 1950s and 1960s:

> the penal lobby could reasonably be said to approximate a policy community with the Howard League ... interconnecting with political elites in a ... closed dialogue.
>
> (1996: 169)

However, by the 1970s and into the 1980s the situation had changed dramatically, with the appearance of groups like NACRO, the PRT, PROP, RAP, Inquest and WIP, with very different views about the nature and purposes of the prison system, some of whom were 'definitely not going to be bound by the "rules of the game"' (ibid.), described by Ryan as an 'issue network with a vengeance!'.

However, it is becoming increasingly difficult to place the various groups within the penal reform lobby along such a continuum, or even to define accurately the boundaries of the lobby itself. While there appeared to be policy community-like features developing during the 1980s and early 1990s, with an ideological convergence between the aims of the three main groups and the priorities of goverment policy under successive Conservative Home Secretaries (around reducing the prison population, developing non-custodial alternatives, etc.),[30] clearly this was fractured by Michael Howard and his 'prison works' ideology. The picture is further complicated by the fact that the Penal Affairs Consortium itself could be seen as possible evidence of a policy community developing within the lobby, with an increasingly diverse range of groups being drawn into concerted opposition to government policy.

Today the situation is much more complex and even more difficult to describe, whether within the framework of policy network analysis or by utilising any other perspective. While there appears to be the potential for the development of a policy community under New Labour, with many charities being drawn into the policy-making process, via committees and working parties, the penal reform lobby is generally cautious about going along this road of cooperation due to a realistic fear that it may lead to cooption and loss of independence.

Update: all change for penal networks

Since the interviews were carried out in 1998/99 there has been significant change within the penal reform lobby. Andrew Rutherford stood down as Chair of the Howard League, a memorable farewell dinner being held at the House of Lords on Thursday 20 January 2000, featuring an inspiring talk by Jerome Miller.He has been succeeded by David Faulkner, whose contribution to criminal justice policy while working at the Home Office in the late 1980s/early 1990s is summarised by Windlesham (1993: ch. 5). Stephen Shaw left the Prison Reform Trust towards the end of 1999 to become Prisons Ombudsman, a post for which ironically he was originally shortlisted when the office was set up, before Michael Howard as Home Secretary rejected the whole short list as being too liberal and supplied his own list of names. The new Director of the PRT is Juliet Lyon, ex-Associate Director of the Trust for the Study of Adolescence. Paul Cavadino recently announced that he would be giving up his role as Secretary and leading light of the PAC to concentrate on his work as Director of Policy with NACRO.

Appendix: organisations currently participating in the Penal Affiars Consortium

Adullam Homes Housing association
Apex Trust
Association of Black Probation Officers
Association of Chief Probation Officers
Association of Members of Boards of Visitors
Bourne Trust
Federation of Prisoners' Families Support Groups
Howard League for Penal Reform
Inquest
Inside Out Trust
Institution of Professionals, Managers and Specialists
JUSTICE
Liberty
National Association for the Care and Resettlement of Offenders
National Association for Youth Justice
National Association of Probation Officers
National Council for Social Concern
National Forum of Care Trusts
National Remand Rescue Initiative
The New Bridge
Payback
Prisoners Abroad
Prisoners' Advice Service
Prisoners' Education Trust
Prisoners' Families and Friends Service
Prisoners' Resource Service
Prison Governors' Association
Prison Officers' Association
Prison Reform Trust
Public and Commercial Services Union
Quaker Crime and Community Justice Committee
Release
RPS/Rainer
Society of Voluntary Associates
Standing Committee for Youth Justice
Standing Conference on Drug Abuse
Suzy Lamplugh Trust
Unlock
Women in Prison

Notes

1. Although Scotland still has one of the highest prison populations in Europe, there are welcome signs of a 'shift in official thinking', according to Clive Fairweather (1999: 24).

2. The interviews, which were recorded and lasted an average of about an hour each, were carried out between 19 November 1998 and 8 January 1999 and were loosely structured around the question of 'the nature and effectiveness of the prisons lobby since 1979'. Three main areas were covered: (a) the development of the organisation itself; (b) the relationships between the various organisations within the lobby, and (c) the relationship between the lobby and government and possible influence over policy-making.

3. According to Ryan and Ward (1992), while RAP's work in the 1970s played an important part in laying the ground for a new consensus on law and order policy within the Labour Party, 'RAP's very success...left it without a distinctive role...active membership and financial resources dwindled in the 1980s; since 1988, when its journal The Abolitionist ceased publication, it has been virtually defunct' (327). Incidentally, Ryan and Ward do flag up the formation of the PAC as an indication of the degree of consensus within the penal lobby (328).

4. Stephen Shaw sees Inquest and Women in Prison as: 'direct lineal descendants of the movement for prison abolition, albeit they are essentially casework oriented' (interview, 3 December 1998). Probably Women in Special Hospitals should be added to this list.

5. Penal Reform International (PRI) was formed in 1989, with Vivien Stern, then Director of NACRO, as its General Secretary, and can be seen as providing 'an increasingly international backcloth to the shape of penal pressure group politics in Britain' (Downes and Morgan, 1997: 117). It should also be noted that the HL has consultative status with the United Nations, with a permanent representative (Christian Kuhn), and increasingly operates on the international stage.

6. In his study of the victims movement, Paul Rock quoted an influential source from the mid-1980s as saying that: 'The standard lobbies...are not very important to the Conservative Government...no Conservative Home Secretary is going to bed shaking and shivering because one of those sorts of groups is actually critical of him' (1990: 227). This clearly indicates the problems confronting the penal reform lobby after 1979.

7. In the 1950s Margery Fry, a judge's daughter, member of the Fry's Chocolate family, and herself once a victim of street robbery, campaigned on behalf of the victims of crime, helping to create the Criminal Injuries Compensation Scheme and which saw later, in the 1970s, the development of Victim Support Schemes, through the efforts of NACRO members based in Bristol.

8. Andrew Rutherford saw the Troubleshooter Project as being: 'quite successful in demonstrating to local authorities and government agencies that there is a will to remove such cases from institutions' (Interview, 19 November 1998).

9. I am sure that the HL would wish to take at least some of the credit for the recent 'controversial decision' that by 2002 'citizenship lessons' will be compulsory in all secondary schools (*Independent on Sunday*, 21 February 1999).

10. Frances Crook also highlighted their work with women in prison as also drawing into the penal lobby a number of women's groups who had not previously expressed an interest in penal affairs.

11. Through reports, briefing papers and the *Criminal Justice Digest*, which has now become the *Safer Society* magazine.

12. There are also five Directorates: Housing; Education and Employment; Research and Development; Policy and Information and Finance and Resources.
13. Tony (Lord) Christopher was a founder member of NACRO and Chairman for 25 years, from 1973 to 1998.
14. Ryan points out that 'as a government-funded agency, NACRO's policies are never going to be too extreme' and that although it has been highly critical of government policy 'there are consensual limits and both sides know the boundaries' (1983: 109). In this case it seems likely that one side, the government, ceased to honour these boundaries, to the detriment of (the funding of) the other.
15. NACRO now widely advertises its role as consultant in implementing the provisions of the Crime and Disorder Act and boasts that it is repeatedly cited in the Home Office guidelines on developing crime and disorder strategies as 'an agency which can provide informed and effective consultancy on implementing these strategies' (*Annual Report*, 1997/98: 15).
16. According to Paul Cavadino 'The PRT was born from the HL. A group of people in the HL felt that it was time to set up a separate organisation just for prisons' (interview).
17. Lord Hurd became Chair of the PRT in January 1997. Significantly, no previous Home Secretary has ever taken on such a prominent role with a campaigning charity.
18. The Home Secretary, Jack Straw, also gave the guest lecture at the HL AGM on 11 November 1998, following the publication of the HL *Annual Report* for 1997/98 which drew attention to the 'excessive number of people in prison'.
19. The idea of the 'campaigning consortium' is not a new one. Between 1978 and 1993 New Approaches to Juvenile Crime, linking NACRO with social work and probation organisations, campaigned to reduce the use of custody for juvenile offenders and successfully prepared the way for the development of intermediate treatment programmes in the late 1980s. Their last publication *Creating More Criminals* (1993), criticised the proposed secure training order as a 'retrograde and damaging measure'.
20. Windlesham is particularly informative on the influential one-day seminar at Leeds Castle in Kent on 28 September 1987, convened by Douglas Hurd, which 'soon came to be recognised as a milestone in the development of policies that had been consciously designed as a part of a system of criminal justice' (1993: 217: see chapter 5). Out of this seminar emerged a whole range of important reforms, which included the Safer Cities programme in which NACRO was a major beneficiary.
21. Lady Jane Ewart Biggs, who was a dedicated penal reformer and chair of NACRO's Mental Health Advisory Committee, died in October 1992.
22. There were further joint manifestos in 1992 and 1995, with another, the fourth, currently in preparation. The first manifesto stated: 'The case for reducing the use of prison is clear.... Many of those we imprison could be dealt with by non-custodial measures, without endangering the public...' (PAC, 1989: 1).
23. Some measure of this changing profile is provided by the prodigious increase in the output of the PAC over this period: a total of 25 briefing papers were

published between September 1994 and May 1997. This output has now slackened.

24. Some confirmation is provided by Brigitte Koch's (1998:) interesting analysis of NACRO (ch. 5), albeit in the context of crime prevention. Indeed, Koch attributes the resignation of Vivien Stern on 3 May 1996 as being 'partly due to frustrations with the Conservative (under Howard) political climate' (1998: 151).

25. The 'Compact on relations between Government and the Voluntary and Community Sector in England' (Cm. 4100, 1998) committed the government to: 'recognise and support the independence of the sector, including its right... to campaign, to comment on Government policy, and to challenge that policy, irrespective of any funding relationship that may exist' (para 9.1). The Government aim was to 'cement and develop our relationship with the voluntary and community sector' (Home Office press release, 098/99, 19 March 1999).

26. The brochure goes on to summarise the methods used as 'inquiring into the workings of the system; informing prisoners, staff, and the wider public; and influencing Parliament, Government and officials towards reform'.

27. As Shaw explained: 'Whitelaw was keen to see the PRT established because he saw as one of our important roles inproving public awareness of the prison system' (interview).

28. Significantly the Crime and Disorder Act of 1998 incorporates an element of restorative justice through the reparation order for young offenders.

29. According to Stephen Shaw, even the PRT, which was set up with a specific focus on reform of the prisons, cannot be seen as simply a single issue pressure group.

30. It was during the period of the late 1980s and early 1990s that Shaw felt that: 'we did have a lot of impact', a point which was confirmed by Douglas (Lord) Hurd himself: 'I spent longer than most Home Secretaries listening to the views of others, namely the voluntary organisations making up the penal reform lobby... I have a particularly vivid recollection of Vivien Stern and NACRO, but they all played a part in educating me and helping to form my ideas... the increased emphasis on crime prevention and victim support are examples' (letter 22 December 1998).

References

Cavadino, M. and Dignan, J. (1997) *The Penal System: An Introduction* (London: Sage).

Coggan, G. (1998) 'PROP, RAP and the lessons of prison history', *Prison Report*, 45:10–11.

Downes, D. and Morgan, R. (1997) 'Dumping the "hostages to fortune"? the politics of law and order in post-war Britain', in Maguire, M. Morgan, R. and Reiner, R. (eds) *The Oxford Handbook of Criminology*, (Oxford: Oxford University Press).

Dunbar, I. and Langdon, A. (1998) *Tough Justice: Sentencing and Penal Policies in the 1990s*, (London: Blackstone Press).

Fairweather, C. (1999) 'Scottish prisons in a changing society', *Prison Report*, 46: 24–5.
Flynn, N. (1998) *Introduction to Prisons and Imprisonment*, (Winchester: Waterside Press).
HMSO (1998) *Compact on Relations between Government and the Voluntary and Community Sector in England*, Cm. 4100 (London: HMSO).
Home Office (1988) *Private Sector Involvement in the Remand System*, (London: HMSO).
Howard League (1997) *Lost Inside: the Imprisonment of Teenage Girls*.
Howard League (1997/98) *Annual Report*.
Koch, B. C. M. (1998) *The Politics of Crime Prevention* (Aldershot: Ashgate).
McLaren, H. (1998) Interview with Stephen Shaw, *Prison Service Journal*, 117: 47–50.
NACRO (1997/98) *Annual Report*.
NACRO (1996/97) *Annual Report*.
NACRO (1995/96) *Annual Report*.
NACRO (1985/86) *Annual Report*.
NACRO (1987/88) *Annual Report*.
New Approaches to Juvenile Crime (1993) *Creating More Criminals*.
PAC (1989) *Joint Manifesto for Penal Reform*.
Prison Reform Trust (1997/98) *Annual Report*.
Rock, P. (1990) *Helping Victims of Crime*, (Oxford: Clarendon Press).
Rhodes, R. A. W. and Marsh, D. (1992) *Policy Networks in British Government*, (Buckingham: Open University Press).
Ryan, M. (1978) *The Acceptable Pressure Group: Inequality in the Penal Lobby: a Case Study of the Howard League and RAP*, (London: Saxon House).
Ryan, M. (1998) *The Politics of Penal Reform*, (London: Longman).
Ryan, M. (1998) *Lobbying from Below: INQUEST in Defence of Civil Liberties*, (London: UCL Press).
Ryan, M. and Ward, T. (1989) *Privatisation and the Penal System* (Milton Keynes: Open University Press).
Ryan, M. and Ward, T. (1992) 'From positivism to postmodernism: some theoretical and strategic reflections on the evolution of the penal lobby in Britain', *International Journal of the Sociology of Law*, 20: 321–335.
Sabatier, P. and Jenkins-Smith H. C. (1993) Policy change and learning: an advocacy coalition approach (Boulder, CO: Westview Press).
Windlesham Lord (1993) *Responses to Crime, Volume 2*, Penal Policy in the Making (Oxford: Clarendon Press).

7
Networking and Crime Control at the Local Level

Adam Edwards and John Benyon

Introduction

The centrepiece of the new Labour administration's Crime and Disorder Act, which received royal assent in July 1998, was a statutory duty for local authorities and constabularies to formulate and implement 'crime and disorder strategies' in each local government district. This provision indicated national government recognition of the central role of local authorities in reducing crime and restoring order at the district level in England and Wales. It was the culmination of a long campaign, fought by local authorities since the mid-1980s, to stake a claim as a principal actor in the policy response to local crime and disorder.

The role of local authorities had been championed most obviously in 1991 in the report by the Home Office Standing Conference on Crime Prevention on *Safer Communities: The Local Delivery of Crime Prevention Through the Partnership Approach.* This report, known as the 'Morgan Report' after the chair of the working group which produced it, specifically recommended a statutory duty on local authorities, 'for the development and stimulation of community safety and crime prevention programmes' (Home Office, 1991: para. 6.9). The Conservative Government of the time rejected this recommendation claiming it did 'not wish to burden local authorities with new statutory duties in this area especially when, as the report recognises, a good deal has been achieved at local level in developing crime prevention programmes within the existing statutory framework' (Home Office, 1992: 1).

Notwithstanding concerns over the fiscal 'burden' of additional statutory duties, there was a clear political agenda in marginalising local authorities from a policy area of growing importance. Municipal Labour authorities had been at the forefront of defining an executive role for local government in crime control prior to the publication of the Morgan Report and had been consulted by the Morgan Working Group. Given this, and the stream of publications on crime prevention emanating from the local government associations (Association of District Councils (ADC), 1990, 1994; Association of Metropolitan Authorities (AMA), 1990, 1993), they were conspicuous by their low profile in Home Office publications promoting 'best practice' in crime prevention (Home Office, 1990, 1993a) and even more starkly in the Government's 'flagship' *Safer Cities* programme, which began in 1988 and was the only major funding programme dedicated to crime prevention work until it was conflated into the Single Regeneration Budget in April 1994 (Home Office, 1993b).

Even without the full support of Conservative Central Government and the initial rejection of the Morgan Report's key recommendation, local authorities cultivated a growing presence in, and expertise about, the local regulation of crime and disorder (Local Authorities' Research and Intelligence Association, LARIA, 1994; ACC/ADC/AMA/Local Government Management Board, LGMB, 1996). In the current context of a Labour central government providing a statutory foundation for this role, this chapter examines the recent, present and future implications of local authority involvement in crime and disorder strategies. It suggests an increased understanding can be developed by reference to broader discourses on the 'reinvention of government' and, specifically, the promotion of 'community governance'. It is argued that while the changing complexion of political leadership at the national level has a critical bearing on the shape of this role and its likely impact, reference to these broader discourses reveals more profound challenges.

In the context of this book, the experience of experiments in community governance, and their particular application to the local control of crime and 'anti-social behaviour', have major consequences for theoretical and practical accounts of networks in criminal justice policy-making. While the reduction of criminal justice policy into its constituent, penal, judicial, probationary, policing and victim support, dimensions further refines the applications of policy network theory, these need to be complemented by an additional, *spatial*, scale of analysis.

The principal contribution of policy networks theory to an understanding of British government has been to reveal, and develop an explanation of, its 'differentiated' character (Rhodes, 1997: 7ff). In these terms, policy networks theory has been used to challenge the 'Westminster model' of British government by indicating the complex system of interdependent relations among policy actors through which any specific policy must be steered for the actual implementation of its objectives (Marsh and Rhodes, 1992a, 1992b: ch.2). This complex of inter-governmental relations has been viewed in terms of *horizontal* relations between public, private and voluntary sectors and *vertical* relations between supranational, national, and local levels (Lowndes, 1993: 134).

Little has, however, been written about the diverse configuration of intergovernmental relations in different 'locales'[1] and, therefore, the *uneven development* of specific policies across territorial jurisdictions. A number of case studies, forming part of the Economic and Social Research Council's Local Governance Research Programme, have begun to address this lacunae in the study of policy networks and intergovernmental relations at the level of local authority districts and 'sub-local' neighbourhoods.[2] The concept of 'community governance' can be seen as a common theme running through these individual case studies and providing a means of operationalising networks theory on this spatial scale.

The substance of this chapter is a discussion of the findings from our research into local strategies for crime prevention.[3] To place these findings in the context of recent historical trends in the development of criminal justice networks, the following section examines the shift away from police-centred crime prevention towards multi-agency strategies for 'community safety' driven by local authorities. These trends are then interpreted through the conceptual distinction between community governance and local government.

From crime prevention to 'community safety'

Apart from placing local authority involvement in crime control on a statutory footing, the other principal legacy of the Morgan Report has been to promote the concept of 'community safety' over that of 'crime prevention'. The Report argued:

> The term "crime prevention" is often narrowly interpreted and this reinforces the view that it is solely the responsibility of the police. On the other hand, the term "community safety" is open to wider inter-pretation and could encourage greater participation from all sections of the community in the fight against crime.
>
> (Home Office, 1991: para. 3.6)

The local authority associations developed the concept of community safety further and suggested an alternative definition:

Community safety is the concept of community-based action to inhibit and remedy the causes and consequences of criminal, intimidatory and other related anti-social behaviour. Its purpose is to secure sustainable reductions in crime and fear of crime in local communities. Its approach is based on the formation of multi-agency partnerships between the public, private and voluntary sectors to formulate and introduce community-based measures against crime.
(ACC/ADC/AMA/LGMB, 1996: 3)

In turn this concept has attracted criticism for its 'extreme vagueness' (Pease, 1994: 687 n11) and support for the discretion it grants local actors to 'fill' this general idea with substantive, possibly 'radical', proposals tailored to the highly localised contexts of crime and disorder (Hughes, 1997: 159). A brief consideration of the many action plans and community safety strategies published by local authorities in recent years suggests, however, a broader significance for community safety than its efficacy in guiding crime reduction. For example, the *Community Safety Strategy for Camden* defines community safety in terms of 'a wide range of activities to reduce crime and the fear of crime':

It includes the physical measures designed to reduce the opportunity to commit crime but it also includes social measures to reduce crime and the causes of crime. This encompasses a wide range of activity including: preventative work with young people, work to prevent further offending, helping the victims of crime, and preventing drug abuse. *Underlying principles include measures to revitalise the local economy, to enable people to access employment and to empower communities to be involved in determining their future.*
(London Borough of Camden, 1996: (i); emphasis added)

The Camden strategy is by no means alone in this extremely broad construction of what community safety can signify (cf. Marlow and Pitts, 1998). What it exemplifies, however, is the use of the community safety concept by some local authorities as a conduit for politically reconstructing the issue of crime prevention as one of social regeneration. This is a development emphasised, in turn, by the Audit Commission report on *Safety in Numbers*, which examined community safety practice supported, predominantly, by grant-aid from the Single Regeneration Budget.[4]

A survey conducted by the local authority associations and the Local Government Management Board in Spring 1996 revealed the extent to which the concept of community safety had been adopted by local authorities nation-wide (ACC/ADC/AMA/LGMB). Based on a response rate of 71 percent of all local authorities, the survey concluded:

> There is a very high level of recognition of community safety among local authorities. Nine out of ten recognise it as a policy area and over half have published policy statements or aims and objectives.
>
> (1996: 5)

The scale and speed of the conceptual and practical reconstruction of crime control and public order undertaken by local authorities is all the more remarkable given their exclusion from crime control policy-making prior to the Crime and Disorder Act. To account for the impact which local authorities have had on the policy response to crime and disorder, through their promotion of 'community safety', we have found it useful to draw upon current debates in the literature on governance.

This literature explores aspects of market and bureaucratic failure in: (i) providing a coherent conception of governing needs; (ii) coordinating the response to those needs; (iii) rendering that response accountable; and (iv) sustaining that response (Thompson *et al.*, 1991; Kooiman, 1993). The transcendence of these failures implies a 'reinvention of government' (Osborne and Gaebler, 1993) and the privileging of 'active citizen' participation in the definition and conduct of governance.[5] In turn, the concept of 'community governance' exemplifies the critique of state and market failure and indicates a means of transcendence (Wolman and Goldsmith, 1992: 22ff; Stoker, 1998: 10–12).

Local government and community governance

As we have argued elsewhere (Benyon and Edwards, 1999: 146–51), community governance can be distinguished from local government[6] in terms of its governing focus, orientation and technique.

The shift in focus

The development of community governance reflects a 'growing realisation of the complex, dynamic and diverse nature of the world we live in' (Kooiman, 1993, p. 35). The complexity of governing problems is a product of their multi-faceted and interdependent, rather than monistic and discrete, constitution. A recognition of this complexity implies a shift in the focus of governing, from separate elements of citizens' 'well-being', such as their access to better education, housing and employment

Table 7.1   Distinguishing local government and community governance: focus, orientation and technique

	Focus	Orientation	Technique
Local government	Delivery of services addressing social problems regarded as monistic and discrete.	Unilateral interventions by single agencies.	Rigid dependence on hierarchical/ Bureaucratic *or* (quasi-) market mechanisms.
Community governance	Managing the problems of citizens' 'well-being' regarded as multi-faceted and inter-dependent.	Multi-lateral interventions by public–private partnerships that recruit active citizen participation.	Flexible deployment of bureaucratic, (quasi-)market *and* networking mechanisms.

Source: adapted from Benyon and Edwards (1999: 146).

opportunities, and increased personal safety, towards the interdependencies between these elements in enhancing well-being. The focus on interdependency suggests an appreciation of the diversity of citizens' well-being; composite elements are configured differently over time and across space implying a need to tailor policy responses to problems of well-being in accordance with the context-specific conditions in which they arise. In turn, this complexity and diversity have a critical bearing on the causal dynamics of governing problems. Given that interdependencies are configured differently over time and across space, governing problems develop at an uneven rate. They do not progress or recede uniformly or in a linear direction (Kooiman, 1993: 37). This, apparently banal observation, nonetheless represents a major challenge to the measurement, interpretation and manipulation of governing problems on the basis of nationally aggregated data (for example: 'unemployment' in 'Britain'; 'homelessness' in 'Britain'; and, of course, 'The' crime rate). The recognition, through community governance, of the uneven dynamics of social–political problems has been at the epicentre of the increasing preoccupation with local 'base-line audits' as a principal vehicle for public policy formulation and implementation.

The shift in orientation

The growing appreciation of interdependencies accounts, in part, for the shifting orientation of local authorities towards other governmental and non-governmental agencies. Recognising the multi-faceted composition of social–political problems implies an understanding of the limits to 'do-it-alone' governing – 'government' – and the need for co-operative arrangements – 'governance'. Given their increasingly complex, diverse and dynamic qualities, these problems are not amenable to unilateral interventions on behalf of functionally specific agencies or departments. It is in this context that the rise of community-based public–private partnerships can be understood and acknowledged as a defining characteristic of community governance (Stoker, 1997, 1998).

The shift in technique

The concept of community governance can also be understood in terms of the governing technique it promotes and how this is distinguished from the technique of local government. The failures of local government can be explained in terms of reliance on either bureaucratic/hierarchical mechanisms, such as central planning, or quasi-market mechanisms, such as compulsory competitive tendering. The rigidity of these mechanisms means they are unable to respond effectively to the complex, diverse and dynamic qualities of social–political problems (Levacic, 1991). Community governance involves a more flexible deployment of governing mechanisms, questioning the ways in which they can be combined and tailored to locally-specific needs and different kinds of governing problem (Frances *et al.*, 1991).

This concern with flexibility accounts, in part, for the interest in 'networking' as a feature of governance. The key characteristics of networking are the informality, trust and reciprocity that it encourages between partners (Stoker, 1999: xviii). As they are less anonymous and/or rule-bound than relations in markets or bureaucratic hierarchies, networks enable protean forms of collaboration which are more responsive to diverse and interconnected social and political needs. However, the informality of networks raises significant issues of accountability, equity and propriety in the absence of objective rules regulating their operation (Stoker, 1998: 17). There may, therefore, be a trade-off between the role of networks in enhancing the governability of social–political problems and their capacity to revitalise local democracy.

Local (police) government and community governance

The distinctions between local government and community governance enable a greater understanding of the dynamics behind the rise of local authorities' role in community safety strategies and the advantages claimed for this approach to governing problems of crime and 'anti-social behaviour'. Crime prevention in England and Wales has conventionally been regarded as the preserve of local constabularies and, despite the substantial financial contribution by local government, police authorities have exercised limited influence over the priorities and operation of police forces: 'the police authorities pay the piper (or more precisely share policing costs with central government) but do not call any tunes' (Reiner, 1992: 237). The 1964 Police Act confirmed this exceptional relationship of constabularies, as public bureaucracies, to the local populations they serve by arguing that Chief Constables should have 'operational independence' from both local authorities and central government as a means of ensuring their 'political impartiality' (Benyon, 1986: 13–19).

However, the rise of crime prevention through community governance has enabled local authorities to acquire a growing influence over the policy response to problems of crime and 'anti-social behaviour'. To understand this greater influence it is useful to compare the focus, orientation and technique of crime prevention through local (police) government and through community governance, as shown in Table 7.2.

Table 7.2 Comparing crime prevention through local (police) government and through community governance: focus, orientation and technique

	Focus	**Orientation**	**Technique**
Crime prevention through local (police) government	Individual criminals and their crimes.	Police operations independent of other (potential) crime control and prevention agencies.	Law enforcement, including: routine uniformed patrolling; rapid response to calls for assistance; and heavy investment in detection.
Crime prevention through community governance	Problems of 'community safety', constituted by a range of crime events and forms of anti-social behaviour, in turn conditioned by other dimensions of citizen well-being.	Multi-agency partnerships including the police, local authorities, probation services and local populations.	Strategic crime prevention, including networking between, and coordination of, partners' preventive efforts combined with other initiatives for neighbourhood regeneration

Source: adapted from Benyon and Edwards (1999: 149).

The shift in focus

The emergence of crime prevention through community governance can be traced back, in part,[7] to work by criminologists in the research wing of the Home Office. The 'new criminologies of everyday life' (Felson, 1998 cf. Stenson, 1993, Garland, 1996: 450ff), argued that conspicuous failures in crime control policy could be attributed to misconceptions about the character of crime. Instead of regarding crime as reducible to the actions of pathological or under-socialised individuals, crime was seen as a normal social fact shaped by the situational opportunities for its commission. Rather than focusing on the 'dispositions' of individual criminals, the 'new criminologies' highlighted the multifaceted dimensions of crime *events* including potential victims, vulnerable targets and the 'everyday routines of social and economic life which create criminal opportunities as an unintended by-product' (Garland, 1996: 451).

The shift in focus was also driven by Home Office research into the severe limits to orthodox police methods of crime control. Contrary to popular belief, analyses of police effectiveness revealed that the simple presence or absence of patrols had a negligible effect on crime patterns (Clarke and Hough, 1980). Moreover, police successes in detecting and clearing-up crimes were overwhelmingly attributable to information provided by the public rather than to police investigations.

Outside the Home Office it was local authorities themselves who were developing the research-based challenge to orthodox crime control. Throughout the late 1980s and early 1990s metropolitan authorities funded local victim surveys which emphasised the concentration of victimisation on already disadvantaged communities least able to withstand the impact of crime. These surveys informed, and were informed by, an emerging school of criminological thought, 'Left Realism', which has played a significant part in unpacking crime events in terms of their constituent relations of victim–offender–formal control–informal control. This 'square of crime' (Young, 1997: 482–91) complements the critical appraisal of crime control through a partial focus on offenders and elaborates an innovative focus on the multi-faceted constitution of crime.

The shift in orientation

On the basis of this research the new criminologies argued for a reorientation of the policy response to local crime away from unilateral interventions by agencies, such as the police, courts and prisons, towards multilateral strategies involving these agencies in partnership with individuals and organisations in 'the community'. A Home Office circular on crime prevention in 1984 expressed the new nostrum of crime control policy:

> A primary objective of the police has always been the prevention of crime. However, since some of the factors affecting crime lie outside the control or direct influence of the police, crime prevention can not be left to them alone. Every citizen and all those agencies whose policies and practices can influence the extent of crime should make their contribution. Preventing crime is a task for the whole community.
>
> (Home Office, 1984: 1)

This circular marked the first official recognition of the role which local authorities, as the institutions in command of many of the key policies and practices that can shape crime patterns, should play in crime prevention initiatives and provoked the first generation of local crime prevention partnerships whose work the Morgan Report was established to review.

The shift in technique

With this reorientation, alternative techniques for combating crime were promoted. In contrast to the purported deterrent effects of intensive police patrols, punitive sentencing and tough prison regimes, the new criminologies of everyday life advocate prevention through increasing the risks of offenders being caught (through improved surveillance), increasing the effort of committing crimes (through 'target hardening') and reducing the rewards of offending (through 'target removal') (Clarke, 1995). Additionally, Left Realist accounts have promoted a concern with 'long-term transformations' as well as 'short-term gains'; 'crime is about social justice gone wrong', inextricably connected to issues of social inequality, citizenship and, therefore, regeneration per se (Young, 1997: 492–4). Notwithstanding significant differences, a common feature distinguishing these alternative traditions of theory and practice is their promotion of governing techniques that are located in the community and require the active participation of local citizens in their implementation.

Initially, 'situational' crime prevention techniques predominated in the approaches of local partnerships, which tended to be led by the police in view of their expertise. However, as local authorities became increasingly involved, the agendas of local partnerships evolved to include the more 'social' crime prevention techniques, embracing the broader issues implied by 'community safety' and concentrating on entire neighbourhoods. The Morgan Report illustrated the breadth of community safety work by providing a sample portfolio of activities. These ranged from the 'improved security and design of residential areas, city centres and car parks' through 'work with offenders and their families' to 'employment and training programmes' (Home Office, 1991: 32).

Networking, power-dependence and local crime control

These conceptual distinctions can clarify the substance of the shift from police-centred crime prevention towards multi-agency experiments in community safety, importing a significant spatial dimension into policy network analysis. They can also distinguish the core discourses that have shaped, and been shaped by, this policy turn. They are, however, insufficient for an understanding of why the policy response to problems of local crime and disorder have been reinvented in the way they have, when they have and where they have. These distinctions are presented as 'abstractions' to organise interpretation of policy change and not as a substitute for explanatory accounts of 'concrete' experiments in community safety.[8]

A concrete analysis of the rise of the community safety movement, and of other policy networks in criminal justice, requires a theory of political power capable of distinguishing the diverse determinations that shape policy change. In his version of policy network theory, Rhodes identifies 'power-dependence' as the motor for explanations of policy change. The essence of power-dependence theory is that:

> Organisations depend on each other for resources and, therefore, enter exchange relationships ... Each deploys its resources, whether constitutional-legal, organisational, financial, political or informational, to maximise influence over outcomes while trying to avoid becoming dependent on other 'players'. It is a complex game, in which the various levels of government are interdependent but where the relationship between them is shifting from pluralistic bargaining to corporatism.
>
> (Rhodes, 1997: 9)

Accounting for the rise of community safety in terms of power-dependence helps define the diverse determinations that can shape its concrete expression in particular locales. The 'new criminologies of everyday life', identified by Stenson (1993) and Garland (1996) as a principal motor of policy responses to local crime and disorder, are part of the 'informational' resource deployed by advocates of community safety in their challenge to orthodox crime control. In turn, the uneven development of community safety across Britain can be explained in terms of the relative capacities of these advocates to articulate the failure of orthodox crime control, present a coherent alternative strategy and define the practical means by which it can be realised. These capacities are, of course, highly variable and are central to the contingent outcomes of the community safety movement in different locales.

There is a danger, however, of overemphasising the causal 'weight' of this resource in driving policy change. The arguments of the new criminologies have resonated with some policy elites in British criminal justice as the resources of law enforcement organisations have atrophied. The failure of orthodox crime control, especially at a time when it was being vociferously championed by the 'conviction' politics of the first Thatcher term of office, created a political vacuum in which alternative strategies and organisations could thrive (Benyon and Edwards, 1997). Nevertheless, the commitment to orthodox crime control has a resilience forged, not least, by the professional interests of criminal justice agencies and the pressure they are able to exert in defending these interests. As a consequence, the process of policy change in local crime control cannot be reduced to the efficacy of community safety advocates. The deployment of informational resources is limited by the material interests of the criminal justice policy networks discussed in greater detail elsewhere in this text. It is with reference to the limits of these material resources, especially those of local constabularies, that a more concrete analysis of why local crime control policy has changed can be developed.

Notwithstanding their emasculation during the successive Conservative administrations of 1979–97, the resources retained by local authorities left them better placed to exploit the failing organisational powers of the constabularies and other criminal justice agencies. Local authorities continue to provide the key welfare (housing, educational, youth and social) services implicated by both situational and social crime prevention techniques. As a consequence they hold the *balance* of organisational power over law enforcement agencies in the local policy response to crime and disorder. Their role in town planning and environmental development gives them substantial constitutional-legal resources, whilst their local revenue raising powers enable them to steer the focus, orientation and technology of local crime control, particularly in the absence of major central government funding for local crime reduction. Finally, their political resource, as democratically elected organisations, enhances the legitimacy of their claim for leadership of local crime control *relative to* law enforcement agencies. Of course, relative to the scale of local crime and disorder problems and to more objective criteria of organisational, legal, revenue raising and, especially, political resources, the governing capacities of local authorities can be seen as weak. They remain, however, the only single agency at the local level which is in command of such a broad range of resources. It is this balance of resources that has *necessitated* the increasing influence of local authorities in crime control policy-making in spite of resistance among some professional interests in the criminal justice system and their political allies at the national level.

The concept of power-dependence can also inform an understanding of the uneven territorial, as well as temporal, development of local crime control policy. Rhodes' emphasis on examining inter-governmental relations within policy networks along a continuum of 'pluralistic bargaining to corporatism' (1997: 9) has particular relevance for explaining the diversity of approaches to crime control through community governance. Different configurations of resource dependency, in the highly varied context of British local governance, will have a crucial bearing on the *capacity*, as well as the inclination, of local authorities and the community safety partnerships in which they are involved to govern in a pluralistic or corporatist manner. If it is accepted that a, if not *the*, principal aim of community governance is to establish 'self-reproducing' or 'durable' partnerships, then leaders of these partnerships will encounter severe limits to their ability to sustain corporatist arrangements. These partnerships will either fail or they will have to, at some point, re-define their relationship to other agencies and, particularly, to the local citizenry. Following this logic, it is to be expected that the character of concrete community safety partnerships will vary over time and between localities between pluralist bargaining and corporatist diktat.

It is in recognition of this diversity that we argue in favour of a power-dependence theory of local crime control in preference to the over-optimistic pluralism of much official discourse on community safety (e.g. Home Office, 1993b) or the tendency to over-generalise partnership practice found in explanations using corporatist theory (Crawford, 1994, 1997). In the remainder of this chapter we draw upon findings from our research into the practice of local partnerships in two outer-estates in the East Midlands to demonstrate the efficacy of power-dependence theory in accounting for the implications of increasing local authority involvement in crime control policy-making.

The practice of networking in local crime control

A key feature of the development of community safety strategies prior to the 1998 Crime and Disorder Act was the absence of any statutory obligation for local authorities and other local actors to work together. As a consequence, the establishment of community safety strategies depended on the response of agencies in particular localities to the exhortations and inducements of national organisations. These included interdepartmental circulars from Whitehall to all chief constables and local authority chief executives, in 1984 and 1990, advice on 'best practice' from the Home Office Crime Prevention Unit and the Home Office sponsored charity, Crime Concern, and the need to demonstrate multi-agency co-operation as a prerequisite of competing for government grant-aid through the City Challenge, Safer Cities and Single Regeneration Budget programmes. In 1991, the Morgan Report found that the lack of a clear statutory responsibility for local government had inhibited developments. Successful multi-agency approaches required the formulation of an overall crime reduction strategy and structure, within which agencies could co-operate.

The research conducted by the authors examined developments in local crime prevention since the publication of the Morgan Report. The study examined the capacity of community safety strategies, as a form of networking, to transcend the perceived failures of crime control through either bureaucratic hierarchies or market provision. It focussed on the practice of community safety partnerships on outer housing estates in two English cities, Leicester and Nottingham, as a critical test of networking and crime control at the local level. Findings from this research are discussed below in terms of four key criteria for governance:

- a coherent conception of governing needs;
- co-ordinating the response to those needs;
- rendering that response accountable;
- sustaining that response.

Coherence and coordination

In the absence of a national strategy for coordinating crime prevention, progress in its local delivery was uneven, as it depended on the initiative shown by agencies in particular localities and their success in competing for grant-aid. Furthermore, developments were erratic, largely because grant-aid provided on a fixed-term basis left particular projects vulnerable to collapse when initial, 'pump-priming', investment ended. A local activist in Nottingham stressed that the existing system did not promote durable partnerships:

> Ultimately, I think you won't resolve the problems without longer-term funding and longer-term strategies and some sense of permanence because the one thing people out there are suffering from, apart from poverty, is instability. . . . It is not so much the level of funding which is the problem as the need for a 'standard flow' of resources.

A related problem was that the existing institutional framework did not promote the co-ordination or coherence of local programmes. The provision of grant-aid on a project-by-project basis, with continued funding dependent on the accomplishment of project-specific targets, meant that individual projects (which together constituted a 'local strategy') frequently had different time scales. Even when funding was secured for all the projects constituting the strategy, divergent time scales sometimes undermined synchronisation and, therefore, the beneficial effects of their integration, as envisaged in strategy 'action plans'.

The impact of the funding regime was often particularly damaging for the co-ordination of community crime prevention strategies aimed at the restoration of order and reductions in crime across whole neighbourhoods. A local government community safety officer in Leicester pointed out to the researchers that a key problem on the estate being studied was putting the crime prevention strategy into practice:

> What you get is people becoming preoccupied with the individual projects. . . . Most of the time they are under extreme time constraints – they have just not got the time to think about what the links are between their project and somebody else's. If you are in a pressured situation and you have to achieve certain outputs within different time scales, then you don't always have the time to do the linking work which sometimes, I feel, is more important than the contribution of specific projects.

These problems have been compounded in longer-term, city-wide, community safety strategies aimed at managing the displacement of crime and victimisation from one neighbourhood to another. As the number of projects expanded, and as the scope of the strategy's geographical and temporal applicability broadened, inter-project coordination became ever harder to accomplish, and management of the overall strategy was often dissipated into project-based interventions. In the existing institutional framework, this dissipation occurred even at the neighbourhood level. The coherence of local crime prevention strategies was also dependent on relations *within* the participating organisations. The 'peripheral' status of crime prevention in the major statutory agencies involved in partnerships – the police and local authorities – has been exacerbated by externally imposed performance criteria.

In the case of the police, forces are assessed annually by HMIC, using performance indicators which emphasise reactive rather than preventive targets for crime control, such as arrest, detection and clear-up rates and response times. If such targets are not met, a force may be denied its 'certificate of efficiency' thus jeopardising its Exchequer grant, amounting to 51 per cent of all constabulary expenditure. HMIC also has the power to 'recommend' changes in a force's objectives and operational practices, in line with the Home Secretary's directions on police efficiency. Since the passage of the Police and Magistrate's Courts Act, 1994, these directives have been issued on an annual basis. While the national objectives have incorporated crime prevention through the partnership approach since 1994, the overwhelming emphasis remains on more easily measurable, quantitative, targets for police *reactions* to crime.

Thus, the police have strong incentives for subordinating their involvement in crime prevention partnerships to the unilateral pursuit of the crime control targets assigned to them. As a police–community liaison officer involved in the Nottingham partnership argued:

> We are being pushed in a certain way, as are other agencies, and it's not necessarily what the government are advocating in terms of the 'need for partnership', rather it is more to do with the performance criteria they are setting for ourselves, probation, social services etc.... police work is now even more about what might happen today and tomorrow, not involvement in 'strategic' crime prevention. It is so a divisional commander can say: 'My burglary arrests are so and so, the number of burglaries are going down, car crime is staying level and we have had so many arrests', that is the consequence of current police reforms. So, I think everything that is happening at the moment seems to be working against partnership – it seems to be putting us back into compartments.

Similarly, the active participation of local authorities in crime prevention projects is inevitably subordinated to the fulfilment of their statutory obligations. This point was emphasised by a community safety officer in Leicester, interviewed during the research:

> It would be easier, internally, to argue that crime prevention and community safety should have more money because we have to do it . . . should we provide clean streets or should we have a community safety project? Well, you know, we have to provide a general level of cleanliness, we are obliged to do that. So it is harder for councillors to allocate resources to things that we don't have to do, however much they understand that its something that we should be doing.

The coordination and coherence of local crime prevention strategies may also be constrained by the internal organisation of partnerships. A common format for partnerships, advocated by the Home Office and Crime Concern, is a four-tiered structure involving a steering group of representatives from all participating agencies; a planning group, including the strategy coordinator and leaders of the individual projects in the strategy; thematic sub-groups, into which the individual projects are placed, such as 'education', 'family' and 'community'; and project groups of all those involved in a specific intervention (Crime Concern, 1992). As the scope of a partnership's strategy expands to encompass a broader range of crime-related problems, and a wider geographical area, there may be problems of managing the increased work load. Partnerships may become increasingly fragmented into particular problem areas of intervention, which enables inter-agency coordination on specific projects but frustrates overall, strategic, coordination. Bureaucratisation often leads to a proliferation of meetings, additional demands on the time and resources of participating agencies, and the consequent collapse of certain projects or even thematic sub-areas of a strategy through lack of support. A police officer seconded to the Leicester Safer Cities Programme, and involved in monitoring the performance of the case-study estate's strategy, argued the organisation of the partnership was a particular problem:

> The problem, as I see it, is the way in which crime prevention partnerships are organised. The project groups tend to work in isolation and don't tend to know what the other groups are actually involved in and where they are at in relation to their particular work and responsibilities.

Accountability

One of the principal arguments for partnerships, and for community governance more generally, is that they facilitate more responsive policy-making, geared towards the needs of local conditions. However, the shift of decision-making responsibilities from elected councillors to multi-agency partnerships has attracted criticism for undermining accountability. Conversely, advocates of the partnership approach argue that it empowers local populations through the opportunities for direct participation in decision-making. Further, they argue that elected local government has not been particularly successful in responding to the competing demands of different neighbourhoods and groups in their populations.

It is useful to distinguish between different modes and types of accountability of crime prevention partnerships. Discussions of local governance have identified two basic *modes* of accountability – the 'top-up' mode, in which service providers privilege the interests of elite policy-makers and funding bodies, and the 'bottom-down' mode in which providers focus on the interests of individual users, groups and communities (Burns *et al.*, 1994: 277). It is also possible to distinguish two basic *types* of accountability – 'political' accountability, which involves conventional concern with the definition and prioritisation of competing policy goals, and 'financial' accountability, which refers to contractual arrangements between funding bodies and service providers, typical of the 'new public management'. The 'value for money' of services provided by local agencies is assessed according to performance criteria set by the funding bodies. Subsequent financial support is conditional on fulfilling the contractual terms (Weatheritt, 1993; McLaughlin and Murji, 1995).

The accountability of local crime prevention partnerships is better understood in terms of these modes and types of accountability than in terms of the institutional location of decision-making in elected local authorities, constabularies or partnerships. Given the reliance of partnerships on non-local sources of funding, their capacity to develop strategies around the interests of local populations is severely constrained. The contractual criteria set by non-local funders impose a strongly 'top-up' mode of accountability on local partnerships. The political accountability of partnerships is also strongly 'top-up' as the definitions and goals of 'strategic' crime prevention are effectively driven by the performance criteria attached to grant-aid by non-local funders. Where such criteria permit a degree of local discretion in deciding strategic goals, partnerships have the capacity to cultivate a more 'bottom-down' mode of accountability. However, the capacity to sustain this mode beyond the involvement of local citizens in defining the initial priorities depends on the coincidence of local citizens' priorities with those of the funding agencies. Where the priorities do not coincide, the credibility of a partnership's commitment to involving local people as equal partners can be jeopardised.

A youth worker involved in the Leicester estate partnership which was studied identified this problem as a key reason for the difficulties encountered by the partnership in addressing the priorities of local residents. At the outset of the partnership, the City Council commissioned a survey of local people to ascertain the principal crime problems and suggestions about what should be done. One of the most favoured suggestions, confirmed at a number of public meetings, was to establish a motor project to work with youths who were involved in car crime and 'joyriding' round the estate.

> At this stage there was a lot of interest and good-will from the residents, but when the council officers presented the draft action plan the motor project was left out. Apparently, the Safer Cities people had rejected this recommendation because it was too expensive and because its outputs were insufficiently clear. So, we had gone through this elaborate rigmarole of consulting the local community only to turn round and tell them they couldn't have what they really wanted. Of course, the goodwill evaporated – I don't think we have recovered from that.

Partnerships have struggled to develop the 'bottom-down' mode of accountability, particularly amongst the heterogeneous populations and cultures which characterise 'high-crime' neighbourhoods, preferring, instead, to 'imagine' such populations as a morally homogenous community of interest. This can be explained to a large extent by the participation of certain kinds of community-based organisations in estate partnerships and the absence of others. In both of the estates studied, tenants' associations, composed typically of elderly residents, were the principal 'community representatives' on the partnerships, whilst young people were conspicuous by their absence. A school teacher involved with the Leicester partnership commented:

> Amongst the teenagers, I suspect their view is that they wouldn't be taken seriously by the partnership and so 'what's the point of getting involved?

Local government officers were aware of the effects of the lack of young people's views, for example, in the priority accorded to the concerns of the tenants' associations with the 'incivilities' associated with 'boisterous' youth gangs and noisy neighbours.

Durability

The difficulties with the 'bottom-down' accountability of partnerships have significant implications for the durability of community governance of crime prevention. A defining feature of governance is the enhancement of governability through the long-term capacity of service providers to 'self-organise' and 'self-reproduce'. The active participation of local 'communities' is vital for the viability of crime prevention partnerships, particularly in view of the constraints on public expenditure. However, this is undeniably the weakest dimension of progress on the partnership approach.

A common view is that populations in high-crime neighbourhoods suffered from a culture of dependency on statutory agencies and are impervious to their own responsibilities for accomplishing reductions in crime and 'community insecurity'. A member of the Nottingham partnership felt it had not been sufficiently successful in reaching ordinary people on the estate:

> I don't think many of them know it exists – I don't think they give a toss whether it exists. We do need to start involving a lot more local people, but I am convinced that apart from half a dozen local people, who are prepared to commit themselves, all local people want to do is dip in and out when something affects them personally.

The low participation was also attributed to the legacy of tensions between local residents and the police. A youth worker on the Leicester estate commented that it was unsurprising to see the absence of young people participating in the work of the partnership:

> As an outreach worker I have difficulties trying to establish trust and credibility with the kids on the estate because they still see me as, you know, part of 'the state'. I mean, yes, there are benefits to the idea of working in partnership, but inevitably we get associated with the police and the housing department who, because of the jobs they have to do, are not exactly popular amongst some groups on the estate who have had 'run-ins' with them before. I think the issue of

trust is behind the difficulties we have had in connecting with young people on the estate.

Partnerships also encounter problems of credibility given the failures of former urban policy interventions – they often suffer from scepticism among local residents, whose expectations have been raised and then dashed by previous, unsuccessful, attempts at regeneration. A local government officer involved with the Nottingham partnership explained that when she began work on the estate people said: 'well, yet again, another person is parachuting in':

> I understand why they thought that...you've got to do more than simply express your commitment: you have to demonstrate, to do things, to build confidence and trust and that is very hard work. They've had enough experience of agencies coming into the area with a great fanfare and then leaving with little impact.

Given the close residential proximity of victims and offenders in high-crime neighbourhoods, it is said that some people decline active participation in crime prevention strategies for fear of retaliation. This was identified as the principal reason for the absence of Asian and African–Caribbean participants by a member of the Leicester partnership, who was the head of one of the schools on the estate:

> With the African-Caribbean and Asian members of the community there is an isolation that hasn't been broken down yet...I feel there is a fear of coming out, certainly after dark, which has prevented their involvement. There is a fear of making oneself known, which comes down to just a basic fear of personal safety and security.... You must remember that the National Front had their headquarters on this estate, so you have got an almost endemic racism at times in certain areas of the estate.

Low participation was also attributed to the lack of confidence, knowledge and skills of local residents and the absence of training and support to prepare them for such active participation. A community safety officer involved in the Leicester partnership argued that:

> You can't just expect community groups to lock into your way of thinking. You don't just empower them by saying 'come to a meet-

ing'. You have got to give them the skills and the knowledge to participate fully and as equally as possible at the meeting.

Having emphasised the importance of training local citizens in the practice of governance, this same officer acknowledged that control over resources was the ultimate factor in the durability of partnerships and the empowerment of local citizens:

> Ultimately the quality and equality of participation is a question of who controls the resources. It is a hard thing to say, but it's true. Local residents can be part of the decision-making process, but come the end of the day, if we say, 'no, we just don't feel that we can employ three youth workers for your estate', they can't say, 'well, we will then'. So, in truth it is not an equal partnership in that sense.

Conclusion: the strategic dilemmas of networking

In the light of these findings it is possible to identify certain strategic dilemmas[9] that are inherent in community safety partnerships and, generally, in networking as a governing technique. Jessop (1997) identifies four strategic dilemmas associated with networking: *cooperation versus competition; openness versus closure; governability versus flexibility; and accountability versus efficiency*. We conclude this chapter with a discussion of these dilemmas and their potential impact on the future development of networking and local crime control.

Cooperation versus competition

It was noted above that trust is a central attribute or 'glue' of networking and the basis on which partnerships or other forms of this technique are reproduced. While, however, networks provide an opportunity for exchange relationships based on trust, they simultaneously create opportunities for short-term, self-interested, competitive behaviour. Network actors are always, therefore, confronted with a dilemma of maintaining inter-organisational trust in the face of incentives for self-interested competition (Jessop, 1997).

These incentives have been particularly prevalent within local community safety partnerships given the dependence on grant-aid and the application of agency-specific performance criteria to the statutory partners. Three specific forms of competition can be identified. First, within local partnerships unsuccessful competition for grant-aid undermines trust amongst statutory, private and voluntary partners and, especially, between the partnership and the local citizenry. Where successful, however, competition provides the necessary catalyst for recruiting partners and establishing the basis for an equitable ownership of the partnership. Secondly, the competitive logic inscribed into the grant-aid process erodes trust between local partnerships and their sponsors at the district-wide level. Competition amongst different neighbourhood partnerships within a district is, arguably, the most virulent challenge to the reproduction of networking as a governing technique. There is a clear incentive for statutory, voluntary and private organisations with an interest in a particular neighbourhood to amplify their problems of crime and disorder to secure scarce resources. The obvious consequence of this is the erosion of trust amongst neighbourhood-specific representatives asked to cooperate at the district-wide level. Thirdly, failure to compete successfully for grant-aid erodes trust between local partnerships and the non-local funding bodies, such that exhortations for 'best practice' or 'best value' from these authorities are subsequently resisted. In turn this jeopardises future attempts at enrolling active citizen participation in local networks.

Conversely, an excessive commitment to cooperation and consensus can foreclose the creative tensions and conflicts that promote learning and enhance the adaptability of networks to their local policy environments (Jessop, 1997). A false unity can be imposed on community safety partnerships, where the lead partners mobilise out any overt conflicts for fear of appearing amateurish to the funding authorities and in the belief that 'unity', however false, equals 'best practice' (Crawford, 1994; Benyon and Edwards, 1999).

Openness versus closure

Networks have been promoted because of their purported adaptability to complex, dynamic and diverse policy environments. To retain this adaptive capacity, networks need to remain open to the influences and lessons of these environments. Yet to manage and manipulate these environments networks have, at some point, to limit the scope of participation in them and the repertoire of interventions by them. A key dilemma here is that closure may lock in members whose exit would be beneficial or block recruitment of new partners necessary for the reproduction of the network. Conversely, openness may undermine the long-term commitment of partners and their collective acceptance of long-term time horizons. The more open a network is, the more potential there may be for short-term opportunism in the (self-fulfilling) case that networks dissolve or involve high turnover (Jessop, 1997).

This dilemma has been particularly acute for local crime control networks and, in particular, community safety strategies. Closure around police-centred strategies concerned, primarily, with situational crime prevention techniques has limited the capacity of local crime control networks to recruit the range of expertise and resources needed for community-based crime reduction. The openness of community safety strategies to a broad portfolio of measures from target hardening security measures through to local economic regeneration projects, enabled these networks to recruit the necessary range of partners. Simultaneously, this openness broadened the scope of community safety strategies to the point that coordination of the constituent projects collapsed. As such, this dilemma is not a simple product of dependence on grant-aid or the absence of a statutory duty compelling recruitment into a local crime control network. Notwithstanding the new statutory duty, and even if this duty had been accompanied by substantial financial assistance (which it has not), networks will continue to encounter dilemmas over the appropriate balance between openness and closure. This problem is particularly important for current, associated, government initiatives in 'joined-up policy-making' for reducing 'social exclusion' (Cabinet Office, 1998; Audit Commission, 1999).

Governability versus flexibility

The essential advantage claimed for networking over bureaucratic and market mechanisms is that they can provide longer term strategic guidance (which is lacking in markets) while retaining sufficient flexibility to adapt to dynamic policy environments (lacking in bureaucratic hierarchies). Networks are, however, constantly torn between an orientation towards long-term guidance or short-term flexibility (Jessop, 1997).

In local crime control networks this dilemma is epitomised by the tension between 'at a distance' guidance on 'best practice' from the Home Office and the provision of discretion to interpret and act upon the locally-specific contexts and conditions of crime and disorder (Ekblom, 1998; Home Office, 1998). The balance of power has, thus far, fallen in favour of 'at a distance guidance' from the non-local funding authorities. Local discretion, whilst acknowledged in principle, has been largely curtailed by the intensive financial and performance monitoring of local crime control networks. For example, grant-aid provided via the Single Regeneration Budget is conditional on quarterly returns from grant holders about their outputs. This process places a significant amount of power in the hands of central authorities which, if anything, has been accentuated by the new statutory duty and its concomitant guidance. Moreover, this new statutory duty has been provided on the basis of 'crime and disorder' and not 'community safety'. A potential consequence of this is the severe restriction of local partnerships' openness to the broad repertoire of initiatives for reducing crime through social regeneration. The potential that was present in the pre-statutory duty community safety movement for subsuming crime control within social regeneration, for 'socialising crime control', is likely to be reversed through the new duty for crime and disorder strategies. In the new duty social regeneration is accommodated only insofar as it reduces crime and restores order, a process which has been called the 'criminalisation of social policy' (Crawford, 1998; Stenson, 1998).

Accountability versus efficiency

As a governing technique, networking has been legitimised principally in terms of its efficiency relative to markets and hierarchies. There are, of course, major dilemmas concerning the political legitimisation of networking. Advocates of networking have identified their potential for revitalising local democracy by enabling the direct participation of local communities in public policy decision-making processes (Burns *et al.*, 1994). Relative to markets, which exclude those with few resources from 'effective demand' and inscribe severe inequalities into political representation, and bureaucracies, which are notorious for their inertia and lack of responsiveness, networks are regarded as a means of operationalising innovations in participatory, 'associative' democracy (Hirst, 1994, 1997). Conversely, critics of networking identify its potential use as 'Trojan horse' for the reassertion of an authoritarian but more 'efficient' and ruthless form of state power (cf. Coleman and Sim, 1998). In these terms networking threatens to promote a further colonisation of civil society by political authorities; a 'statisation of the private sphere' (Jessop, 1997).

Alternatively, networking has the potential to reverse this 'statisation of the private sphere' by 'privatising politics'. Mike Davis has most eloquently articulated this latter dilemma in his political economy of Los Angeles (1992). In this, Davis describes the consequences of empowering certain residential communities with greater decision-making responsibilities. He found that home owner's associations in one predominantly white neighbourhood, West Hills in the San Fernando Valley, used their influence over land-use planning decisions to exclude the involvement of ethnic minority residents and other social groups they found 'bad...[and] very slummish' (Davis, 1992: 153–4). Clearly the empowerment of local citizens in decisions about crime control has the potential for a dangerous privatisation of politics ranging from bigoted constructions of 'community' to outright 'vigilantism' and punishment beatings of suspected offenders.[10]

These four, by no means exhaustive, strategic dilemmas suggest that networking presents as many problems for public-policy and social science as it does resolutions for the limits to longer-standing state and market techniques for governing complex social–political problems. Examining the tensions and conflicts produced by these dilemmas and possible methods for their reconciliation provides a fertile ground for social and political research into local crime control. Conversely, crime control provides a critical test of networking as a governing technique and 'associative' approaches to the revitalisation of democracy.

Notes

1. Giddens uses the term 'locale' to refer to specific 'time-space' configurations such as 'London', the 'South East', 'England', 'Britain', 'Europe' etc., in the 'last decade', 'post-war period', 'modern epoch' etc. (1984:110–61). In terms of criminal justice policy networks 'locale' provides a concept for thinking about, for example, intergovernmental relations between actors involved in sentencing policy and how their interaction in London could differ from that in Durham or even how this interaction could differ across jurisdictions within London or any other town or city. As such, the concept of 'locale' enables a further disaggregation of governing processes to reveal and account for *diverse outcomes* of a common policy initiative.

2. The Local Governance Programme includes case studies of, *inter alia*, health, education, housing and economic regeneration policies in different localities. The key findings from these studies are provided in Stoker (1999).

3. This project also formed part of the Local Governance Programme. The authors acknowledge the support of the ESRC for its completion (reference number: L311253035).

4. The Audit Commission Report was released in February 1999.

5. In the current context of both American and British Government, the idea of the 'Third Way' and 'joined –up' policy-making have been used to signify the substance of this 'reinvention'. Clearly there is an affinity with these ideas and the concept of 'community governance' which also emphasises the 'interdependencies' among policy actors within and between policy networks. We, however, prefer the concept of community governance for the purposes of specifying experiments in 'joined-up' policy-making at the local and sub-local levels which also emphasise the centrality of active citizen participation in the policy process (see below).

6. Community governance can also be distinguished form the idea of 'local governance' in terms of its orientation toward active citizen participation rather than just 'inter-agency' partnerships.

7. In anticipation of the criticism that this account of the forces driving crime prevention through community governance overstates the importance of ideas, we draw upon 'power-dependence' theory (below) to specify the other, material, determinants of policy change in this area.

8. There is an analogy here with macro-theoretical accounts of the purported shift from 'Fordist' to post-Fordist political economies (Jessop, 1994; Peck and Tickell, 1994), in which the characteristics of 'Fordism' and 'post-Fordism' are not presented as mirror reflections of social reality but as tendencies which have a diverse, context-specific, expression in 'concrete' political economies. On the 'critical realist' epistemology of abstraction and concrete analysis see Jessop (1982: 213–20) and Sayer (1992: 85–117).

9. Jessop (1997: n18) defines a strategic dilemma as a situation in which: 'Agents are faced with choices such that any action undermines key conditions of their existence and/or their capacities to realise some overall interest'.

10. For a detailed examination of 'vigilantism' and crime control in the UK see Johnston (1996).

References

ACC/ADC/AMA (Association of County Councils, Association of District Councils, Association of Metropolitan Authorities) (1997) *Crime – the Local Solution: Proposals for Community Safety and Crime Prevention* (London: Local Government Association).

ACC/ADC/AMA/LGMB (Association of County Councils, Association of District Councils, Association of Metropolitan Authorities, Local Government Management Board) (1996) *Survey of Community Safety Activities in Local Government in England and Wales* (Luton: LGMB).

ADC (1990) *Promoting Safer Communities – a District Council Perspective* (London: ADC).

AMA (1990) *Crime Reduction: a Framework for the Nineties?* (London: AMA).

Audit Commission (1999) *Safety in Numbers: Promoting Community Safety* (London: Audit Commission).

Benyon, J. (1986) 'Policing in the limelight', in Benyon, J. and Bourn, C. (eds) *The Police: Powers, Procedures and Proprieties* (Oxford: Pergamon Press).

Benyon, J. and Edwards, A. (1997) 'Crime and public order', in Dunleavy, P., Gamble, A., Holliday, I. and Peele, G. (eds), *Developments in British Politics 5* (London: Macmillan Press – now Palgrave.

Benyon, J. and Edwards, A. (1999) 'Community governance of crime control', in G. Stoker (ed.), *The New Management of British Local Governance* (London: Macmillan Press – now Palgrave.

Burns, D. *et al.* (1994) *The Politics of Decentralisation: Revitalising Local Democracy* (London: Macmillan).

Cabinet Office (1998) *Bringing Britain Together* (London: Cabinet Office, Social Exclusion Unit).

Clarke, R. V. (1995) 'Situational crime prevention', in Tonry, M. and Farrington, D. (eds), *Building a Safer Society: Strategic Approaches to Crime Prevention* (Chicago: The University of Chicago Press).

Clarke, R. V. and Hough, M. (eds) (1980) *The Effectiveness of Policing* (Farnborough: Gower).

Coleman, R. and Sim, J. (1998) 'From the dockyards to the Disney store: surveillance, risk and security in Liverpool city centre', *International Review of Law Computers & Technology*, 12(1): 27–45.

Crawford, A. (1994) 'The partnership approach: corporatism at the local level?', *Social and Legal Studies*, 3(4): 497–519.

Crawford, A. (1997) *The Local Governance of Crime: Appeals to Community and Partnership* (Oxford: Clarendon Press).

Crawford, A. (1998) *Crime Prevention and Community Safety: Politics, Policies & Practices* (London: Longman).

Crime Concern (1992) *Family, School and Community: Towards a Social Crime Prevention Agenda* (Swindon: Crime Concern).

Davis, M. (1992) *City of Quartz* (London: Vintage).

Duclaud-Williams, R. (1993) 'The governance of education: Britain and France', in Kooiman, J. (ed.), *Modern Governance: New Government–Society Interactions* (London: Sage).

Ekblom, P, (1998) *Community Safety and the Reduction and Prevention of Crime – a Conceptual Framework for Training and the Development of a Professional Discipline* (London: Home Office).

Felson, M, (1998) *Crime and Everyday Life*, 2nd edn (Thousand Oaks, Ca: Pine Forge Press).

Frances, J., Levacic, R., Mitchell, J. and Thompson, G. (1991) 'Introduction', in Thompson, G., Frances, J., Levacic, R. and Mitchell, J. (eds), *Markets, Hierarchies and Networks: The Co-ordination of Social Life* (London: Sage).

Garland, D. (1996) 'The limits of the sovereign state: strategies of crime control in contemporary society', *The British Journal of Criminology*, 36(4): 445–71.

Giddens, A. (1994) *The Constitution of Society* (Cambridge: Polity).

Hirst, P. (1994) *Associative Democracy: New Forms of Economic and Social Governance* (Cambridge: Polity).

Hirst, P. (1997) *From Statism to Pluralism: Democracy, Civil Society and Global Politics* (London: UCL Press).

Hogwood, B. (1995) 'The integrated regional offices and the single regeneration budget', *Commission for Local Democracy, Research Report No. 13* (London: CLD).

Home Office (1984) *Circular 8/84: Crime Prevention* (London: HMSO).

Home Office (1990) *Partnership in Crime Prevention* (London: HMSO).

Home Office (1991) *Standing Conference on Crime Prevention: Safer Communities: The Local Delivery of Crime Prevention Through the Partnership Approach* (the Morgan Report) (London: HMSO).

Home Office (1992) *Home Office Response to the Report: 'Safer Communities – The Local Delivery of Crime Prevention Through the Partnership Approach'* (London: Home Office).

Home Office (1993a) *A Practical Guide to Crime Prevention for Local Partnerships* (London: HMSO).

Home Office (1993b) *Safer Cities Progress Report, 1992/1993* (London: HMSO).

Home Office (1998) *Guidance on Statutory Crime and Disorder Partnership's* (London: Home Office Communications Directorate).

Hughes, G. (1997) 'Policing late modernity: changing strategies of crime management in contemporary Britain', in Jewson, N. and MacGregor, S. (eds), *Transforming Cities* (London: Routledge).

Jessop, B. (1982) *The Capitalist State* (Oxford: Martin Robertson).

Jessop, B. (1994) 'Post-Fordism and the State', in Amin, A. (ed.), *Post-Fordism: A Reader* (Oxford: Blackwell).

Jessop, B. (1997) 'The governance of complexity and the complexity of governance: preliminary remarks on some problems and limits of economic guidance', in Amin, A. and Hausner, J. (eds), *Beyond Market and Hierarchy* (Aldershot: Edward Elgar).

Johnston, L. (1996) 'What is vigilantism?', *British Journal of Criminology*, 36(2): 220–36.

Jones, T., Newburn, T. and Smith, D. (1994) *Democracy and Policing* (London: Policy Studies Institute).

Kooiman, J. (1993) 'Governance and governability: using complexity, dynamics and diversity' in Kooiman, J. (ed.), *Modern Governance: New Government–Society Interactions* (London: Sage).

LARIA (Local Authorities' Research and Intelligence Association) (1994) *Research for Policy: Proceedings of the 1994 Annual Conference of LARIA* (Newcastle-upon-Tyne: LARIA).

Levacic, R. (1991) 'Markets and government: an overview', in Thompson, G., Frances, J., Levacic, R. and Mitchell, J. (eds) *Markets, Hierarchies and Networks: The Co-ordination of Social Life* (London: Sage).

Liddle, M. and Gelsthorpe, L. (1994) *Inter-Agency Crime Prevention: Organising Local Delivery*, Police Research Group Crime Prevention Unit Paper 52 (London: Home Office).

London Borough of Camden (1996) *The Community Safety Strategy for Camden* (London: Borough of Camden).

Lowndes, V. (1993) 'The other governments of Britain: local politics and delegated administrations', in Budge, I. and McKay, D. (eds), *The Developing British Political System: the 1990s*, 3rd edn (London: Longman).

Marlow, A. and Pitts, J. (eds) (1998) *Planning Safer Communities* (Lyme Regis: Russell House Publishing).

Marsh, D. and Rhodes, R. A. W. (eds) (1992a) *Policy Networks in British Government* (Oxford: Clarendon Press).

Marsh, D. and Rhodes, R. A. W. (eds) (1992b) *Implementing Thatcherite Policies* (Buckingham: Open University Press).

McLaughlin, E. and Murji, K. (1995) 'The end of public policing? police reform and the "new managerialism"', in Noakes, L., Levi, M. and Maguire, M. (eds), *Contemporary Issues in Criminology* (Cardiff: University of Wales Press).

Osborne, D. and Gaebler, t. (1993) *Reinventing Government: How the Entrepreneurial Spirit is Transforming the Public Sector* (Massachusetts: Addison-Wesley).

Pease, K. (1994) 'Crime prevention', in Maguire, M., Morgau, R. and Reiner, R. (eds), *The Oxford Handbook of Criminology* (Oxford: Oxford University Press).

Peck, J. and Tickell, A. (1994) 'Searching for an new institutional fix: the after-Fordist crisis and the global–local disorder; in A. Amin (ed:), *Post-Fordism: A Reader* (Oxford: Blackwell).

Reiner, R. (1992) *The Politics of the Police* (Hemel Hempstead: Harvester Wheatsheaf).

Rhodes, R. A. W. (1997) *Understanding Governance: Policy Networks, Governance, Reflexivity and Accountability* (Buckingham: Open University Press).

Sayer, A. (1992) *Method in Social Science: A Realist Approach*, 2nd edn (London: Routledge).

Stenson, K. (1993) 'Community policing as a governmental technology', *Economy and Society*, 22: 373–89.

Stenson, K. (1998) 'Displacing social policy through crime control', in S. Hanninen (ed.), *Displacement of Social Policies* (Jyvaskyla: Sophi Publications).

Stoker, G. (1997) 'Local government in Britain after Thatcher', in Erik-Lane, J. (ed.), *Public Sector Reform* (London: Sage).

Stoker, G. (1998) 'Public–private partnerships and urban governance', in Pierre, J. (ed.), *Partnerships in Urban Governance: European and American Experience* (London: Macmillan).

Stoker, G. (ed.) (1999) *The New Management of British Local Governance* (London: Macmillan Press – now Palgrave).

Thompson, G., Frances, J., Levacic, R. and Mitchell, J. (eds) (1991) *Markets, Hierarchies & Networks: the Coordination of Social Life* (London: Sage).

Weatheritt, M. (1993) 'Measuring police performance: accounting or accountability?', in Reiner, R. and Spencer, S. (eds), *Accountable Policing: Effectiveness, Empowerment and Equity* (London: Institute of Public Policy Research).

Wolman, H. and Goldsmith, M. (1992) *Urban Politics and Policy: a Comparative Approach* (Oxford: Blackwell).

Young, J. (1997) 'Left realist criminology: radical in its analysis, realist in its policy', in Maguire, M., Morgan, R. and Reiner, R. (eds), *The Oxford Handbook of Criminology*, 2nd edn (Oxford: Oxford University Press).

8
Liberty: Networking Criminal Justice in Defence of Civil Liberties, 1979–99

Mick Ryan

Introduction

This chapter focuses on the role of liberty in networking to defend and enlarge our civil liberties in criminal justice matters in England and Wales, and to a lesser extent, Northern Ireland. This focus is partial, yet at the same time, and paradoxically, amorphous.

It is partial in the sense that it does less than credit to Liberty's many endeavours; its work in matters of civil justice, for example, is only mentioned *en passant* where it helps to delineate the boundaries of our current inquiry. It is amorphous in the sense that alongside its role in monitoring the operation of the criminal justice system per se, an undertaking which brings it into contact with a whole range of other advocacy groups, such as the Howard League for Penal Reform, as well as professional groups such as the Magistrates' Association, Liberty also contests matters relating to criminal justice policy as they arise across a whole range of quite discrete, or at best contingent lobbies, say the travellers' lobby, or the lobby for gay and lesbian equality.

After a short, early history which is intended to highlight some of Liberty's enduring political and organisational characteristics, its activities will then be ordered in the language of policy scientists with a special interest in policy networks. Given the complexities and extent of Liberty's activities in a polycentric political order this ordering is far from absolute and will require some 'funnelling down' to isolate criminal justice issues as such.

This will be followed by an empirical overview of the patterning of Liberty's lobbying activities in criminal justice matters during the period of successive Conservative governments between 1979 and 1997. The tactical, strategic and organisational dilemmas which confronted Liberty during these years will be addressed, and then some assessment made of its lobbying activities under New Labour. References to other, related groups such as Justice and INQUEST, will be made and the increasing globalisation of Liberty's networks signalled, as will significant shifts in its strategy, and what these might tell us about the underlying dynamics of policy networks.

Background

Liberty, or the National Council for Civil Liberties (NCCL) as it was mostly referred to in the period we are discussing, was set up as small, politically non-aligned organisation in the 1930s. Its initial role had been to monitor police behaviour at demonstrations in the 1930s, a concern prompted by the use of agents provocateurs by the police at rallies organised by trade unions and the unemployed during the tenure of the National government. (Lilly, 1984: 1–33) However, it soon broadened this remit to monitor the rise of Fascist organisations and the policing of Mosley's Blackshirts in the context of the Public Order Act (1936)(Dyson, 1994: 13–16).

During the Second World War it took on board the issue of press and broadcasting censorship and the operation of tribunals which had been set up to process conscientious objectors, and while not (surprisingly perhaps) actually campaigning against internment, it nonetheless sought to monitor the treatment of detainees during the office of the wartime Coalition government. (Lilly, 1984: 34–63)

In the 1950s its major campaign was to defend the rights of the mentally ill and its contribution to overturning the outdated Mental Deficiency Act of 1913 with the passing of the Mental Health Act (1959) by Macmillan's Conservative Government is widely recognised (Lilly, 1984: 74–81). It also intervened through the courts to justify the rights of groups like CND to hold peaceful protests. This public order focus carried over into the 1960s after Labour returned to power in 1964 with the rise of the anti-Vietnam war movement, student protests and the issue of immigration which was accompanied by the rise of racism. This was to become even more marked in the 1970s with the rise of the National Front. The public order issues surrounding the Front's activities and the deteriorating situation in Northern Ireland – including its impact on policing the mainland during what were also troubled industrial times – was to occupy an increasing amount of Liberty's energies as the unsettled seventies came to a close (Lilly, 1984: 82–151).

It would be reasonable to infer from this short history that as a politically non-aligned organisation Liberty had, up to and including the 1970s, some success in challenging the power of the British state in the courts and/or lobbying and networking to confront (and influence) both wartime Coalition governments, and then later, successive Conservative and Labour administrations on issues as diverse as public order and the rights of the mentally ill as the major parties alternated in office and constructed the postwar consensus.

This inference is not wholly inaccurate, though it skates over some uncomfortable truths. The first is that at times the organisation was in some disarray with declining membership and was heavily in debt (Dyson, 1994: 38–49). It was therefore far from being the effective organisation that our historical sketch suggests. Second, and sometimes contributing to this disarray, for most of the period in question Liberty's active membership was very much centre Left. This was seen in some quarters to undermine its credibility as a politically non aligned or all party organisation with the capacity to deal even handedly (and influence) governments of all political persuasions. Some prominent public figures resigned from the Executive as a result of these worries (Dyson, 1994: 23–27). These resignations and debates about sensitive issues, e.g. internment in Northern Ireland in the early 1970s, sometimes caused a public stir and split the organisation from top to bottom (Dyson, 1994: 57).

Liberty was thus, and continues to be, a potentially volatile organisation. Currently, it has a membership of over 5,000. This includes a good number of lawyers, and also trade unionists who become members through local branch (or national) affiliation. But how are we to understand how it operates? How does it fit into the heuristic framework of policy scientists?

Liberty and its networks

It is important to say at the outset that characterizing Liberty's work in the language of the policy scientist with a particular interest in policy networks presents some problems.

In the first place, policy scientists often work on groups or policy networks which relate to one, two or three at most, departments of state covering a limited number of policy areas. Liberty has a much wider focus. During the period between 1979 and 1997, for example, it worked at various times, to a whole range of departments from the

Department of Employment on issues of women's employment and trade union rights, the Department of Health on the rights of mental patients, to the Home Office on asylum seekers and the rights of prisoners, the Lord Chancellor's Office on rights of audience and so on. The list of 'client' departments and policy areas is almost endless.

Furthermore, and this is our second and related difficulty, while the unifying theme underpinning all this across the board activity is the defence and enlargement of our civil liberties much of Liberty's lobbying and networking is not centred on either the making or the implementation of criminal justice policy per se. Far from it in fact. So we shall need to tailor this analysis of Liberty to meet our brief, to narrow our concerns down, though few of Liberty's networks are totally discrete.

Thirdly, policy scientists are also keen to categorise lobbies or policy networks (Rhodes and Marsh, 1992). For example, those lobbies or networks which contain relatively few, stable, tightly organised groups sharing common goals among a disciplined membership, groups which together have easy access to government departments are defined as policy communities, while those which contain a variety of somewhat diverse groups, some of which are poorly resourced and who float in and out of the policy-making process are known as issue networks. Liberty of course, operates across a number of lobbies or policy networks, and to establish where some of these might be located along the community – network continuum would take a good deal of research.

True, in some lobbies one can sense where they might be located. For example, Liberty is frequently lobbying where groups like MIND have a well-established presence in a reasonably stable, well accessed lobby which is perhaps more of a policy community than an issue network. On the other hand, the lobby against the trespass provisions in the Criminal Justice and Public Order Act (1994) displayed more of the characteristics of an issue network.

However, these examples raise a fourth problem, which is that while policy scientists are keen to categorise in this broad fashion they are also keen to suggest the need to disaggregate lobbies or policy networks, say between insider and outsider groups (Rhodes and Marsh, 1992: 9). So where does a relatively recently established and poorly resourced group like WISH fit into the mental health and penal lobbies respectively? And what sort of player is Liberty in this company? Again, mapping these disaggregations is surely possible, but only after extensive research.

These then, are some of the real problems which do not arise when policy scientists pick – as they often do – on lobbies or policy networks where the players are few and where the policy focus is relatively narrow and often technical, say sea defences or nuclear power, and where client departments are limited in number (Sabbatier and Jenkins-Smith, 1993).

A comprehensive analysis of Liberty from the point of view of policy scientists is, therefore, a longer-term project requiring an understanding that a good deal of its activities are about networking outside of criminal justice per se. In other words, it needs to be appreciated that defending civil liberties necessitates a much wider brief involving, for example, various branches of civil law such as employment law which for many years discriminated against women.

Having made this important caveat, however, Liberty is nonetheless clearly very active in the criminal justice network, trying to both influence policy and monitor its implementation throughout the criminal justice system, from policing through the courts to the administration of punishment in the penal system. After sketching in the legislative background since 1979, I shall then map out this activity before going on to make some assessment of Liberty's achievements between 1979 and 1997, and identify emerging strategies.

Networking criminal justice, 1979–97

One of the defining characteristics of the Conservative ascendancy was the proliferation of criminal justice legislation. There were measures, for example, to reduce the scope for trial by jury and enable police to enter households in hot pursuit. Changes in sentencing practices which led to prison overcrowding and increasingly repressive prison regimes were also introduced. There was a whole raft of Acts which brought trade union activities, such as picketing, further within the ambit of the criminal law and also two very controversial measures to regulate demonstrations, the Public Order Act (1986) and Criminal Justice and Public Order Act (1994), the most recent of which criminalised trespass in certain circumstances. There were also two Royal Commissions prompted by miscarriages of justice which reported in 1983 and 1993 respectively. Throughout this period too, the Prevention of Terrorism Act (1974) was constantly revised and renewed which had implications for both the mainland and Northern Ireland, as did moves to abolish the right of silence in both jurisdictions.

The material is available to trace in some detail Liberty's attempts to secure safeguards in just about all of these areas. However, I am more concerned here to map out the broad patterns of its lobby operations rather than looking at the detail of how it sought to influence this or that piece of legislation.

Professional lobbies

Liberty is often involved with lobby groups whose members, or at least some of their members, are directly charged with operating the criminal justice system. It has lobbied, for example, with the Bar Council and the Law Society on the right to silence and issues around legal aid. (Liberty, 1993a) In these particular contexts there is a good deal of overlapping membership. Prominent members of the Bar Council, for example, have been members of Liberty's Executive and/or are members of its working parties on particular issues. In 1992 Liberty also organised an Independent Civil Liberties Panel on Miscarriages of Justice in July 1992 which not only brought in the legal professions, including the Crown Prosecution Service(CPS), but also involved the ACPO and the NAPO. (Liberty, 1992a)

This professional constituency might seem to be Liberty's natural milieu, and to an extent it is. However, Liberty's activities in monitoring the implementation of criminal justice policy often brings it into direct and critical conflict with many of the professional groups involved. Given its criticism of the almost unlimited powers of Chief Constables (Spencer, 1985), its attack on the Police Complaints Authority (Liberty, 1993b), its highly critical report in 1994 on the work of magistrates (Liberty, 1992b), its demands for a radical overhaul of the higher judiciary,[1] then it is hardly surprising that it is often as much in conflict with some of these groups as working with them. It is at odds with either the policies (or practices) which these groups are asked to administer, or more uncomfortable for some of the professionals, critical of the way in which they are being implemented. Apparently, Liberty has more involvement with, is often more in sympathy with, its contingent advocacy lobbies than those professional interests who are charged with operating the criminal justice system. Indeed, many people become involved with Liberty just because they believe the activities of these professional groups – and not just the policies they administer – need to be monitored.

It is perhaps worth mentioning here by the way that many of the professional groups referred to above, around police, judiciary and the probation service, for example, were struggling with the demands of what has been described as the 'revolution in governance' during the Conservative ascendency, increasingly subject to the Audit Commission and/or under direct government pressure to either contract out or re-model their practices in line with the three Es, Economy, Efficiency and Effectiveness (Rhodes, 1997). While groups like Liberty and INQUEST were, it is true, similarly forced to better account to their sponsors such as the London Borough Grants Committee for the effectiveness of their service delivery, and significantly so in some cases, as non-governmental organisations the overall impact of the new managerialism on their practices was marginal in comparison.

It is important to remember that many of these professional groups were subject to another kind of pressure after 1979. Not only were their members charged with administering an ever-changing criminal law, aspects of which they sometimes strongly disagreed with, but also the manner in which they delivered their own services came to be challenged as successive governments sought more accountability and greater efficiency savings through the new public management initiative.

Advocacy groups

In addition to working with those professionals who actually run the criminal justice system Liberty often works closely with advocacy groups who monitor its activities from the outside.

For example, during the course of the late 1970s and early 1980s prison regimes became more repressive and attracted the interest of a whole range of new and more vocal groups like the prisoners' union PROP, the RAP and the PRT, groups which alongside the more established lobbyists like the Howard League and NACRO sought to combat the growing segregation and militarisation in the system. Liberty was very much a part of this lobby. It gave evidence to Parliamentary Select Committees on prison medicine, helped to bring to public attention the appalling state of Holloway Prison's C Wing, campaigned vigorously against prison secrecy and criticised the role of Boards of Visitors and the operation of the parole system while at either end of our time frame it made submissions to both the May and Woolf enquiries into the prison system.

This high level of involvement encouraged Liberty's attempt to set up a National Prisons' Project in the mid-1980s. While it was stressed that Liberty's special contribution was to be its legal expertise there is no doubt that had the Project ever secured funding for three workers its role was always going to be rather more than simply that of legal advisor or facilitator to what was by then an already crowded penal lobby. It intended to help set the agenda.

The failure of the Project to find sponsors led to a scaling down of Liberty's involvement in prison issues, though it has remained closely allied to the penal lobby. For example, it was recently asked to advise the Howard League on a possible challenge to the Government's use of imprisonment for juvenile offenders. Liberty gave legal advice, but significantly did not seek to mobilise around this issue. It is also keeping up its interest in monitoring deaths in custody through its work with INQUEST and occasionally turns up at the Penal Affairs Consortium, but generally speaking its involvement with the penal lobby is currently more modest than it once was.[2]

Contingent lobbies

Not all of Liberty's work in defending civil liberties around the criminal law involves groups – professional or advocacy groups – which belong to the criminal justice network as such. It is frequently involved in other networks and other interests, trade unionists, travellers, gay and lesbian rights activists and so forth in seeking to influence legislation or overturn judicial decisions which it judges will either curtail or criminalise established liberties.

Sometimes this involvement has not amounted to much, simply the subject of a few round table meetings followed by a legal briefing or challenge and/or a joint press statement or Parliamentary briefing. At other times it became the source of a more sustained campaign.

There is a constant tendency for a group like Liberty to get sucked into these contingent lobbies, they often express the wider social and political concerns of the day. Take, for example, Liberty's involvement in the gay and lesbian rights lobby.

In the 1980s Liberty also became more actively committed to monitoring gay and lesbian rights across a whole range of areas – though again not *just* the criminal law over such matters as the age of consent – and appointed its first gay and lesbian rights officer. At this point Liberty became more involved in the gay and lesbian policy network as one of its participant groups. Questions therefore need to be asked, for example, about how Liberty stands in relation to Stonewall and Outrage. It is arguably no longer just a legal advisor or facilitator for such groups, a role it often adopts when it brushes against other lobbies. Of course, its legal advice makes its contribution distinctive, but with the appointment of a dedicated worker with a brief to open up new areas of work in the struggle to secure equality for gay and lesbian rights this was never intended to be Liberty's only contribution. Again, it was intending to help set the agenda (Dyson, 1994: 49–50). But this level of commitment to a contingent lobby is rarely sustained over a long period of time. Rather, it ebbs and flows.

Liberty and Justice

The tension that Liberty's activities can sometimes generate within the legal profession is in marked contrast with the low key style of Justice the other main advocacy group monitoring the operation of the criminal justice system for abuses of civil liberties in the United Kingdom and Wales. Perhaps mostly because its 1,500 or so members are almost exclusively barristers and judges, Justice has tended to lobby *inwards* seeking to engage those in power in a sometimes closed dialogue rather than lobbying *outwards* and engaging in public campaigns with contingent lobbies.

To give some examples from our period in the debate leading up to the Criminal Justice Act(1991) which heralded a major change in sentencing policy, Justice set up its own small committee to review sentencing – chaired by the Vice-President of the Magistrates' Association – which received oral evidence from civil servant David Faulkner, generally regarded as the architect of this Act, and also from another senior Home Office official (Justice, 1989). Justice was also a prominent player in the debate over mandatory life sentences. It gave evidence to the House of Commons Select Committee on the subject, publishing its own report, Sentenced for Life(1996) and was prominent in seeking changes in the Lords where it is very well connected.

The fact that Justice is constitutionally an 'all party' group whereas Liberty is a 'non- party' group, perhaps helps to explain some of the contrasts in lobbying style. Justice is not in business to publicly embarrass governments, Conservative or Labour. Having made this point, however, Justice has long been associated with working to overturn miscarriages of justices, prioritising those involving more serious offences such as rape or murder. Indeed, until recently it is arguable that in the public mind Justice was mostly associated with this work by way of Petitioning the Home Secretary. True, Liberty set up its own more extensive helpline on miscarriages of justice and really prioritised this issue in the late 1980s following concern over Guildford Four and the Birmingham Six, but it was arguably late in the game.

There are also other significant differences between the groups. Justice, for example, originally founded to monitor the South African apartheid trials in the 1950s, has retained an international/Commonwealth human rights flavour to its work. Liberty does not have this remit and is largely home-based, being more inclined than Justice to burrow away into some of the key, politically sensitive issue of the day, the struggle over police accountability and Northern Ireland being two cases in point.

While these differences in style and substance are important there is clearly significant, and arguably developing, overlap as Justice broadens its brief. Furthermore, both are keenly aware that securing civil liberties in Britain requires an increasingly global perspective, though as ever their contributions are not quite the same.

The global network

Although Britain played an important part in drawing up the European Convention of Human Rights in the late 1940s the Convention was not incorporated into UK domestic law. Furthermore, UK citizens and supporting organisations were not entitled to petition the European Court of Human Rights (ECHR) in Strasbourg for the redress of grievances under the Convention until 1969. Since that date individuals and organisations have made use of this channel to challenge governments, employers and the British courts.

Liberty increasingly resorted to the ECHR after constant rebuffs from unsympathetic Conservative governments.[3] True, this channel had been used on occasions against Labour governments before 1979, but the tendency to use it has increased significantly and Liberty has been involved in some very high profile cases involving the criminal justice system. For instance, in 1991 it helped to successfully challenge the legality of the re-detention of two prisoners serving discretionary life sentences (Wilson and Gunnell), and in 1997 there was an unsuccessful challenge to the House of Lords ruling to uphold the criminalisation of sado-masochistic practices between consenting adults (Spooner). Liberty was also involved with Human Rights Watch and IINQUEST in the partly successful petition to the ECHR against the British government in 1995 into the Gibraltar killings and the use of inquests to investigate deaths involving the police more generally.

As a direct consequence of its success in 'looking to Europe for assistance in defending civil rights in Britain' (Spencer, 1988: 7). Liberty also affiliated to the International Federation of Human Rights. This enabled it to address the United Nations Human Rights Commission on the Stalker affair in February 1988. More recently it has used the Commission's quinquennial review of Human Rights in the UK to bring together a whole range of groups, including several black groups who monitor the operation of the criminal justice system, to report on recent government abuses of human rights, including those of the disabled (Liberty, 1996).

Justice does not attach as much strategic importance as Liberty does to working these particular European channels, but it has nonetheless stepped up its activity on these fronts, and with some notable successes. For example, at its prompting the ECHR unanimously held that juveniles (Hussain and Singh) convicted of murder and detained at Her Majesty's pleasure were entitled to an independent hearing about their release dates (Justice, 1996b: 16–17). Justice had also been closely involved with Liberty in the earlier, successful ECHR challenge over re-detaining discretionary life prisoners (Thynne, Wilson and Gunnell) (For an account of this intervention, Windlesham, 1993: 347–403). It was less successful with its challenge over the right to silence (Murray) (Justice 1996: 19) Justice too, reported to the United Nations Human Rights Committee on the Elimination of Racial Discrimination which was critical of the British Government's race relations legislation, the absence of a Bill of Rights (Justice, 1996a: 18–19), and to INQUEST's satisfaction given its particular brief, supported an independent inquiry into deaths in police custody (Justice, 1996: 39 – 40).

Liberty against the Conservative ascendency, 1979–97

What influence Liberty did have on governments before 1979 was inevitably partly conditioned by Britain's long post-war social democratic consensus. Once this was challenged by the rise of the New Right, which by the late 1970s and 1980s had successfully promoted its own brand of authoritarian populism, anti-libertarian measures came thick and fast; attacks on freedom of assembly through successive Public Order Acts (1986 and 1994); the steady increase in police powers with the 1984 (PACE) and subsequent Criminal Justice Acts (1987,1988, 1991); restrictions on trade union membership (GCHQ) and other trade union activities such as picketing; tighter immigration controls; the passing of Section 28 (Local Government Act, 1988) to limit the promotion and understanding of gay and lesbian relationships and restrictions on reporting Sinn Fein and other prescribed organisations. Liberty lobbied strongly on just about all of these measures, through a variety of channels, and often with the strong support of other advocacy and professional groups. However, it was mostly unsuccessful, securing only minor concessions. Its one or two victories at the European Court of Human Rights were exceptional.

The rise of the New Right and Liberty's ensuing political impotence had a major impact on the organisation. In the first place, Liberty's determination to defend trade union rights led to some very public squabbles in the early 1980s. One Executive member resigned over its stance on the banning of trade unions at the government's communications headquarters, GCHQ, alleging among other things, that the organisation was over reliant on financial sponsorship from the radical GLC (Dyson, 1994: 54).

The trade union issue divided Liberty even more bitterly when its own interim report into the policing of the bitter 1984 miners' dispute was said to have damaged the miners' case by upholding 'the right to work'. In response to this criticism members of the inquiry broke away to complete their final report independently (Dyson, 1994: 56). In the aftermath of this very public debacle Liberty's General Secretary Larry Gostin resigned, claiming that Liberty had been taken over by the Left, a view that would not have surprised certain Conservative MPs who had publicly berated Liberty for being partisan (Dyson, 1994: 56). Gostin had previously been in trouble with the Executive when it was revealed by the Guardian that his staff had given advice to a member of the National Front whose flat had been raided by the police.

This sort of public bickering had a very direct effect on Liberty's morale. Membership dropped, staff lost jobs and the always difficult task of securing grants become even more difficult. Traditional funders backed off and at one stage an emergency appeal was needed to keep the organisation afloat (ibid, 57).

It is easy to detect the sense of defeat and political isolation that Liberty's beleaguered staff felt after these self-inflicted wounds and almost a decade in a hostile political climate. In a speech to members Sarah Spencer observed that:

> 'We have had no alternative but to acknowledge that the public re-elected the government for a third term.... And we have been forced to ask ourselves what this means for us. ... whose raison d'être since 1934 has been to lobby and cajole governments to defend and extend the very liberties which are so profoundly under attack. In reviewing the implications for us, as we have been, we have noted the significance of the government's reaction did not follow a strenuous public debate about the treatment of civil liberties. ... Civil liberties, despite the government's record, have been marginalised as an electoral issue'.
>
> (Spencer, 1988: 1)

This realisation that the Conservative hegemony was so strong, that its agenda on civil liberties was of little interest to the public at large, led to major changes at Liberty which began to re-define its strategy and its image.

Re-thinking strategy and tactics

The thrust of Liberty's re-thinking was the realisation that as a civil liberties group it was always reacting to events, rather than setting the agenda. This inevitably gave it a very negative image. It was always 'against' this or that police activity, or court ruling, or 'against' this or that piece of government legislation. And never had it been more 'against' than during the years the of Conservative ascendency. However, while this stance was (and is) inevitable up to a point – that is to say, there is a way in which all civil liberties organisations come into being 'against' state incursions into civil society – this constant, piecemeal, defensive reaction never really addresses the need for a positive, coherent framework of rights.

This had made the job of defending civil rights against Conservative attacks an uphill task. What was needed instead, therefore, was a campaign to create a popular culture of rights. This was the *positive* agenda that the organisation needed to develop and assert. Liberty's new General Secretary Andrew Puddephatt argued that members had to:

> recognise that there has been a fundamental shift in our political culture. Voters demonstrated in the election that in the end they will not support policies which were more 'against' than 'for'. It is no longer enough to express our concern about developments in society that threaten civil liberties. We need to offer a *Positive* vision as to how fundamental human rights and freedoms can be guaranteed. If we do not offer this vision, someone else will. As in any sphere of life, Liberty is in competition with other organisations for members, for funding, for press coverage. Unless we are positive . . . we are going to lose out.
>
> (Puddephatt, 1992)

This strategy, the need to establish a popular culture of rights, required important strategic and tactical changes. Liberty had to carry its message well beyond the confines of the political decision-making process, to do more than deliver a succession of narrow expert briefings. Members were told by its General Secretary that securing its new agenda:

> means more than trying to influence Parliament. That comes at the end of the process. First of all we need to win over public opinion. . . . The best way of doing this is through high profile public campaigning, it involves a broad range of activities, public meetings,

letter writing, campaigns.... demonstrations.... Above all, we must actively encourage people to be active in defence of their freedoms and not rely exclusively on others.

(Puddephatt, 1991)

But more particularly, the vehicle to translate this new positive concern for rights into practice was to be a new Bill of Rights and the incorporation of the European Convention of Human Rights into British law. Securing this crucial strategic goal would clearly have implications for criminal justice, a point we shall return to later.

This new strategy was sold to Liberty's rank and file in the late 1980s and early 1990s. Liberty's officers were brutally frank about the organisation's precarious position, arguing that its traditional methods – the lucid Parliamentary brief, the authoritative submission to this or that committee of enquiry – had made it difficult to recruit more members and to secure new financial sponsors. Successive General Secretaries pointed out that campaigning organisations like Amnesty International and Greenpeace had not only edged Liberty out in terms of public recognition but also even more importantly, had mobilised popular support around the issues they were concerned with in a way that Liberty had singularly failed to do.[4]

Furthermore, campaigning on such issues, and this was to be strongly reinforced when the anti-roads lobby mobilised against Twyford Down and environmental campaigners like 'Swampy' became national heroes, showed that there was a whole generation of young activists out there who *did* care about their rights. If Liberty as going to flourish as an organisation and put civil or human rights on the agenda then it needed to attract just these people, or at the very least, work closely with them. So, in addition to its alliances with the great and the good on issues like the right to silence Liberty by 1994 had begun to:

'forge links and alliances with a new constituency of young people – rock bands, sound systems, travellers and squatters groups, hunt saboteurs and environmental protesters. There is an enormous and developing movement of young people who are not aligned to any political party who are active and who are committed to non-violence and are conscious of their rights; they are people who cherish their personal sovereignty and are willing to do something to defend it; they are people who have become painfully aware of the lack of enforceable rights in our society...

(Puddephatt, 1994)

Finally, there is also evidence that Liberty's officers were increasingly aware that there was a growing interest in what they had traditionally taken as 'their patch', that in opposition to the Conservative ascendency groups like Charter 88 were beginning to emerge and interest, among others, the Labour party.[5] True, There was more to Charter 88 then its Bill of Rights, and that Labour under Neil Kinnock was ambivalent about simply incorporating Human Rights into the constitution. Nonetheless, the beginnings of the revived social democratic agenda was beginning to take shape and Liberty could hardly be left behind, could not fail to acknowledge that the marketplace was changing.

Advocating with the tide

The election of the Labour Party to government in May 1997 with a huge Parliamentary majority and a determination to modernise the United Kingdom's constitutional framework has helped to secure Liberty's new strategy on human rights.

It was always unlikely, however, that Liberty would get all that it wanted. For example, while the incorporation of The European Convention on Human Rights into domestic British law has now been secured with the Human Rights Act (1998) – it followed the Government's White Paper, Bringing Rights Home (Home Office, 1997) – Liberty has long argued for an additional Bill of Rights to reinforce the Convention which it argues is far from perfect (Liberty, 1997a). The Labour government opposed this, and was similiarly reluctant to adopt protocols 4, 6 and 7 which Liberty argued would at least strengthen the existing Convention. There is also government opposition to setting up a separate Human Rights Commission (Liberty, 1997b).

But perhaps the most important and obvious point to make here is that Liberty's *broad* strategy on human rights is now in the political mainstream, it is part of New Labour's agenda. Alongside groups like Charter 88, Justice, the British Institute for Human Rights, the Public Law Project and the Centre for Public Policy Research, Liberty finds itself at the table talking to, and being consulted by, the Ministers (and their officials) most directly involved, including both the Home Secretary and the Lord Chancellor.

That tensions and disagreements have arisen over human rights legislation perhaps reflects the simple fact that the Labour Party is a recent convert to the idea of incorporating the European Convention. The idea that judges, traditionally drawn from the upper reaches of our society, might be given a pivotal role in defining our rights is not something that has always appealed to British social democrats. (Liberty it has to be said, has not always supported incorporation on the same grounds).[6] So there has been a learning process with Labour in dialogue which might best be described as an advocacy coalition with the groups mentioned above at its core.[7]

Liberty can claim to have been an important member of this coalition. It was particularly active, for example, in Labour's own rights campaign and organised a one day conference at the House of Commons on the implications of incorporation at the request of the then Labour spokesman on constitutional issues, Graham Allen.[8] At this point in Labour's learning curve, there is probably some truth in John Wadham's claim that Labour and Liberty were both singing from the same hymn sheet.[9] However, this probably marks the high point of Liberty's influence on Labour's thinking in the run up to the 1997 General Election and Lord Irvine's approach, as we have already indicated, is arguably less ambitious.

It goes without saying that the incorporation of the ECHR into domestic law will make governments more sensitive to civil liberties when legislating in the area of criminal justice. It would also make legal challenges to government over the application of such legislation far easier to mount for groups like Liberty who do not always have the resources to follow the time consuming procedures involved in getting cases to Strasbourg, or indeed, to raise these matters with the United Nations Human Rights Commission.

Conclusion

The election of a Labour government has clearly revitalised the civil liberties and contingent lobbies, or at least those groups within those lobbies which occupy a centre left perspective. After nearly 20 years in the political shade groups like Liberty and INQUEST, for example, see the opportunity for a dialogue with government, a dialogue which starts from certain broadly accepted social democratic assumptions, and one which is already well underway.[10] After a year of New Labour in office one of Liberty's officers observed that:

> 'One of the most obvious differences is that our work is having a much more direct impact. The cautious optimism which we expressed shortly after the election...has been borne out. We are less dependent on criticizing the government through the press,

because they're prepared to meet us and hear what we have to say. We're consulted on policy proposals at a much earlier stage.

(Liberty, 1998: 3)

These remarks should not give the impression that either of these groups is likely to secure all the changes they would like or that they will not on occasions, and probably quite soon, be at loggerheads with the new Labour government'. Far from it. For example, Liberty took strong exception to what it saw as the conflation of civil and criminal law in the Crime and Disorder Bill (1998); is currently networking with other groups such as the Bar Association and the Law Society to fight the government over the reform of Legal Aid and its plans to limit the right of jury trial. Liberty is also not convinced that Labour is genuinely committeed to open government following its legal action against the former MI6 officer David Shayler.

Nor should the impression be given that in this (and other) areas of government policy that pressure groups per se have suddenly been given access to decision-makers where previously none existed. This would be misleading. Pressure groups have continued to have access to governments, it is simply that many of those on the centre left of the social democratic consensus were, while not wholly excluded, at least effectively marginalised.

To take criminal justice policy particularly, as groups like Liberty were excluded so groups like the Adam Smith Institute, starting first with its pioneering Omega Report (1984) Privatizing Criminal Justice, and then its later report *The Prison Cell* (1987), were on their way in (Ryan and Ward, 1989). Among professional groups, ACPO's influence and public profile grew as that of groups like the NAPO declined. As the New Right saw the electoral advantage to be gained by stressing the rights of victims over those of offenders so groups like the Prison Reform Trust and NACRO were edged out and new groups like the National Association of Victims Support Schemes were actively promoted. In Liberty's contingent lobbies, say on trade union rights, much the same pattern was at work as the arguments of groups like the National Association of Freedom were established and arguably had as much influence as the TUC or Liberty in redefining trade union rights.

This is not to say that these right of centre groups determined policy, indeed, in some cases they fought to frustrate it, as did the Magistrates Association over certain sentencing measures in the Criminal Justice Act (1991). Nor is it to suggest that the traditional and simple left – right continuum tells the whole story. The impact of the women's movement, for example, on how issues like domestic violence and rape were processed in the criminal justice system, was interwoven with the rise of the Victims Support (Ryan and Ward 1992). But it is to argue that many of the more high profile pressure groups were moving with the ideological drift of government, indeed, *they helped to chart the detailed course that of that drift*, just as Liberty is attempting to in the new climate.

Liberty's recent history is, therefore, testimony to the role of ideology in defining the parameters and players in any given network. Policy scientists, it is true, have always acknowledged this role in seeking to explain how networks change. (Atkinson and Coleman, 1992; Rhodes and Marsh, 1992) In my view, however, they seriously *understate* its paramount importance in certain lobbies, possibly because they have studied too short a policy cycle,[11] or possibly because they have concentrated too much on lobbies which are somewhat narrow and technically defined and where change is often the outcrop of technical education and persuasion and not largely driven by ideological predisposition and wider social movements. More detailed and discrete studies of Liberty's work, touching say on its involvement in networks around women's rights and gay and lesbian rights rather than focusing on the somewhat amorphous criminal justice network, would in my view confirm this limitation and restore normative issues of *value* and *prescription* to the study of networks in policy science over and above issues of *process* which have arguably gone too far.

Finally, and conversely, it is at least arguable that in some respects policy scientists have *overstated* the impact of the much heralded 'revolution in governance'. Lobby groups like Liberty have been directly affected by this revolution, it is true. It was, for example, forced (alongside other groups) to make its own service delivery far more efficient and accountable, and has vigorously contested the civil liberties consequences of the drive for 'value for money' in contracting out legal aid and improving the efficiency of court services. However, the effect of these changes on the overall patterning of its networks has so far been modest.

The fact that government is being 'hollowed out', that the delivery of services such prisons, court security and other criminal justice services are being hived off to, and/or shared with the private sector, or responsibility for their operation being 'pushed downwards' to local authorities and/or the Audit Commission should not obscure the important fact that *central government is still responsible for determining many matters of policy and principle which underpin the criminal justice system;* its involvement is by no means just restricted to auditing, monitoring, or even, arguably more important, coordinating through audit the performance of its component parts. The Human Rights Act (1998) is the paradigm example.

In seeking to influence these policies and principles Liberty continues to operates much as it always has done, across a complex and layered series of advocacy networks and professional networks, many of which from time to time, and crucially in some cases, intersect with government. This intersection with the centre, as Foucault reminds us, is fairly routine across all policy areas (Foucault, 1982). The fact that policy scientists wish to define government as a many layered or 'polycentric', as now comprising of a 'multiplicity of centres', may be something of a conceptual breakthrough in some circles (Rhodes, 1997), but for Liberty it simply reflects the complex reality of its day-to-day lobbying of Parliament, judiciary and the adminstration, a complex practice which I have attempted to describe.

Of course, what applies to Liberty's practice in the civil liberties lobby might not be true of all lobbies, and things may change, but that is another matter for another time.

Notes

1. On several occasions, but formally in 1991 (see note 6).
2. In 1997 Liberty worked with INQUEST to arrange a training session for lawyers on the work of coroners. It also secured funding to take controversial inquest cases to the ECHR.
3. Liberty sometimes gives direct legal support to people or organisations appearing before the ECHR, or alternatively, may submit a third party or Amicus Brief to the court if it regards the issue being considered is of special significance to civil liberties.
4. The challenge of organisations like Greenpeace and Amnesty was touched in Andrew Puddephatt's AGM address in 1991.
5. Puddephatt was keen to network with Charter 88 from late 1980s. (interview with John Wadham July 1997, London).
6. Liberty's 1991 AGM which endorsed its current policy on a Bill of Rights also carried a motion calling for reform of the judiciary to include more working class people and a better representation for ethnic minorities.
7. I have borrowed the term 'advocacy coalition' from American political science. See, for example, Sabatier (1988) 'An advocacy coalition framework of policy change and the role of policy orientated learning therein', *Policy Sciences*, 21: 129–68.
8. Interview with John Wadham, op.cit.
9. Interview with John Wadham, ibid.
10. For details of INQUEST'S new dialogue with government, particularly the Lord Chancellor's department, see Annual Report, 1998 p. 6, 7 (INQUEST, London).

11. Sabatier's call for more longitudinal studies of the lobby has a real resonance here, P. Sabatier(1991) 'Toward better theories of the policy process', *Social Science and Politics* June (1991), 147–56.

References

Adam Smith Institute (1987) *The prison cell* (London: ASI).

Adam Smith Institute (1984) *Omega Report* (London: ASI Research).

Atkinson. M. and Coleman, W. D. (1992) 'Policy networks, policy communities and the problems of governance', *Governance*, 5: 154–180.

Dyson, B. (1994) *Liberty in Britain* (London; Civil Liberties Trust).

Foucault. M. (1982) 'Afterword: the subject and power', in Dreyfus, H., Rabinow, D. and Michel Foucault, Michel (eds), *Beyond Structuralism and Hermeneutics* (Brighton: Harvester).

Home Office (1997) *Bringing Rights Home*, Cmnd 3782 (London: HMSO).

Justice (1989) *Sentencing: A Way Ahead* (London: Justice Educational and Research Trust).

Justice (1996a) *Annual Report*, pp. 16, 17 (London: Justice).

Justice (1996b) *Sentenced for Life* (London: Justice).

Liberty (1992) *Unequal before the law: sentencing in Magistrates Courts in England and Wales 1981–1990* (London: National Council for Civil Liberties).

Liberty Annual Review (1993a) (Liberty: London).

Liberty (1993b) *Review of Police Disciplinary Proceedings* (London: National Council for Civil Liberties).

Liberty (1996) Agenda Issue no. 17 (London: Liberty).

Liberty (1997) *Parliamentary briefing on the Human Rights Bill* (London Liberty).

Liberty (1998a) *Newsletter (Summer)* (London: Liberty).

Lilly, M. (1984) *The National Council for Civil Liberties*: The First Fifty Years (London: Macmillan).

Puddephatt, A. (1991) AGM address (Liberty: London).

Puddephatt, A. (1992) AGM address (Liberty: London).

Puddephatt, A. (1994) AGM address (Liberty: London).

Rhodes, R. A. W. (1997), *Understanding Governance* (Buckingham: Open University Press).

Rhodes, R. A. W. and Marsh, D. (1992), *Policy Networks in British Government* (Oxford: Oxford University Press) and Smith, M. J. (1993), Pressure Power and Policy (London: Harvester).

Ryan, M. and Ward, T. (1989), *Privatization and the Penal System: the American Experience and the Debate in Britain* (Milton Keynes: Open University Press).

Ryan, M. and Ward, T (1992) 'From positivism to postmodernism: the penal lobby in Britain, *International Journal of the Sociology of Law*, 20: 172–205.

Sabatier, P. (1991) 'Towards better theories of the policy process', *Social Science and Politics*, June: 147–56.

Sabatier, P. and Jenkins-Smith, H. C. (1993), *Policy Change and learning: an Advocacy Coalition Approach* (Boulder, CO: Westview Press)

Spencer, S. (1985), *Called to Account* (London; NCCL).

Spencer, S. (1988) AGM address, unpublished manuscript.

Windlesham Lord (1993) *Responses to Crime*, pp. 347–403 (Oxford: Oxford University Press).

9
The Victims Lobby
Sandra Walklate

Introduction

> The final strand in the new punitiveness is the rise and rise of the
> crime victim. Since the mid-1970s there has been a growing emphasis
> on the neglect and invisibility of the victim of crime in the adminis-
> tration of justice. The trumpeting of crime victim wrongs has been
> useful to anyone wishing to make an electoral appeal on law and
> order issues. Although at a common sense level one might have
> thought that it is because crimes do have victims that anyone ever
> cared about crime in the first place, the 1970s rediscovery of the
> victim has certainly fed into 1990s punitiveness...and with a ven-
> geance! The results? A greatly increased fear of crime, daily demands
> for stiffer sentences, and a steep increase in levels of criminological
> nonsense...
>
> (Carlen, 1996: 53)

> The impact of Victim Support on criminal justice was all the more
> remarkable given its non-statutory position, voluntary sector status
> and volunteer dependency. The newcomer organisation was able to
> effect change in police attitudes and practice, inspire the CPS to
> review its practices in this context, persuade the courts to surrender
> space and resources to accommodate victim support work, and the
> probation service to take on new responsibilities in relation to vic-
> tims as well as offenders.
>
> (James and Raine, 59: 1998)

While it is possible to take issue with the analysis of the role and impact
of Victim Support offered by James and Raine above, what is beyond

dispute is the increasing voice and space which has been given to issues relating to victims of crime since the late 1970s. What is of particular interest is to understand why this space has become increasingly available, who is seen to (legitimately) occupy it, and what influences (if any) this voice has on criminal justice policy. As the quote above from Carlen suggests, the answers to these questions may not solely lie within the organisations associated with crime victims. Indeed, as we shall see, the answers to these questions may also vary according to what kind of victim of crime is under consideration.

In order to explore these issues more fully this chapter will: first, offer a brief overview of the historical emergence of concerns about the victim of crime; secondly, address the underlying political processes which have given space to victims' interests; thirdly, analyse, through the use of two case studies, the increasing complexity of both understanding and characterising those interests; and finally, we will consider whether or not it is possible to talk in terms of a victims lobby. However, before addressing these issues it will be useful to say something of a more general nature about the changing characteristics of British politics and the policy-making process since 1945.

Policy, politics and process

The post-war years have often been characterised as years of consensus, both socially and politically. In some respects it is difficult to dispute this view given the key concerns of the first post-war decade. Certainly re-building a 'land fit for heroes' constituted an appropriate mechanism of social cement during that decade which could be identified in a whole range of policy initiatives and concerns. Arguably there were a number of principles underpinning those concerns; but one, that of 'social citizenship', is of particular interest to this discussion.

Marshall (1948) offered a seminal historical analysis of the emergence and development of citizenship in England and Wales. Historically, he argued that citizenship in the eighteenth century was centred on debates around civil rights, in the nineteenth century centred around political rights, and in the twentieth century, social rights. Marshall argued that these social rights, set in motion at the turn of the twentieth century under the guidance of Lloyd George, achieved their ultimate expression in the formation of the Welfare State. The policies associated with the formation of the Welfare State are largely attributed to the guiding influence of Beveridge. Those policies, put together under his guidance, were intended to provide protection from the five great social diseases: 'disease, squaloar, ignorance, idleness, and want'. In order to extend this protection to (potentially) all members of society, he introduced the principle of insurance. This became the key mechanism whereby social rights could be extended to all citizens. Indeed, while there was some social and political dissent around the introduction of this principle, which in reality did not extend social rights but rather demonstrated, 'that such rights are not social rights at all but merely the individual contractual entitlements that arise from a contractual relation' (Garland, 1985: 246), the view that the late 1940s and 1950s were largely a time of social and political consensus is a legitimate one.

As we shall see, it is against this backcloth of predominantly consensual welfarism, that the more contemporary concerns for the victim of crime emerged. In order to understand that emergence, it is also valuable to consider the relevance of the changing nature of the general political climate and associated policy-making process.

The inception and formation of the Welfare State and its associated principles were put in place at a time when government was clearly discernible as 'Government'. Put fairly simply, the idea of Government alludes to a set of principles in which it was believed that the 'leader knows best', that there was accountability through the electoral process, a belief in a strong cabinet, and a clear adherence to parliamentary democracy. (These characteristics are sometimes referred to as the 'Westminster' model of politics.) However as Rhodes (1997: 4) states:

> Since 1945 the institutions of British government have experienced at least two revolutions. The post war Labour government built the welfare state and its institutions , but these survived barely three decades before a reforming Conservative government sought to redefine most and abolish many. Allegedly the Westminster model no longer works.

The revolutions of which Rhodes (1997) speaks have been felt in all aspects of the policy-making process including criminal justice policy. One key to understanding the radical policy changes which Rhodes (1997) discusses can be seen in the shift from 'government' to 'governance'. To explain: the notion of government is characterised by the Westminster model; the notion of governance, however, is less clear. Rhodes (1997) argues that governance is broader than government: 'governance refers to self-organising intraorganisational networks' (ibid.: 53) in which the boundaries between the public sector, the private sector, and the voluntary sector are constantly shifting and opaque.

Arguably, it is this notion of the policy-making process which is embedded in the quote from James and Raine with which this chapter began.

It can be argued that the movement from government to governance has been accompanied by shifting understandings of accountability and citizenship. Under a system of governance organisations are no longer characterised by mechanisms of accountability to the state, and citizens are much more likely to be viewed as consumers or customers of services. Services offered by an increasingly differentiated range of organisations. This is part of a process which Garland (1996) has characterised as 'the responsibilisation strategy' in the criminal justice arena leading to the emergence of 'corporate grey areas' (Crawford, 1994). In other words a process which has extended the responsibility for crime and crime prevention to a disparate range of public, private and voluntary organisations for whom the lines of accountability are far from clear yet who wield an increasingly important influence on the distribution of monies and resources especially at a local level. In some respects it is within the space between these 'corporate grey areas' (ibid.) in which the concerns for the victim of crime has grown.

From a point of view, the impact of changes such as these has resulted in increasingly complex organisational networks which inform the policy making process in general, and criminal justice policy in particular. One possible consequence of such a process is that we have moved from an absence of voices speaking for the victim of crime to one in which there are an increasing number of voices claiming to speak for such victims. This chapter will be concerned to map some of these changes by connecting them to the changing nature of citizenship and examining the consequent viability or otherwise of the governance thesis. In order to this we shall turn to a brief historical appreciation of the changing nature of citizenship and the emergent concern with the victim of crime in the first instance.

The politicisation of the crime victim, 1945–75

It was against the backcloth of the formation of the Welfare State and its associated understanding of social justice and citizenship that it is possible to map the concerns and influence of Margery Fry. She was an active criminal justice campaigner in the 1950s , who campaigns on behalf of both the crime victim and the offender. Indeed it was her commitment to the notion of compensation for the victim of crime which informed the formation of the Criminal Injuries Compensation

Board (CICB) in 1964. Rock (1990: 66) offers this analysis of these interconnections:

> In her last formulation of the problem, compensation would represent a collective insurance provided by society. All taxpayers would be regarded as subscribers. All taxpayers were at risk of becoming victims. Since the state forbade citizens arming themselves, it should assume responsibility for its failure to provide protection.

Such a formulation clearly builds on the principle of insurance embedded in the Beverage proposals of 1945 implying the notion of a contract between the victim of crime and the state. This contract implicitly assumed a very positive image of the crime victim as the innocent party. An idea which became embedded in the version of the CICB established in the 1960s. However it must be remembered that the CICB was established to address the perceived needs of the victims of violent crime who could demonstrate that they were the innocent party to the events which happened to them. This narrow remit, and the symbolic construction of the innocent victim contained within it, are part of what Miers (1978) has referred to as the politicisation of the victim. Indeed it is important to note that such concerns were debated, and the CICB put in place, in the absence of exploring what crime victims might want and in the absence of any organisation offering a voice to victims' concerns. As Mawby and Gill (1987) pointed out, victims of crime could already be treated under the NHS if injured or claim benefit if unable to work; so in comparison with victims of violent crime in other countries their perceived needs were already well-catered for. Yet the victim of (violent) crime became an important symbolic rhetorical and political device in extending the protection offered by the state to all its citizens. In this respect Waller (1988) has referred to the CICB as a 'trail blazer' followed in later years by much of the rest of Europe.

With the establishment of the CICB (and its perpetuation of the distinction between the deserving and the undeserving in enshrining the notion of the innocent victim within its remit) it is possible to argue that the final brick of the Welfare State, cementing the power and the regulatory potential of the state, had been put in place (see Mawby and Walklate, 1994: ch. four). A regulatory potential which it is possible to discern from the concept of social citizenship on which the Welfare State was founded. This conceptualisation of citizenship defined the boundaries of what were considered to be public matters from private ones; for example, it was seen to be legitimate to view the innocent victim of violent crime as a public matter, but not legitimate to view what might have been the equally innocent victim of 'domestic' violence as such. Such issues were very much a private concern in the 1950s. However these boundaries, and the concomitant notion of citizenship shifted in the next 20 years as did the nature and influence of the victim of crime on the policy making process. Yet nevertheless the symbolic power of the image of the victim, especially for political purposes was soundly put in place.

The politics of the crime victim, 1975–95

The late 1960s saw the emergence of two significant developments which were to make their presence felt in the criminal justice arena with respect to the victim of crime. The first of these was the formation of the Bristol-Victims Offenders Group. A short-lived organisation which paved the way for the founding of the National Association of Victim Support Schemes from the Bristol Victim Support Scheme in December 1973. The second was the feminist movement. The first Women's Refuge was opened in Chiswick in 1972 and the first Rape Crisis Centre in London in 1976. These developments, whilst tangential at the time to mainstream criminal justice policy concerns, nevertheless marked the beginnings of a discourse around issues concerning criminal victimisation which arguably bore fruit towards the end of the time period under discussion here. Some brief comments on each of these strands will be offered here.

Initiatives emanating from the feminist movement did not have criminal victimisation per se at the forefront of their concerns. They were more concerned to encourage women towards equality and empowerment in all spheres of life. Such idealistic aims notwithstanding, it became clear when addressing the specific issues of rape and 'domestic' violence that much could be achieved from focusing more narrowly on improving the response of the criminal justice system to such events. Consequently feminist informed campaigns and organisations (like for example, Women Against Violence Against Women) directed some of their energies towards changing the law and its practice. It is, however, a moot point, as to the extent such campaigns were successful in their own right. The 1980s did see the introduction of considerable changes in practice by police forces in particular towards rape 'victims' and 'domestic violence. However, the impetus for such changes in the context of rape in particular, arguably lay with the public outcry which followed a fly on the wall documentary of the Thames Valley police handling of a rape case in 1982 rather than the influence of feminism. In the aftermath of this broadcast Home Office 25/1983 outlined how rape investigations might be handled more appropriately. Continued pressure for change for maintained by the Women's National Commission, a government advisory body leading ultimately to many police forces having put in place rape suites by the end of the decade following recommendations in Home Office circular 69/1986.

For many police forces the recommendations contained in Home Office Circulars 25/83 and 69/86 to put women in touch with other support groups meant one support group: Victim Support. This was somewhat in the face of the fact that workers in Rape Crisis Centres emanating from the feminist movement had a longer history of involvement with, and expertise in, supporting women who had been raped. Some explanations for this preference have cited political considerations as the underlying reason (see for example, Radford and Stanko, 1991). Indeed, it is clear that the perceived political neutrality of Victim Support was influential in its early acceptance by both the Home Office and police forces (Corbett and Maguire, 1987; Rock, 1990). A similar pattern is discernible in relation to 'domestic violence' (see below) what is clear is that Victim Support came to be seen as the organisation for victims of crime by the early 1990s, the question is why?

As has already been suggested Victim Support had rather humble origins in Bristol in the early 1970s but from 1975 to 1995 became the fastest growing voluntary organisation that that sector has probably ever seen (for example, it grew from one scheme in 1973 to over 300 in England and Wales alone in 1990; there being separate organisations for Scotland and Northern Ireland). Moreover Victim support secured Home Office funding in the 1980s when government ideology and financial uncertainty were leading other areas of public service to a curtailment of service delivery and a reduced level of state involvement. This event is not solely explicable in terms of the neutrality of this particular organisation; though, as Rock (1990) has accurately observed, the fact that the victim of Victim Support was an androgynous victim did, as we shall see, have considerable influence. The underlying philosophy of the organisation was also important.

Victim Support represented a community based voluntary movement at a time when the government was sounding the 'trumpet voluntary'. It constituted a response to the victim of crime which was built on an intent to reintegrate the victim into the community; not to create dependency. It was a voluntary response which emphasised individuals helping other individuals from within their own community. This vision of self help melded well with the unfolding theme of active citizenship associated with the general political tenor of this decade. The, then, Prime Minister, Margaret Thatcher had as one of her personal gaols the elimination of the 'dependency culture'. In these senses then Victim Support was very appealing. Moreover, the economic circumstances of the 1980s, demanding economy, efficiency, and effectiveness in all aspects of public expenditure, leant an additional logic to looking for alternative sources of service delivery. This search for such alternatives had translated into the 'cult of the customer' (Edgar, 1991) by the early 1990s. As Conservative MP Sir Ian Gilmour remarked; 'under this philosophy everybody is a consumer and the world a giant supermarket. Life is nothing but a prolonged pursuit of groceries whereby one chooses education from Tesco's and local government from Sainsbury's'.

This construction of the citizen as a consumer marked a significant re-orientation of the understanding of citizenship from that of the 1950s. It carried with it a view of the citizen who not only has rights but also had responsibilities. Responsibilities which could be played out in and by organisations like Victim Support (part of the responsibilisation strategy identified by Garland, 1996, and referred to earlier). Indeed, important endorsement was given to this organisation, in the context of responding to victims of crime, not only in its receipt of government funding in 1986 but also in the conditions which were attached to that funding: the provision of services to women who had been raped. In this sense it is possible to argue that via Victim Support the state co-opted those issues which had been raised by the feminist movement and also silenced a potentially highly critical political voice. However, it also makes sense to situate decisions such as these within the broader extension of the consumerist notion of citizenship referred to earlier and reflected in a wide range of service delivery processes; perhaps epitomised in the criminal justice system in the publication of the first Victims Charter in 1990 (for a fuller discussion of this see Mawby and Walklate, 1994).

To summarise: by 1990 Victim Support had gained considerable stature and influence in the formulation of government policy and in representing the voice of the victim of crime; a voice which was largely absent during the 1950s. Indeed the work of this national organisation was heralded as the expert agency in promoting the interests of the crime victim and led the way in sponsoring 'demonstration projects' concerned with the extension of victim oriented services: families of murder victims; the victim/witness in court; children as victims of crime; racial harassment. The range of this agenda certainly highlights the extent to which, by the end of the 1980s, Victim Support had come to be seen as the support agency in England and Wales wielding considerable influence on government policy. Indeed in many respects the extension of this organisations work into what might be called these more 'exotic' areas has transformed its ability to deal with much of its initial bread and butter work; the burglary victim.

Moreover the nature and extent of the influence of this organisation also stands as testimony to the changing character of the influences on the policy process; the process of governance as opposed to government. As Rock (1998) reports the Home Office frequently referred to the national officers of Victim Support for consultation and advice in relation to policy initiatives which might impact upon victims of crime. Indeed, Rock (1998) quotes a Home Office official, responsible for victim's policy as saying: 'We have tended to operate through Victim Support [in] dealing with the smaller groups. . . . There's just a few groups that are specialised in some areas, and even they want very much to be allied with Victim Support.' In this sense understanding what might be referred to as the micro politics of the policy-making process would be pertinent.

To take this view as the explanatory framework for these developments however, would constitute an analysis akin to a still portrait. It is the case that, as the work of Rock (1990, 1998) aptly demonstrates, that the linkages and networks between government officials and other parties campaigning for the interests were clearly present and influential. The questions remains as to whether such a micro political analysis is a wholly adequate one with which to understand emergent concerns about the victim of crime. The 'lobby' for victims' interests is neither as simple nor as straightforward, in contemporary terms as the foregoing analysis might suggest. In some respects the neutral, androgynous victim of Victim Support has lost some of its predominance and in that process of loss there has emerged an increasingly diverse range of voices making claims on the victim of crime in relation to some issues but not in relation to others. The two case studies which follow are intended to illuminate both the diversity and the complexity of what might be called the contemporary victims lobby.

Responding to 'domestic' violence

As was indicated earlier, much feminist campaigning during the 1970s was focused on male violence towards women. While those campaigns much preferred to talk of survivors rather than victims, they also clearly demonstrated the inadequacy of the general policy response to women as victims of violent crime. However, there has been a remarkable change in policy rhetoric (if not practice) on this issue since the Association of Chief Police Officers denied the need for any change in their role to the Parliamentary Select Committee hearings on Violence in Marriage in 1975 to Home Office Circular 60/1990 which demanded changes be instituted. The questions remains; what processes underpinned this change in direction?

It would be difficult to deny that the role of feminist researchers and campaigners did not have some influence in putting 'domestic' violence on the policy agenda. What the precise nature of that influence was, however, is much more difficult to determine. It is certainly the case that feminist informed research documented the nature and extent of violence against women in the home and clearly demonstrated police, and other criminal justice agencies, unwillingness to respond positively to such incidents (see, for example; Dobash and Dobash, 1980; Faraghar, 1985; Edwards, 1989). However, the vocal presence of Erin Pizzey and the formation of the Women's Aid Federation 1974 notwithstanding it was not until the mid-1980s that the Women's National Commission appeared to be instrumental in encouraging government to address some feminist concerns about the criminal justice agency response (Smith, 1989). This resulted in Home Office circular 69/1986 which recommended that procedures for helping victims of sexual assault should also be employed in responding to victims of domestic violence.

While this circular did not offer any explicit policy directive on domestic violence some police forces, most notably the Metropolitan Police took their own initiatives. Leaning heavily on (not wholly validated) North American informed policy responses to domestic violence, the Metropolitan Police encouraged the use of a positive arrest stance and the development of the dedicated domestic violence unit as a way of overcoming some of the criticisms of the criminal justice agency response inherent in circular 69/1986. This was to set the scene for circular 60/1990 which was both telling and far reaching in placing domestic violence squarely on the policing agenda.

Many police forces have subsequently followed the Metropolitan Police model in one form or another and contemporarily a police manager would find it very difficult to justify not having some sort of 'dedicated' response to domestic violence in place. What has actually changed on the ground as a result of this level of police activity is not altogether unequivocal (Grace, 1995; Hoyle, 1998) and is not of central concern here. What is of more interest is to consider why such policy considerations came to fruition at this particular time.

Arguably, the underlying logic to this process has three dimensions. The first is associated with the rising influence of consumerism in the public service sector already commented on above (see also Jefferson, *et al.*, 1992). The second lies in the need to secure public consent for the policing task in the light of increasing evidence of declining public confidence (Radford and Stanko, 1991). The third lies not so much with the feminist movement or the Women's National Commission but with the increasing involvement of Victim Support in such cases (Victim Support, 1992). Unlike Canada, there has been no feminist voice with the ear of policy makers (Rock, 1988) and in the absence of that voice the presence of Victim Support has been a substitute. Arguably, of all these influences, the most telling has been the policing drive for customer satisfaction.

Policy responses to domestic violence are still undergoing monitoring, evaluation, and refinement. Much is made of inter-agency working in this area. Yet the initiatives emanating from the feminist movement, especially those concerned with refuge provision, remain for the most part left to haphazard, local authority, financial support. In other words, whilst the policy agenda has focused on changing the law (criminal and civil) and its implementation; real practical support is far from being in place. Thus lending strong support to the notion that while some voices may have been heard those voices have not necessarily been responded to in a meaningful and effective way. The commodification of the citizen as a consumer has been a much more overriding concern (cf. Offe and Ronge, 1975). It was this, and its surface manifestation in the search for efficiency and value for money in the public sector during the 1980s, which facilitated the reconstruction of the citizen as a consumer and through which the questions raised about women and policing were given space to emerge. This, alongside the reported decline in public confidence and satisfaction with the police (Reiner, 1992), constituted the generative mechanisms which contributed to the marginalisation of feminist concerns and the centralisation of the androgynous victim of Victim Support. This process highlights the importance of understanding not only the nature and impact of potential policy *networks* (whose influence seems to have been of significantly less importance in the context of domestic violence) but what mechanisms might be underpinning the policy *agenda* (Wilkes, 1995). The commodification of the citizen as a consumer seems to have been a significant contributor in this case. The influence of a logic such as this is not so clearly discernible when a different victim is considered: the families of murder victims.

Responding to murder

Recognising the particular grieving problems associated with the families of murder victims is not an easy nor a straightforward process. Depending upon the nature of the murder itself, of course, members of the victim's family may, on the one hand, be the prime suspects in the police investigation or, on the other hand, may at least have to wait until such an investigation has been completed before they can enter into funeral arrangements. Both of these sets of circumstances arguably interfere to a considerable extent with what might be considered to be a 'normal' grieving process. For reasons such as these it is possible to see that responding to people grieving under these circumstances has its own associated difficulties. Nevertheless, as Rock (1998) documents, support systems for families grieving in this way have been in place for some considerable time.

The Compassionate Friends was formed in 1969. This organisation was intended to help families grieving for the death of a child and from its connections an organisation known as Parents of Murdered Children grew in the mid 1980s. This organisation emerged from a recognition within existing members of The Compassionate Friends that there were distinctive difficulties which parents of murdered children had in coming to terms with what had happened to their child and the subsequent impact of that event. Parents of Murdered Children began life in 1984 as a separate part of The Compassionate Friends. By 1990, however, this group had established itself as an autonomous organisation. Rock (1998) documents the detailed process which resulted in this outcome. What is interesting for the discussion here the potential relationship that may or may not have existed between these developments and those emerging from within Victim Support.

Victim Support had originally established itself as an organisation primarily concerned to offer short term practical and emotional help to the victim of crime from within their own community. However, by the mid-1980s it was also clear that some schemes were already dealing with families of murder victims. An event, which by definition, required much longer term involvement and arguably the kind of skilled support that Victim Support volunteers were unlikely to possess. In the light of these developments in 1988 the national organisation established a two year demonstration project in Essex, Merseyside, Sheffield, and South

London, funded by the Home Office, to examine Victim Support's work with families of murder victims. There were a number of different outcomes as a result of this project in improving both police and volunteer responses to such victims (see Rock, 1998: 184–6), not least of which was that by the end of 1993 Victim Support had received 626 murder referrals. One key outcome was the recognition given to Parents of Murdered Children as a significant self help group in this area. They had been invited, by Victim Support, to sit on the advisory board to this demonstration project and were subsequently also invited, along with Victim Support to submit evidence to the House of Lords Select Committee on Murder, Manslaughter and Life Imprisonment in 1989. The relationship between these two organisations became a more formal partnership in 1993 with the two partners agreeing to a three year project designed to examine the neatness of fit between the work of the two groups. It is at this juncture that Parents of Murdered Children became SAMM (Support After Murder and Manslaughter).

As Rock (1998) documents SAMM has continued to evolve as an organisation but not in a clear and/or unidirectional fashion. The 1990s have seen the emergence of additional organisations who claim to speak for the victim of crime. of particular note are Justice for Victims and Victims' Voice. These groups present themselves as considerably more vociferous on issues such as victims' rights, the political implications of which Victim Support and its associated satellite groups have shunned. The emergence of these more vociferous groups have taken a particular toll on groups like SAMM as the process of victim politicisation has become more acute; an impact which has been felt not least in terms of increasing media demands being made of groups like SAMM. However, largely as a result of SAMM's relationship with Victim Support it has managed to maintain its, albeit fragile, position as a voice for families of murder victims. Rock (1998: 330) puts it this way:

> Ministers were certainly advised by their officials in August 1994 that they should pay more heed to SAMM than to Justice for Victims, and that they should attend SAMM's launch to promote an association that was reasonable in the face of competition from one that was not. Although the campaigning Justice For Victims might have overshadowed SAMM in the summer of 1994, it was said, SAMM was the more constructive, rational, and cohesive association *whose propriety was guaranteed by Victim Support.*

(My emphasis)

The achievements of the voluntary sector in this area of lobbying for victims' interests should not be undervalued. At least by the end of the 1990s the needs of families of murder victims were being considered from the moment the event occurred through to the support offered to them through the Witness Support Schemes (another initiative starting life as a Victim Support demonstration project) now operating in many Crown Courts. At the same time the Probation Service is now charged with the responsibility of soliciting the views of victims of serious crime (including murder) when 'their' offender is under consideration for release. (For a fuller discussion of this development see Nettleton *et al.*, 1997). From the point of view of the victim all of these changes are of potential benefit in recognising their distinct needs of the criminal justice process. What remains to be established in this particular context is how to make sense of the emergent nature of these concerns and the impact that they have had.

Arguably the substantive area of murder, and the responses to the 'secondary' victims of murder which have emerged since the late 1960s, represent a further articulation of the 'powerful motif' of the victim discussed by Bottoms in 1983. That motif leads Rock (1998: 321) to suggest;

> For decades penal reformers and policy-makers in England and Wales were haunted by the spectre of angry victims of violence, the victim-vigilantes who would storm out like latter-day sans-culottes to wreak a terrible revenge and undo all their liberal reforms.

Yet self-evidently this has not been the case, despite the fact that anger rather than anxiety is a key emotional response to victimisation (see Ditton *et al.*, 1999). While it is clear that the Victims of Crime group does articulate the views of an 'angry victim', in relation to policy it is a view which has been heard but not responded to. In this particular context it would appear that the key relationships and networks led by Victim Support have wielded a considerable influence to date on managing and constructing what has to be seen to be a reasonable response to the families of murder victims. In this respect the links between organisations and people have shown themselves to be very effective gatekeeping mechanisms. So arguably in relation to this issue it is the policy *networks* which have mattered to date rather more than the logic of the policy *agenda*.

Conclusion: policy networks, agendas and processes

As the quote from Carlen, cited at the beginning of this chapter, aptly illustrates, the image of the crime victim has been used increasingly to justify a punitive stance on law and order. Successive Home Secretaries now feel able to invoke such imagery without compunction. Such rhetorical devices, however, while valuable in invoking support for a change in policy orientation towards offenders have not necessarily been translated in policies which are simultaneously more victim oriented. The various incarnations of the Victims' Charter notwithstanding, there has been little movement in the direction of victims' rights which could be compared, for example, with those which have been put in place in the United States. This is not to imply that much has not been achieved, nor is left to be achieved, by fully implementing the 'good practice' implications of the Victims' Charter recommendations. However, as hopefully this chapter has suggested, not all of those achievements can necessarily be attributed to the presence or absence of a victims' lobby. Indeed, one of the major improvement for the victim of (violent) crime, the CICB, was arguably put in place in the complete absence of an identifiable victims' lobby as such.

Yet overall it has to be said that services for, and the consideration of, the victim of crime has been considerably improved since the inception of the CICB in 1964. A key player in that process of change has been the presence and development of Victim Support and the ability of its national officers to win the ear of government. In this respect, for the victim of what might be called conventionally understood crime, the emergent process of governance has yielded some benefits. Through the back door of governance those campaigning for the victim of crime have had an opportunity to be heard. However, what hopefully this chapter has also demonstrated is that understanding the shift from Government to governance, is not a sufficiently powerful enough explaination through which to understand fully the whole picture of the shifts in pattern and emphasis with respect to criminal victimisation which has occurred over that same time period.

This chapter has also argued that in the context of 'domestic' violence processes other than policy networks underpinned the development of that policy agenda; whereas in responding to families of murder victims, a policy network analysis might well prove to be much more fruitful. What is clear is that there is no simple nor straightforward analysis to be made of the 'victims' lobby' per se but nevertheless there has been a gradually increasing political and policy awareness that the victim of crime is someone who is centrally affected by crime and to whom appropriate support should be directed.

One common thread to this argument throughout has been the way in which the crime victim, whether constructed as the innocent victim of violent crime in the 1960s, the consumer of police services in the 1980s, or the secondary victim in the 1990s, has been increasingly and consistently been invoked in the political domain as the symbolic person about whom we should all care. The use of the crime victim in this way is, of course, a matter of politcal expediency. Expediency which has on occassions benefitted the victim (as with the formation of the CICB) and has on other occasions been much more about punishing the offender as Carlen correctly observes. It is a moot point whether or not the victims' lobby, such as it is, in this context has had any real power or influence. The changing political and economic context would have appeared to be the underlying drivers for some responses to victimisation and not for others. Appreciating the complex ways in which some voices are heard at some points in time and yet not at others constitutes the real challenge for those who might be more persuaded by the governance thesis.

References

Carlen, P, (1996) *Jigsaw: The Politics of Youth Homelessness* (Buckingham: Open University Press).

Corbett, C. and Maguire, M. (1987) *The Effects of Crime and the Work of Victim Support Schemes* (Aldershot: Gower).

Crawford, A. (1994) 'The partnership approach to community crime prevention: corporatism at the local level?', *Social and Legal Studies*, 3: 497–519.

Ditton, J., Farrall, S., Bannisrer, J., Gilchrist, E. and Pease, K. (1999) 'Reactions to victimisation: why has anger been ignored P', *Crime Prekution and Community Safety: an International Journal*, 1(3): 37–54.

Dobash, R. and Dobash, R. (1980) *Violence Against Wives* (Shepton Mallett: Open Books).

Edgar, D. (1991) 'Are you being served?', *Marxism Today* May: 28.

Edwards, S. (1989) *Policing 'Domestic' Violence* (London: Sage).

Faraghar, T. (1985) 'The police response to violence against women in the home', in Pahl, J. (ed.), *Private Violence and Public Policy* (London: Routledge and Kegan Paul).

Farrall, S., Bannister, J. Ditton, J. and Gilchrist, E. (1997) 'Questioning the measurement of the 'fear of crime', *British Journal of Criminology*, 37(4): 658–79.

Garland, D. (1985) *Punishment and Welfare* (Aldershot: Gower).

Garland, D. (1996) 'The limits of the sovereign state', *British Journal of Criminology*, 36(4): 445–71.

Grace, S. (1995) 'Policing domestic violence in the 1990s', *Home Office Research Study*, no. 139 (London: HMSO).

Hoyle, C. (1998) *Negotiating Domestic Violence: Police, Criminal Justice, and Victims* (Oxford: Clarendon Studies in Criminology).

James, A. and Raine, J, (1998) *The New Politics of Criminal Justice* (London: Longmans).

Jefferson, T., Sim, J. and Walklate, S. (1992) 'Europe, the left, and Criminology in the 1990s', in Farrington, D. and Walklate, S. (eds), Offenders and Victims: Theory and Policy (British Society of Criminology, ISTD).

Marshall, T. H. (1948; 1981) *The Rights to Welfare and Other Essays* (London: Heinemann).

Mawby, R. and Gill, M. (1987) *Crime Victims: Needs, Services and the Voluntary Sector* (London: Tavistock).

Mawby, R. and Walklate S. (1994) *Critical Victimology: the Victim in International Perspective* (London: Sage).

Miers, D. (1978) *The Politicisation of the Crime Victim* (Abingdon: Professional Book).

Nettleton, H., Walklate, S., and Williams, B. (1997) *Probation Training with the Victim in Mind* (Keele: Keele University Press).

Offe, C. and Ronge, V. (1975) 'Theses on the theory of the state'. *New German Critique*, 6 (autumn): 139–47.

Radford, J. and Stanko, E. (1991) 'Violence against women and children: the contradictions of crime control under patriarchy', in Stenson, K. and Cowell, D. (eds), *The Politics of Crime Control* (London: Sage).

Reiner, R. (1992) *The Politics of the Police* (London: Harvester Wheatsheaf).

Rhodes, R. W. (1997) *Understanding Governance* (Buckingham: Open University Press).

Rock, P. (1988) 'Governments, victims and policies in two countries', *British Journal of Criminology*, 2801): 44–66.

Rock. P. (1990) *Helping Victims of Crime* (Oxford:

Rock, P. (1998) *After Homicide: Practical and Political Responses to Bereavement* (Oxford: Clarendon).

Smith, L. (1989) *Domestic Violence* (London: HMSO).

Victim Support (1992) *Domestic Violence: Report of an Inter Agency Working Party* (London: Victim Support).

Waller, I. (1988) 'International standards, national trail blazing, and the next steps', in Maguire, M. and Pointing, J. (eds), *Victims of Crime: A New Deal?* (Milton Keynes: Open University Press).

Index